2002 GEMS

of
Educational
Wit & Humor

P. Susan Mamchak
Steven R. Mamchak

PARKER PUBLISHING COMPANY
West Nyack, New York 10995

10 9 8 7 6 5 4 3 2 1

Library of Congress Cataloging-in-Publication Data

Mamchak, P. Susan
   2002 gems of educational wit and humor / by P. Susan Mamchak
and Steven R. Mamchak.
     p. cm.
   ISBN 0-13-489683-1
   1. Education—Anecdotes. 2. Education—Humor. I. Mamchak,
Steven R. II. Title. III. Title: Two thousand and two gems of
educational wit and humor.
LA23.M35 1994   93-47894
370′.207—dc20   CIP

ISBN 0-13-489683-1

Parker Publishing Company
Career & Personal Development
West Nyack, NY 10995

Simon & Schuster, A Paramount Communications Company

Printed in the United States of America

Contents

B

C

D

E

F

G

H

I

M

N

O

P

xvii

S

T

U

V

W

X

Y

Z

Introduction: Getting the Most Out of This Book

Certainly, there are places where wit and humor are out of place and are even to be avoided. But for you, the active, front-line educator headed toward the turn of a new century, they are very few indeed. Rather, we have a myriad of opportunities and occasions where a shared laugh, a wisely reflective comment, or an insightful quip are not only welcome and appropriate, but can go a long way toward establishing a cooperative rapport, gaining the confidence and support of the audience you may be addressing, or directing and focusing the thoughts of your listeners. This is true whether the situation occurs in the classroom, at an after-dinner speech where you are the featured speaker, before a group of parents at a school-sponsored affair, during an in-service session where you may be a presenter or lecturer, or in front of an audience of the general public. As you elaborate on the educational scene with which you are so intimately familiar and about which you have such a deep and personal knowledge, humor becomes a valuable link to your audience.

"Laugh, and the world laughs with you;/Weep, and you weep alone," wrote Emma Wheeler Wilcox close to one hundred years ago. Almost a century later, that statement remains as true as ever. Whether in a formal and expansive speech, a classroom learning situation, an address to faculty or parents, or in an article you will write for the school newsletter or that professional journal, the use of wit and humor in appropriate proportions will get your audience, your "world," to laugh with you, sympathize with you, see with you, understand with you, agree with you, and even act as you would have them act. We honestly believe that there is not an educator anywhere who does not appreciate how powerful an educational tool wit and humor can be.

Of course we understand that, as educators, the witty and humorous material we use must be "appropriate" both to the subject we are addressing and to our positions as professional educators. We are educators, and our intent and purpose is to educate those we touch, enhancing our presentations with material that is at once dignified, clever, truly amusing, befitting the subject we are discussing, and bespeaking the educational world with which we are so familiar.

It is our contention that *2002 Gems of Educational Wit and Humor* is precisely the type of volume that you can use to find the materials you need for your educational speaking and writing tasks. Whether you need a story to break the ice with a new group or a witty and insightful comment with which to end that article, we are certain that you will find the "gem" you need within the pages of this book.

Yes, we believe that you have come to the right place. As the title implies, here are over TWO THOUSAND ENTRIES from which to choose—all of them highly reflective of today's educational scene. To help you find precisely the right material for your particular needs, they are listed in encyclopedic fashion under general topics listed A to Z. Even a cursory glance at the Contents will convince you of the incredible range of topics and situations that are covered and will certainly start you on a path to the exact material you need. Moreover, since every entry in this book has been garnered and written and prepared *by* educators *for* educators, you can use anything here with the assurance that it will appropriately reflect upon the dignity of your audience and your status as a respected educational leader.

Get the most you can out of this book. Use it to help you present a memorable lesson to a class . . . to gain virtually instant rapport and support from that audience you will be addressing next week . . . to find something that will help you make your point in that article or essay you are writing . . . to allow those parents to see how well you understand the "Human Comedy" which is so much a part of the world of modern education.

In short, use this book for each and every occasion where you wish to add humor and wit that is both fitting and satisfying. Use it to make a powerful point, get a laugh, start a process of thought and reflection, and give a presentation that will both please you and prove memorable for your audience.

This is a book of wit and humor about education in all its myriad aspects. In a very real sense, therefore, it is a book about you and your world.

May that world be a happier place for your use of it.

P. Susan Mamchak
Steven R. Mamchak

A

Absent

1

"Were you absent yesterday?" asked the teacher.

"I got poison ivy all over my arms," answered the student, "and my mom couldn't find any bandages to cover them. Not only was I absent yesterday; I was absent without gauze!"

2

On a field trip to a nearby country estate, a group of five boys decided to go swimming in the lake and left their clothes on the bank, where they were "stolen" with many a giggle by another group of students. An hour later, four of the group girded around with twisted shrubs and leaves, arrived at the school bus. "Where's Johnson?" asked the teacher in charge.

"He was the last one out of the lake," answered one of the swimmers, "and by then, the only leaves left were poison ivy, so I guess you'd have to say that Johnson is absent without leaf."

Absenteeism

3

"We need this budget request for repairs," the principal told the school board. "Why, conditions in our school have gotten so bad that we have an absentee rate of eighty percent!"

"Eighty percent!" shouted a board member. "How can children stay away like that?"

"Children?" answered the principal. "I'm talking about the teachers!"

4

"I checked my records," the teacher told the class, "and you were ALL physically present the day I reviewed for the test. Then how do you account for the miserable grades on the exam?"

Volunteered one student: "Mental absenteeism?"

Absent-Minded

5

I know a principal who was so absent-minded that one day he left his office and taped a note to the door saying, "Be back in fifteen minutes. Please make yourself comfortable." When he got back from his errand he read the note and then sat down to wait for himself to return!

6

"I heard a report on the radio this morning," the driver's ed teacher told the class. "It reported that in our state a person is run over every twenty-six minutes!"

"I don't think it's my fault!" exclaimed one student. "I don't even remember taking the car out this morning!"

7

"Young man," said the teacher, "I think you are a bit absent-minded."

"Why do you say that?"

"Because," answered the teacher, holding up the student's test paper, "it is evident that your mind was absent from every answer you wrote!"

8

"I think I'm getting absent-minded," stated one teacher to her friend.

"Why do you say that?"

"Yesterday, I drove home, parked in the driveway, got out, and then I kissed the car door and slammed my husband!"

Absurd

9

Near the school was a store that sold only candles, every shape and type imaginable. Once, it caught fire during the school day, and the teacher had to deal with thirty requests that the class be allowed to walk down the street to blow it out!

10

Someone once defined "absurd" as doing something over and over again that is clearly impossible. Ever since I heard that, I can't help feeling "absurd" every time I tell my students to make certain that their homework is neat and clean!

11

Webster defines "absurd" as "so unreasonable as to be laughable." I'm going to recommend that to the Child Study Team as a classification for seventh graders!

Abuse

12

The frazzled teacher picked the spitballs out of her hair, dabbed at the bubble gum that stuck to her skirt, looked down at her ink-covered shoes, then turned to her friend and said, "You know, I'm firmly against child abuse, but I'm also getting tired of being abused by children."

13

"Thelma Jones!" said the teacher, "I just saw you writing in your English text with a crayon! Are you abusing that book?"

"Oh, no, teacher," answered Thelma, smiling, "I'm just giving it that 'lived-in' look!"

Accent

14

Said the visiting New England teacher to her Southern colleagues, "As I entered your school this morning, two things struck me. One, of course, was your most beautiful and charming southern accents."

"And what was the second," drawled a Southern educator.

"A spitball!"

15

A student arrived in school from a foreign country. She spoke English, but with such a heavy accent that her teachers were having a difficult time understanding her. One teacher came up with the idea of letting her watch "talk shows" on TV in order to improve her speech. Now she speaks almost perfect English, except that every time she leaves the room, she says, "We'll be right back after these important messages!"

Accidents

16

"Come quick!" the excited student told the school nurse, "This is an emergency!"

"What is it?" asked the nurse as she grabbed her medical kit.

"In science class, one of the kids just swallowed a tadpole, and we think he's gonna croak!"

17

"I can't understand how the accident happened," the student told the driver's ed teacher. "After all, I had the right of way!"

"Yes," replied the teacher, "but the other driver had an eighteen-wheeler!!!"

18

In the faculty lunch room, one teacher dropped his fork and said to his colleague, "You know, I can't prove it, but I think that every time they have an accident in the home ec department, it gets served to us as a 'Faculty Special.'"

Achievement

19

"It's not that I want to exaggerate my achievements," the potential candidate for superintendent told the school board.

"It's just that when you've accomplished as much as I have, it's so hard to be modest!"

20

"Young man," said the principal, "school has been in session less than a month, and you have managed to break every rule in the student handbook! Now, what kind of behavior do you call that?"

Answered the student, "An unprecedented achievement?"

Adjectives

21

"According to the dictionary," the teacher told the class, "the adjective 'TAWDRY' means, 'cheap and tasteless.' Now, who will use it in a sentence?"

Volunteered one student, "Our cafeteria serves TAWDRY sandwiches!"

22

"Now," said the science teacher as she stood over the dissected amphibian, "who will give me an adjective that will describe this frog?"

One student swallowed hard and answered, "Hopefully, 'DEAD.'"

Admonishment

23

Two students were given the job of painting the scenery for the school play. Soon, there was paint everywhere and they had gone through two gallons for a job that should have taken a pint. Finally, a teacher approached them.

"I must admonish both of you," said the educator, "for your injudicious use of the medium."

"Gee, thanks," replied one child, "I was afraid we was usin' too much paint!"

24

"Do your parents ever admonish you?" asked the teacher.

"No," said the first grader, "but if I'm bad I get a lickin' with the wooden spoon!"

Adolescence/Adolescent

25

"Come on," said the mother to her teen-aged son, "let's go clean your room."

As the door to the room was pushed open, an array of dirty socks, pizza crusts, and various unidentifiable objects met their view.

"Gosh, Mom," said the lad, "where do we start?"

Lowering her head, Mother began, "Let us pray . . . "

26

"Until a year ago, I never had an auto accident on my insurance records."

"What happened a year ago?"

"My teenager learned to drive!"

27

Believe it or not, there are people around who never make mistakes. They are called teenagers, and if you don't believe me, just ask one of them!

28

Adolescence is a stress-filled and often devastating time of transition from child to young adult. It is only in retrospect, when one is securely established as a middle-aged adult, that it becomes a time of wonder to which we long to return.

Adult Education

29

Ask any parent—having children is the greatest adult education that life has to offer!

30

"I want to sign up my parents for adult education," the teen-aged student told the registrar. "I keep trying and trying, but they still refuse to see things my way. Maybe you guys can set them straight!"

31

A man walked into a local high school where adult education classes were held. He walked up to the principal and said, "Excuse me, could you tell me when adult education starts?"

"Certainly," replied the principal. "The minute you graduate; the very minute!"

Adults

32

"Yes," said the English teacher, "to 'ADULTERATE' something means to make it impure; to contaminate it."

"I knew it!" one student exclaimed. "I knew that sooner or later you ADULTS would mess up everything!"

33

Little Janette and Martin had been assigned as work partners in the classroom. They fought constantly, however, and not a bit of work was getting done. Finally, the teacher called them to his desk.

"Janette and Martin," he said, "I want you to go back to your seats and think about an adult way to handle your difficulties. Then come back and tell me the adult thing to do."

The children were back in less than ten minutes.

"Have you thought of the adult way to behave?"

"Yes," they said together, "we want a divorce!"

Advice

34

The teacher invited a very rich business person to speak to the class. Naturally, the class asked the secret of his success.

"When I was just starting out," said the wealthy business owner, "my father sat down with me and gave me a great deal of advice about the business world."

"And his advice made you what you are today," stated one student.

"Yes," said the rich man, "that and his gift of three million dollars in negotiable bonds . . . "

35

"Did you get any advice when you started teaching?" the young educator asked the elder.

"Certainly. I was told never to smile; never to get involved with my students, never to get bogged down through loving the children, and to teach the subject and leave it up to the students as to whether or not they learn."

"How did this advice help you?"

"Simple," the elder teacher replied, "I did the direct opposite of everything that was advised and have had a happy and productive life in education ever since!"

Affluence

36

"I hear we have a really rich kid in kindergarten," said one elementary school teacher.

"Yes," answered the kindergarten teacher. "There he is over in the sandbox with his personal secretary."

37

"Jenkins came into teaching from a very affluent family," said one teacher.

"How do you know that?"

"Well, for one thing, she's the only one around here who hires temporary office workers to do her grades and final averages!"

Age Levels

38

"I'm past forty," said the teacher to the first grader. "What's your age?"
Answered the smiling tot, "Computer!"

39

"What do you think is the best age?" asked the teacher.
Answered the disgruntled student, "Just old enough to have passed this course!"

40

"Now that you have reached the age where all your children have graduated from school, how does it feel?"
"Wonderful! I'm actually looking forward to discovering if there's life after the PTA!"

41

Of course, there was the grandfather who visited the school and told the class that the secret of old age is to be born a very long time ago!

Aisle

42

The teacher asked the student, "Why were you in the aisle of the auditorium during the principal's speech?"
Answered the child, "It was the only place with enough room to lie down and sleep."

43

The teacher asked the students how the class might be improved.
Wrote one youngster, "Designate one aisle as an express lane to the door when the bell rings!"

Allowance

44

"When I was your age," ranted the father, "I didn't get an allowance; I worked for my money!"

"When you were my age," said his son, "there were a lot fewer people around to compete for jobs!"

45

"Mom, could you raise my allowance a hundred dollars a week?"

"What!" exclaimed the mother, and there followed a lecture on economy and children's allowances.

"Well, Mom, since you feel like that, I withdraw my request, and since I've been so reasonable, I'm certain you won't mind slipping me a few bucks so I can go to the movies."

46

"And what do you call an allowance in your home?" asked the teacher.

Answered one student, "A family quarrel!"

Alumni

47

One of the alumni of our school has become rather famous. You see, he was out swimming when he was attacked be a great white shark and lost part of his thigh. A doctor on the scene was able to replace the lost tissue using the thigh muscle from a German shepherd.

I'm happy to report that now he is perfectly fine, can walk and run well, and the only trouble he has is when he passes a fire hydrant!

48

The social studies teacher asked a student in her class, "Who originated the philosophy of 'Win at Any Cost'?"

"I don't know his name," answered the pupil, a boy on the school's football team, "but it's got to be one of the guys on the alumni!"

Amateur

49

The coach had built up a head of steam as he addressed the football team.

"Aim for that goal," he orated, "strive for that goal; even if you are in terrible pain; even if you're bloody and injured; even if you're in the worst kind of misery and agony . . . "

At which point one player leaned over to another and said, "Shouldn't somebody tell him that we're only amateurs?"

50

The home ec class invited a professional pastry chef to the school for a demonstration. The results were absolutely delicious, but the entire home ec room was a mess with pots, pans, flour, and sugar scattered from one end to another.

"How am I ever going to get this clean?" mused the teacher.

"Don't ask me!" stated the pastry chef. "I am a professional baker but an amateur cleaner-upper!"

Ambition

51

Said the class bully to the new student, "I'm gonna pound you into dust; I'm gonna mop up the floor with you; I'm gonna grind you up into hamburger!"

Whereupon, the new kid let loose an uppercut that knocked the bully across two desks.

"Sorry about that," said the new student to the downed bully. "While I admired your ambition, I simply could not agree with your goals."

52

The teacher sent a student to get something from the janitor. The child returned shortly and reported that the janitor had been asleep in his office.

"Why didn't you wake him up?" asked the teacher.

"What?" replied the student. "Who am I to interfere with the fulfillment of a fellow human being's chief ambition in life?"

America

53

Isn't it wonderful that here in America every child is born with life, liberty, the pursuit of happiness, and a healthy percentage of the national debt?

54

"Do you think that TV has affected our students' view of American history?" one social studies teacher asked a colleague.

"I don't know; why do you ask?"

"Because on my last test, one student wrote that he had no idea who won the Revolutionary War because the TV set broke down at the most interesting part!"

55

Questions about America from a second-grade class:

"Can you buy a 'Suit of Happiness' at a clothing store?"

"What do you do with the Bill of Rights if you're left-handed?"

"If we're one nation, invisible, how come I can see you?"

Angels

56

"What are you making?" the art teacher asked the small student.

"I'm making an angel," replied the pupil.

"But, at least half of each wing is missing."

"That's OK, the angel is flying economy class this trip!"

57

"I got a part in the class play," the child announced as she slammed the front door.

"It's an important part," she yelled as she pulled the cat's tail and knocked over a vase of flowers.

"Teacher said it was type casting!" she continued as she took the rattle from her baby brother, sending him into a wail.

"Guess what?" she asked as she arrived in the kitchen after having tracked mud through the entire house.

"What?" sighed her frazzled mother.

"I'm an angel!"

Angles

58

As one student wrote in his math report, getting through life is a lot like geometry—to fully appreciate it, you have to know all the angles!

59

One student who truly hated math sat with a particularly downcast look one Monday morning.

"What's the matter?" asked the teacher.

"Yesterday in church I was reading this book," replied the pupil, "and it said that there were ANGLES in Heaven! Gosh, you can't get away from this math stuff anywhere!"

Animals (See Nature; Pets)

Annual (See Yearbook)

Anonymous

60

Written on a desk top:

If you can't remember who wrote the book,
There's no need to worry or fuss;
When the English teacher asks you, say,
"It was written by A NON Y MOUS!!!"

Said the student to the school librarian, "Where can I find a book about the life of a guy named ANONYMOUS? You know, the one who wrote all those poems!"

Anticipation

62

ANTICIPATION is HOPE sitting over a slow fire.

63

"I'm sorry I charged the defensive line all by myself, Coach," said the young player. "I was carried away by the anticipation of victory!"

"That's OK, Son," said the Coach. "It's just that now you're about to be carried away by the ambulance from City General Hospital."

Antiques

64

"What is an antique?" asked the teacher.

"Anything," replied the student, "that is impossible to dust!"

65

"Who can explain antiques?" asked one teacher.

"It's like this," answered a colleague. "My grandmother bought it, my mother threw it out, and I'm selling it to my daughter for her apartment. That's an antique!"

Anxiety

66

"So you see," said the teacher, "too much anxiety and stress can make a person ill."

"I knew it," whispered one student to another. "I knew there was a perfectly good reason why I was sick of school!"

Then there was the student in home ec class who suffered an anxiety attack while preparing pancakes. I guess you'd say it was a case of "mind over batter."

Appearance

68

"What day is it, Mr. Jones?" asked a student.

"You know how to find that out," answered Mr. Jones, indicating the calendar on the wall.

Instead, the child rose and stood before Mr. Jones' desk.

"Black tie with red stripes," murmured the child. "It's Tuesday!"

69

"Hey, Ms. Aarons," asked a student, "who is that ugly woman standing by the door?"

"That," replied the teacher, "is my sister!"

"Isn't it wonderful," returned the student with a gulp, "how there is absolutely no family resemblance whatsoever!"

70

"You know," the teacher told the failing student, "we give you textbooks to carry for other reasons besides keeping up appearances!"

Appreciation

71

On Teacher Appreciation Day, one student brought her teacher a box of homemade brownies.

"Those brownies were the best I ever tasted," the teacher told the student later in the day.

"Glad you liked them," said the student. "You'll get a box a week if my grades start going up!"

"How can I show you how much I appreciate all the extra help you've given me," said the student as the late afternoon sun sank behind the horizon.

"Simple," answered the teacher. "Go home and let me take some aspirin and put my feet up!"

Aquarium

73

"Did you see any big fish during your class trip to the aquarium?"

"I'll say," answered the student. "I took a Polaroid of one fish who was so big that when the picture came out of the camera, the photo weighed three pounds and ten ounces!"

74

"How will you explain why you weren't in school yesterday?"

"I'll say my family went to the aquarium."

"But the aquarium is closed."

"Sounds a little fishy, huh?"

Arena

75

"Suppose you had a boxing arena," said the math teacher, "and there were ten people in the audience and then fifteen more showed up. What would you have?"

Answered one student, "A really rotten card of boxing!"

76

One district reconditioned an old field house behind the high school. Soon the argument began as to what it should be called.

"We should call it 'The Old Field House,' because that's what it was!"

"Let's call it 'The High School Sports Building,' because that's what it's for!"

"Whatever we call it," chimed in someone, "we should put the word 'ARENA' after it, because then we can charge five bucks more per ticket!"

Argument

77

"Let me put it this way, I certainly admire the way you can draw such an extensive argument from a basis of such sheer ignorance!"

78

"What can I do," said one educator, "to put an end to this argument between us?"

"Well," said the other, how about saying, 'Yes, you are absolutely right!'"

Arithmetic

79

"Now," said the math teacher, "suppose I had a fifty-dollar bill in one pocket and a one-hundred-dollar bill in the other pocket, what would I have?"

"Around here," said one street-wise youngster, "if you were wise, you'd have one hand in one pocket and one hand in the other!"

80

"If you had four candy bars, and I asked you to give me half of what you had, how many would I have?"

"None," said the small child, "'cause I don't like you, and I ain't givin' you none!"

81

"Yesterday, you told us we was gonna look for the lowest common denominator."

"Yes."

"My father says that they had him lookin' for that when he was in school! You mean, all this time has gone by and they ain't found it yet?"

Art

82

Said the art student, "Where do you think I should hold my first exhibit?"

Answered the art teacher, "Have you considered the City Institute for the Blind?"

83

"What a magnificent example of modern art!" exclaimed the teacher.

"My painting?"

"No! This rag on which you've been wiping your brushes!"

84

The elementary school art class was taken to an exhibit of modern art. The moment they entered the hall, they were assailed by vivid colors all over the walls.

One young tyke scampered up to the teacher.

"I ain't been nowhere near the paint jars," the child fumed, "I didn't do it, and I AIN'T GONNA CLEAN IT UP! You got that?"

85

"I'm interested," said the art teacher to a person who had just purchased a landscape at a local gallery. "What made you buy that particular painting? Was it the brush technique or the use of pastel colors or the brilliant shading . . . "

"Actually," said the purchaser, "it's just the right size to cover the hole that my two-year-old put in the wall!"

Asphalt

86

"What if you owned an acre of land in the middle of a great city?" the science teacher asked. "What would you do to it to aid the ecology?"

"Easy question!" said one student. "I'd cover it with asphalt, turn it into a parking lot, and give a couple bucks of the profit to some environmental group!"

87

"I'm worried that the principal might be getting a bit overconfident."
"Why do you say that?"
"Yesterday they painted new parking-space lines on the asphalt, and the principal says, 'Mine by Divine Right'!"

Assemblies

88

The visitor to the school watched as a person walked down the hall wearing a baseball-catcher's mask, an umpire's chest protector, football shoulder pads, and a hockey player's shin guards.

"My goodness, is that person going to officiate at some sporting event?"

"Not at all," answered a teacher. "That's our vice-principal, and he's just been put in charge of discipline at the school assembly!"

89

The child packed a water pistol, a slingshot, and fifty wads of paper into his school lunch box.

"You are NOT taking that to school, young man," said Mother.

"Have a heart, Mom!" the young boy implored. "How often do we have an assembly?"

Assignment (See also Homework)

90

"What do you mean, you've had complaints?" the irate teacher asked the principal. "I have taught these children American history as few other teachers could have; I've taught them about pre-Columbian days, the colonists, the Civil War, and just last week, we started the Western Movement. What is wrong with that?"

"Nothing," said the principal, "but you were assigned to teach a math class!"

91

"Do you remember that one student in your class last year who always caused trouble?" the principal asked the teacher.

"I certainly do," replied the teacher.

"Do you remember how pleased we were when the family moved, and you insisted on buying me dinner to celebrate?"

"I sure do."

"Well, here's twenty bucks for my half of the meal. The family moved back, and I've just assigned the kid to your class!"

Attire

92

"In order to succeed in life," affirmed the classroom lecturer, "one must always have the proper attire!"

"At last you're talking my language!" exclaimed one young man from the back of the room. "What do you like best, steel-belted or radials?"

93

One teenager to another: "That's what I like about her clothes; they are so bad they refuse to go out of style!"

94

"We have a great home ec teacher. She even found a use for clothes left over from the thirties and forties."

"Really? What?"

"She wears them to school!"

Audience

95

While school plays are not supposed to be the height of dramatic endeavor, this one was soooooo bad that several of the teachers and parents in the audience began to rise to spend time waiting in the hallway.

Backstage, one young actor ran to the teacher.

"This is wonderful," she said. "I looked out at the audience, and they're giving us a standing ovation—AND WE AIN'T EVEN FINISHED YET!"

96

"What a wonderful audience," said the speaker. "I particularly want to thank you for your patience. I know I've been a little long, but thank you for choosing to listen."

"Fella," yelled someone from the audience, "They won't serve us dinner until you are finished talking. We were choosing to eat!"

Austerity

97

"I know the district is on an austerity budget," said the science teacher, "but I would hardly call two safety pins and a jackknife a dissection kit!"

98

"Remember," said the teacher, "money cannot buy you happiness!"

"Yes," replied one student, "but you can be miserable in SUCH comfort!"

Automobiles

99

If you want to talk about gasoline economy, ask any teenager how he or she manages to get the car into the garage with less than half a cup of fuel left in it!

100

"My car is in the 'newborn' class," said the teacher.

"What do you mean?"

"Every time I'm with it, it's got a rattle!"

Aviation

101

"I understand that you don't travel by airplane."

"That's right."

"Get airsick, huh?"

"Oh, no. It's just that the trip to the airport is so long that I usually get carsick!"

102

It was the child's first trip by air, and he had been talked through it several times, including being told how courteous the flight attendants were and all the little courtesies the airline provided.

Once on the plane, he spotted the airsickness bag and asked what it was. When he was told, he stared at it in disbelief.

"You mean they put it in a bag for you to take home? That's carrying courtesy a little bit too far!"

Awards

103

"I got an award in school today!" shouted the child as he tracked mud across the living room carpet, knocked over a vase that spilled water all over the floor, and pushed open the kitchen door leaving two smudged handprints.

"For what?" his exasperated mother asked.

"Neatness!"

104

At the assembly, the student received an award and was asked to say something.

"Well," said the child, "I really don't deserve this award . . . "

The student paused for a second; then continued, "But, I really don't deserve the detention Mrs. Melendez gave me, either, so I guess I'll just have to take both!"

105

"I'd like to give each of you an award," said the teacher as she placed a cookie on each child's desk. "It isn't much, but it is a token of my deep gratitude for your efforts."

"If this is an award for her gratitude," said one student as he stared at the cookie, "I'd hate to see what we'd get if she were merely thankful!"

Awkward

106

Tommy Jones was the most awkward child in my class, and I made up my mind to talk to his parents about it at our upcoming Parent's Night.

On that occasion, I stood at my door and greeted the parents. Suddenly, there was a commotion down the hall, and I watched as a tall, thin, man picked himself up from the floor, bumped into two oncoming parents, upset a table with handouts on it, and finally stumbled down the hall to my door.

"Mr. Jones?" I ventured.

"Yes," he answered, "how did you know?"

107

At the end of the school year, Mother insisted that she accompany her child to school to present the teacher with a small gift.

"And don't forget to say something complimentary to your teacher," she told her offspring.

They arrived at school, presented the gift, and stood in an extremely awkward silence. Finally, Mother nudged the child and whispered, "Say something nice!"

"Ms. . . . Ms. . . . Sierra . . . , my . . . my mother and I want you to know that you really don't smell, even if you do sweat a lot!"

108

The teacher had a private talk with one boy whose awkwardness was the talk of the class. He literally could not walk down an aisle without bumping into someone or upsetting something.

"Think about what you're doing," said the teacher. "Understand where you are going and what you want to do, and then figure out the best way to get there or do the thing BEFORE you move."

"Ma'am," said the hapless student, "I know perfectly well where I'm going and how to get there, it's just that my arms and legs refuse to get the message!"

B

Babysitters/Babysitting

109

I almost had one of my students as a babysitter for us this past weekend. I promised that I'd rent movies at the video store and keep the refrigerator stocked with pizza and soft drinks. Everything was going fine, until she found out that I intended to leave the baby home!

110

"I think this babysitter must be in demand," said the husband as he hung up the phone.

"Why do you say that?" asked his wife.

"She told me she'd get back to us—just as soon as she checked OUR references!"

111

"Do you charge much for babysitting?"

"Let me put it this way: I honor Visa, MaterCard, and American Express!"

Bachelor

112

While visiting a college campus, an alumnus remarked on the large number of female students who thronged into a lecture hall designated as "Shakespeare 101."

"What makes Shakespeare so attractive to all these young women?" mused the visitor.

Replied the guide, "The professor who teaches it is young, handsome, and a bachelor!"

113

A colleague was trying to convince his friend of the joys of marriage.

"Just think," he continued, "you would have someone to share your trials and tribulations."

"But I have no trials or tribulations," commented the bachelor.

"Well," fumed his friend, "if you got married, you would have!"

114

"Can you give me one good reason why you're still a bachelor?"

"Everybody I asked said 'No.'"

Bacteria

115

"Noelle," said the science teacher, "I think you are going to get an award."

"I am? For what?"

"I just saw your locker; the award will be for the best growth of bacteria on school premises!"

116

"How do we know that bacteria always come in large masses?" asked the teacher.

"Well," answered one child, "I never heard of anyone getting A MEASLE."

117

From a student's report:

That lake was so polluted, if you fell into it, you could walk to the other side on the bacteria!

Bait (See also: Fishing)

118

While out ice fishing, the man noticed a boy with a huge pile of fish. He went over to the lad and asked, "Son, what is the secret of catching so many fish in this old water?"

The boy spit something into his hand and answered, "Keep your bait warm!"

119

The school forensics club was about to begin its afternoon meeting when the doors burst open and in walked a student wearing wading boots, an old hat with several hooks and lures dangling from it, a creel at his side and a fishing rod in his hand.

"What," asked the forensics' coach, "are you doing here?"

"A fellow told me this was the place where they had de bait!"

Balance

120

On summer vacation, I saw an act where this man would balance anything the audience threw to him. He must have had fifty items balanced perfectly on his nose, chin, and forehead. Afterward, I asked him how he did it.

"This is just my summer job," he answered. "During the year, I'm a teacher (principal/custodian/superintendent), so this sort of comes naturally."

121

The teacher visited his ex-student in the county jail.

"I thought you said that life was a balance; a matter of give and take?" said the ex-student.

That's right," replied the teacher, "but when the appliance store won't GIVE you a TV set, that doesn't mean you can TAKE it at three in the morning!"

Bankrupt/Bankruptcy

122

"Wait a minute! Yesterday you told me that you were on the verge of bankruptcy, and now you say that you just burned a fifty-dollar bill?"

"Well, it was either burn the fifty-dollar bill or pay it!"

123

"So you're going bankrupt, eh? Why did you decide to do that?"

"I thought it was time when the credit-card companies wrote me a letter demanding that I make them beneficiaries in my will!"

124

"We're going to have to think about going bankrupt," the spouse told his mate. "There's only enough money left to pay the electric company or the doctor."

"Try paying the electric company; the doctor can't turn off anything!"

Barometer
(See also: Inclement Weather)

125

The student came forward and stared at the instrument on the teacher's desk. "We'll have some lowering clouds this afternoon with rain by nightfall that should clear off by morning."

"Wonderful!" exclaimed the teacher. "You can tell all that by looking at my barometer?"

"Well," returned the student, "that and listening to the local radio station on these earphones."

126

One science class hooked up a barometer to a computer so they could get automatic readings about weather conditions.

"I think this coming storm is going to be quite powerful," said the science teacher. "I just asked for a forecast, and it told me to grab my dog, Toto, and get ready for a ride!"

Baseball

127

I wouldn't say that our school has a poor baseball team, but they've been living in the cellar so long, the team color is green mold!

128

I wouldn't say that our school has a poor baseball team, but we're the only club around that can get three strike-outs on six pitches!

129

Said the coach to the freshman player, "We have to get you a cap. What size is your head?"

Answered the student athlete, "I'll let you know when the stats come out!"

130

Coach!" shouted the young player, "did you see how I slid into home plate? I was great! I did it just the way you told me to!"

"It was fine," said the coach, "except for the fact that it usually isn't done when you are coming UP TO BAT!"

Basketball

131

Was I a good basketball player? Let me put it this way. Do you know how all those players have numbers like 98 and 79? Well, mine was one and two-thirds!

132

"For the second half," the coach told the school basketball team, "I've asked the custodian to turn down the lights so they won't disturb your sleep as much as they did in the first half!"

133

The principal's car broke down, so she was very late getting to the basketball game. When she arrived, she found the team engaged in a loud and joyous victory party.

"Don't tell me we finally won a game!" she exclaimed to the coach.
"Better than that!" he shouted. "The other team never showed up!"

Beard

134

There's nothing wrong with a beard; it's just the outside of what used to be inside a couple of weeks ago.

135

"You know," one student said to the bearded teacher, "my father had a beard exactly like yours; I mean it was EXACTLY like yours, but he shaved it off."

"Too hot for him?" wondered the teacher.

"No, one day I just held a mirror in front of him, and he saw how ugly it really was!"

Beatnik
(See Generation Gap)

Bees

136

"Now," said the teacher, "who can tell me what a beekeeper does?"

Answered one student, "He goes about his work and keeps himself buzzy."

137

"And, what do bees produce?"

"Fathers."

"Fathers? No, they produce honey."

"Right! And that's what my Mommy calls my Daddy!"

Beginner (See also: Kindergarten)

138

Two mosquitoes arrived at a nudist colony.

Said the younger to the elder, "I'm only a beginner; teach me where to start!"

139

The garage desperately needed cleaning. Said young Paul, "I'll do it; there's nothing to it. All you need is a good plan, and I'm an expert planner!"

An hour later, Mom went out to the garage to find Paul, exhausted, lying on a pile of junk.

"I thought you were an expert planner?" stated Mother.

"I am!" returned Paul. "The trouble is that when it comes to hard work, I'm only a beginner!"

Behavior

140

"On our way up the ladder of success, why should we be kind to everyone we meet?"

Answered one student, "Because we can never tell who we're going to run into on the slide down?"

141

"Take me, for instance," said the teacher. "I have very few personal faults."

"True, sir," commented one student, "and you certainly do manage to get a great deal out of them!"

142

If, at first, you don't succeed—you can always start another business when you get out of bankruptcy court.

143

"Your behavior," the teacher told the student, "is infantile, regressive, completely lacking in morality, and totally reprehensible!"

"Oh, thank you," replied the student, "it's so nice to have one's strong points recognized!"

144

If you have relatives who are always bragging about what a perfect child they have, give the kid a set of drums for his next birthday.

Bell

145

Did you hear about the student who entered the school's variety show and played a kazoo while beating on a bell with a hammer?

Everybody said his act was a humdinger!

146

"Excuse me," said the minister to the man as he left the church, "you're a teacher, aren't you?"

The man stared in amazement. "Yes, I am, but how did you know? This is my first time here."

"Just a guess," continued the minister, "plus the fact that every time the church bell rang, you shouted, 'OK, you guys, let's quiet down and get to work!'"

Benefits

147

"Do you think you'll enjoy teaching here?" the new teacher was asked.

"I thought so, but I just read the contract, and now I'm not so sure."

"Why? What did you read?"

"One of the 'benefits'—is long-term psychiatric care!"

148

"Honest, Ma'am," said the child, "I didn't know; honest I didn't!"

"Well," said the teacher, "you are, after all, only a child, and you'll learn, so we'll forget about it this time."

When the teacher left the room, the student looked at the ceiling, smiled widely, and said, "Ah, the benefits of being young and inexperienced!"

Biceps (See: Muscles)

Bickering (See also: Argument)

149

"I don't see why my friend and I should be punished," the student told the principal, "just because we tossed a few words back and forth between us!"

"It's not for the words," commented the administrator, "it's for the alphabet soup they happened to be in at the time!"

150

"My mother and father have not had an unkind or nasty word between themselves in the last five years," the student told the teacher.

"That's wonderful!' the teacher said. "What's their secret?"

"Simple," the pupil replied, "that's how long they haven't spoken to each other!"

Big Shot

151

"Harry thinks he's such a big shot, he tells everybody how good he is!"

"That's for sure! He's the only person I know who personally broadcasts boast to boast!"

152

"Remember," the teacher told the class, "the best advice I can give you is to be yourself."

"Excellent advice for me," said the class big shot, "but what about the others in the room?"

Bill of Rights

153

"So the Bill of Rights gives us the right to bear arms," the social studies teacher told the class.

The next class period, five students were sent to the office for going topless!

154

"If the Bill of Rights gives us freedom of assembly, how come I gotta go down to the auditorium and watch some old guy talk about bugs if I don't want to?"

Biology

155

"Professor," one student asked, "I've always wanted to know—do animals laugh?"

"Listen," commented the teacher, "any species that watches human beings . . . "

156

"What're you studying?" little brother asked big brother.

"Biology," the elder brother replied.

"What's that?"

"Something you won't need for another five years."

Birds

157

"Class, what is the meaning of the proverb, 'A bird in the hand is worth two in the bush'?"

Asked one student, "From whose viewpoint, the human's or the bird's?"

"In class, we did a science experiment," said the student. "We had this French hen, and we fed her only on breadcrumbs."

"What happened?"

"She laid a croissant!"

"She eats like a bird . . . "

"But, she's at least fifty pounds overweight!"

" . . . known as the vulture!"

Birthdays

160

With the help of several parents, the class was giving a surprise birthday party for their teacher.

"Are we going to serve the cake out on the front lawn?" asked one child.

"Of course not; why do you ask?"

"Because," answered the child, "if we light all those candles in here, the fire alarm will go off for sure!"

161

"How many candles should we put?" asked one child about the cake the class was preparing for their teacher's birthday.

"Just put one of those kind that goes out and then relights," said another student. "Then we can watch her blow and blow until she faints!"

Blame

162

Many people have faced situations where they have not accomplished what they have set out to do. The only time you have really failed, however, is when you begin to blame other people for your mistakes.

163

"Son," said the father, "sure you have troubles. Everybody has troubles. What you have to do is learn to handle them like a MAN, just like I did all my life!"

So, the young man took his father's advice, went home, and blamed everything on his wife!

Blues, The (See also: Depression)

164

"So you've got the blues, eh?"

"I wouldn't say that. It's just that I have this feeling that if I keep climbing and struggling upward, some day I'll reach bottom!"

165

"Of course you don't know what the blues are," the boy told his little brother, "you've ALWAYS been a failure!"

166

"You're really blue about losing your job, huh?"

"Look, lots of people have been replaced by a computer, but do you have any idea how it feels to be replaced by a calculator and an electric pencil sharpener?"

Board of Education
(See also: School Board)

167

"You're mean!" said the first-grader to the teacher. "You wait! You'll be sorry!"

"Why?" asked the teacher. "Are you going to beat me up?"

"Better than that. I'm gonna run for the Board of Education! Then you'd just better watch out!"

"And, who is the Board of Education?" asked the teacher.

"We is the bored of education!" the class chanted.

169

"What is a Board of Education?"

Answered one student, "That which my father applies to the seat of knowledge!"

Books

170

"Did you enjoy that author's last book?" the English teacher asked.

"That was his last book!" exclaimed the student. "Thank goodness he's not writing another!"

171

"Book titles are often misleading," the English teacher explained. "Do you see this? It's a legal paper drawn up by a lawyer; it contains about twenty thousand words. Do you know what it's called?"

"A BRIEF!"

172

The ailing teacher sent a thank-you note to her class for the gift they had sent.

"Thank you," the note read, "for the trip to distant lands and different people."

"I don't understand," said one child. "All we did was give her a book . . ."

Bosses/The Boss

173

"That home economics teacher is really into her work."

"Why do you say that?"

"I saw her yesterday, and she was buttering up the principal."

174

"Don't tell me I have cafeteria duty again this year unless you want to see a grown woman cry," the teacher told her principal.

"Please, I can't stand to see an adult cry," said the principal.

Then the administrator took out a handkerchief, tied it around her eyes and said, "You have cafeteria duty again this year!"

175

"Remember," said the social studies teacher, "to be the boss of any business, you need to work hard and be brave and courageous!"

"And," came a voice from the back of the room, "being the boss's kid don't hurt none either!"

Botany

176

"Why is gardening such a good hobby?"

"It's one of the few ways in which anybody can improve his lot nowadays!"

177

"I hear the gardener got fired because he bore a resemblance to his plants?"

"Yes, they were both potted on the job!"

Boxing

178

Coach to student between rounds:

"You have to understand, you get credit for a no-hitter only in baseball!"

179

"When I was on the boxing team in school, I was known as a colorful boxer."

"Why, because of your antics in the ring?"

"No, because the black and blue of my bruises went so well with the red of my blood!"

Boys

180

"I thought, 'My little boy is growing up, and unless I spend some quality time with him, I'm going to miss it.' So, I took off a day, and I spent that whole day, from sunrise till bedtime alone with my little boy . . . just us two . . .

"Gosh, did that ever cure me!"

181

If there is something, a book or song or movie, that you really, truly love; and you want it spoiled forever, just share it with a teenaged boy!

182

"Son, I think I've figured out what you're going to do in life. You're going to be one of America's foremost astronauts."

"Why do you say that, Dad?"

"Because, Son, I know of no one who takes up space better than you!"

Brain/Brains (See also: Intelligence)

183

"Who can tell me why the brain has so much knowledge in it?"

"Because," one student called out, "so few people bother to take anything out of it!"

184

"Jones," said the professor to the argumentative student, "I'd like to have a battle of wits with you some day, but right now you have only half your ammunition!"

Brick

185

"Surely you exaggerate about the need for repair of the school," said the superintendent. "Why, if you'd just get that graffiti off the bricks, everything would look fine."

"I can't take that graffiti off those bricks," said the principal.

"Why not?"

"The graffiti's the only thing holding up the wall!"

186

"What an unusual paperweight," said the visitor.

"That's a brick from the old school building that was given to me by the people of this community," said the principal.

"How wonderful! Who presented it?"

"I'm not sure. You see, it was tossed through the front window of my house from a passing car!"

Brothers and Sisters

187

"You're ugly," shouted the boy at his sister. "You're a real dog!"

"Yeah!" called the boy's playmate, "Woof! Woof!"

Whereupon, the girl's brother knocked his friend flat!

"Hey," he said, looking down at his prone playmate, "She's MY sister; not YOURS!"

188

Sister was truly angry with her little brother, and she had cornered him in a room where there was no escape.

"Now, you're going to get it!" threatened the sister.

"Wait a minute," pleaded the brother. "You're my sister, and I'm your brother. Just think of all I've done for you over the years!"

They say his broken nose should heal quickly.

Buckle

189

"I want you to take these textbooks home and buckle down . . . buckle down!" the teacher told the third-grader who was having some trouble with his studies.

"I can't," he sobbed, "the men in my family all wear suspenders!"

190

"I believe in the 'BUCKLE THEORY,'" the boy told his older brother.

"What's that?"

"A buck'll keep me from telling Mom what time you got in last night!"

Bunny

191

When her pet rabbit had a litter, one of the cafeteria workers asked the principal, "Would you like a bunny?"

"No," she answered, "but I will take that slice of cakie over there."

192

The child brought in his pet rabbit for show and tell.

"You know," remarked the teacher, "rabbits really multiply fast."

"Not this dumb bunny," said the child. "He can't even use a calculator!"

Business

193

"Always remember," the local businessman said as he addressed the high school class, "that America is the land of the free . . .

" . . . or at least the substantially discounted!"

194

At a public meeting, the school district's business administrator was addressing a group of parents.

"I want to assure you, ladies and gentlemen," she said, "that the finances of our school system are as sound as our country's economy."

"Oh, no!" proclaimed one parent. "How will our children ever get an education!"

195

"I don't think the new business teacher is very well qualified."

"Oh? Why do you say that?"

"Well, I asked him what he thought of Dun and Bradstreet, and he told me that the shops and restaurants were better at Fourth and Main!"

196

"Today's speaker," the business teacher told the class, "started out on a shoestring, and now, less than a year later, he has doubled his investment!"

"Big deal," whispered one student to another. "So he's got two shoestrings; what I want to know is can he afford the shoes to go with them?"

Bus Driver, The School

197

The classic definition that has been around for at least three decades: A school-bus driver is an individual who USED to like children.

198

The principal watched as a school bus unloaded its screaming, boisterous contents. Then he went up to the bus driver.

"I really must congratulate you," said the administrator. "You remain perfectly calm and serene with all those children yelling and making noise. Why, the noise level in this bus must be all but intolerable!"

The bus driver looked up and said, "Oh, I'm sorry! Were you speaking to me? Just a moment, and I'll turn on my hearing aid."

199

Two teachers were at the mall, when a fight broke out between a number of people who had been waiting in line for a store to open. Out of the crowd came a small woman who waded into the combatants, threw several to the ground, put a wrist lock on another, grabbed one more by the scruff of her neck, and, in less than a minute, had completely restored order.

"Martial arts expert?" queried one teacher.

"No," answered the other, "school-bus driver!"

Buses

200

One teacher was notoriously afraid of flying. In fact, when she was selected to participate in an International Educator's Convention in Paris, France, she told everyone that she would be honored to go, if they could just figure out a way of sending her there by school bus.

201

The buses for the school trip were chartered, and they were complete with every luxury, including a "rest room" on the bus itself.

About an hour on the road, one student came up to the teacher in charge.

"Gosh, Mrs. Goodhand," said the youngster, "it's really neat having a bathroom right on the bus!"

"Oh," the teacher smiled, "have you had occasion to use it?"

"I'll say," the child replied. "The minute we left school, we locked Billy Kravitts inside, and he hasn't bothered us at all!"

Butter

202

The two colleagues were at lunch in the teacher's cafeteria.

"Harry, ever since you took up golf, you've become obsessed with the game. Golf, golf, golf! That's all you think about morning, noon, and night! Golf!"

"Really, Jim, I think you exaggerate," said Harry as he broke open a dinner roll. "Oh, and would you please pass the putter."

203

The home ec teacher entered the room to find two students, one holding a spatula and the other covered head to toe with butter. She stood there aghast.

"It's OK, Ma'am," said the student with the spatula, "Ginny wants a new bike."

"What's that got to do with this mess?"

"Well, we heard another teacher talking, and she said that every time you buttered up the principal, you got whatever you wanted, so . . . "

204

Two students were in line in the cafeteria.

"A good question would be, 'Is this really butter?'"

"A better question would be, 'Is this really food?'"

Cabbage (See also: Money; Vegetables)

205

The sign in the school cafeteria read, "Today's Special, CABBAGE SOUP!"

"It's obvious," said one student to another. "There must be an all-out campaign to discourage students from becoming vegetarians."

206

The teacher took her class to visit a farm. They stood at the edge of a vast field. Before them, rows of green stretched to the horizon.

"Look at that," the teacher told her class, "acres and acres of cabbage growing in the sun, ready for harvest!"

One small student turned to another and whispered, "Well, I guess we know what the cafeteria will be serving next week, don't we?"

Cadet

207

The youngest cadet at military school had had a particularly bad day. He had been "chewed out" by several older cadets, failed room inspection, forgotten his homework, missed supper, and had to walk an hour's punishment duty. Now, he literally dragged himself back to the dorm.

On his way, he ran into the commanding officer of the school who took one look at the bedraggled youth and said, "Son, is there anything I can do for you?"

"Well, Sir," replied the cadet, "if the Commander can remember what it's like to be my age, could I please have permission to cry?"

208

"Mom," asked the young boy, "did any of our family come from Poland?"

"No, son," Mother answered, "our heritage is Italian-American, but why do you ask?"

"In this brochure," continued the lad, "it says that all cadets at the military school are 'spit and P-O-L-I-S-H,' and since we ain't Polish, that means I don't have to go!"

Cafeteria

209

"Please understand," said the principal to the cafeteria manager, "I'm not saying that your food is starchy, but two students told me that the reason they couldn't put back their trays was that when they went to get up, their knees wouldn't unbend!"

210

"Madam," said the judge, "you claim your husband tried to kill you by putting poison in the food you both ate?"

"That's correct, Your Honor."

"But, if he poisoned the food you both ate, wouldn't he become ill as well?"

"You don't understand; he's a teacher, and he eats every day in the school's cafeteria, so NATURALLY HE'S IMMUNE!!!"

211

Down the hall of the school came a figure inside a silvery fire-fighter's coveralls, wearing rubber gloves, boots, and with the entire head covered except for a small piece of glass that allowed for vision.

"My goodness, is there a fire?" someone asked.

"Oh, no. That's just Ms. Jones getting ready for cafeteria duty!"

Cake
(See also: Dessert)

212

Two students were put in charge of refreshments for the upcoming visit of a local artist to the school. The two pupils were beside themselves wondering what to serve.

Then they found out that the visitor was a sculptor, and that solved the problem.

They served marble cake!

213

"No, Jenkins, the cafeteria does not call it pound cake because you could pound a three-penny nail into solid concrete with it!"

214

"Oh, yes," the cafeteria manager told the teacher, "baked meat loaf and chocolate cake are the two finest dishes we prepare."

"Really," said the teacher, "which one is this I'm eating?"

Calculus

215

"Well," said the registrar to the student who was trying to decide which courses to take, "would you like to have calculus?"

"Gosh, no!" said the prospective pupil, "my father had them on his feet, and he had to go to a doctor to get them taken off!"

216

"I'm going to push someone from a ten-story building," the math teacher said as she created the problem. "I want to know how long will it take before he hits the ground. For this, we'll have to use calculus."

"Ten stories!" whispered one student to another. "I wouldn't be that calculus kid for anything!"

Camera

217

After her third trip to the store only to find that her photos had not yet been developed, the young girl turned to her friend and said, "I feel just like Snow White!"

"What do you mean?"

"Some day my PRINTS will come!"

218

"Unless you take me to the ball game on Saturday, I'm gonna tell Pa that you were driving the car without permission!" the little boy told his teenaged brother.

"Go ahead!" replied the older sibling. "Everybody knows what fibs you tell! The question is, will anyone believe you with your record?"

"Actually," the younger brother smiled, "the question is will Pa believe the photo I took of you in the car with YOUR Polaroid?"

Camp (See also: Summer Camp)

219

Letter from camp in the Why-Parents-Get-Gray Department:

"Dear Mom and Dad,

Just a note to let you know that after they sucked out the poison from the snake bite, my leg felt much better. They didn't kill the snake. His name is Bruce. I feed him every day. Can I keep him?"

220

When the foursome made camp for the night, one man stepped forward and addressed the rest.

"I have a bow and arrows, my hunting knife, and my skills as a woodsman," he said. "I will bring us dinner!" And with that he strode off to the north into the woods.

He returned about an hour and a half later with four huge venison steaks that were enjoyed by all, along with many comments about the hunting prowess of their friend.

The next morning, as they broke camp, another of the group spotted a man walking through the woods.

"Hi!" he said, "are you a camper around here, too?"

"No, I live nearby," said the stranger. "In fact, I run a little specialty butcher shop in the mall about a mile and a half north of here."

Cane

221

"Let's have a little lesson in economics," said the teacher. "Harris, suppose you went to the local supermarket and found that the price of sugar had risen to fifty dollars a pound?"

"Easy," replied Harris, "I'd start raising cane!"

222

When the teacher returned after a leg injury, he used a cane. Two of the more mischievous students in the class were quick to observe this.

"What you gonna do?" asked one. "You gonna steal his cane?"

"Naw," said the other, "I'm going to wait till he's at lunch, 'borrow' the cane, and take it down to the wood shop and saw off a quarter inch. He won't fall down, but I'm really going to enjoy watching him wonder why his limp is getting worse!"

Capacity

223

"I'm getting an A plus in all my subjects," one student told the new kid in class, "so I can help you with anything!"

"But," the new kid told a companion when the first child had left, "I just saw that kid's test paper, and he got an F."

"He's like a lot of people," commented the other. "He has a higher capacity for imagination than for achievement!"

224

"I don't care how long it takes you to learn this," said the teacher. "I have an amazing capacity for patience."

"That's good," remarked the student, "because I have an amazing capacity for ignorance!"

At the end of the school year, a boy appeared before the teacher's desk. He took five peeled bananas and shoved them into his mouth all at once. When the lad had finally swallowed, the teacher spoke.

"Besides showing a tremendous capacity for bananas, what was that all about?"

"School is almost out," said the boy, "and I didn't want you to forget me over the summer!"

Carnival/Circus

226

"What did you do yesterday?" one child asked a classmate.

"Went to the carnival at the mall . . . "

"I thought you didn't like carnivals."

"I don't," the youth replied, "but Dad was so impossible, I had to take him!"

227

"Nowadays," the teacher told the class, "most circuses and carnivals play only in auditoriums in major cities. The day of the sand-lot circus is over."

"That's terrible!" said one student. "If you're an average kid living out in the country, where are you going to run away TO?"

228

A Flea Circus was one of the attractions of the carnival side show.

"Wow, Dad!" said the child, "I wish we had something like that."

"Take a good look at Ruff when we get home," the father remarked. "We might not have a Flea Circus, but he certainly provides us with a Flea Surplus!"

Cars (See also: Automobiles)

229

The family took a trip to a nearby city with the specific intent of purchasing a family car. Once they arrived in the city, however, they found it all but impossible to find a parking space.

After they had circled one block for almost half an hour, one of the children spoke up.

"I have an idea," the child said. "Why don't we just buy one that's already parked!"

230

Dad took his teenaged son out on the road for a driving session.

The boy, exuberant about driving, shouted, "Out of the way! I own the road! I own the road!"

"Pull over to the side!" the father ordered. "I own the car! I own the car!"

231

The teacher claimed that her new car had a certain "lifetime quality" about it.

"Does that mean you'll be keeping it forever?" joked one colleague.

"No," replied the teacher, "just making monthly payments for eternity!"

Cash

232

"Oh, no!" exclaimed the teacher to his friend as they stood in line to pay for a purchase, "I left my credit cards at home! What am I going to do?"

"But," remarked the friend, "your purchase can't be more than two dollars. Why don't you just pay for it in cash?"

"What?" replied the educator. "And have the clerk wonder if my credit rating is bad?"

233

Then there was the teacher who paid cash for everything. It wasn't that he distrusted credit cards; he just loved to watch the clerks go crazy trying to handle actual money.

234

"Do you know that rich kid in my class?" asked the teacher. "Well, today we had a charity collection for the County Old Folks Home."

"Oh," asked a colleague, "did the kid give a large cash donation?"

"No," answered the teacher, "he tried to convince them to take me!"

Cats

235

As one teacher informed her class, we could all take a lesson from the cat. You won't find a cat crying over spilled milk, will you?

236

"Can you name three animals in the cat family?" asked the teacher.
"Sure," answered the student, "my cat, Dewdrop, and her two kittens!"

237

"Billy," Mother asked, "did you put lemonade in the cat's dish?"
"Yes, I did. How did you know?"
"I could tell. The cat was being a real sourpuss!"

Cause/Causes

238

The Town Hall was issuing permits to solicit for charity. A young man came up to the counter and asked for such a license.
"And, for what cause will you be soliciting?" asked the clerk.
"Cause?" the young man repeated. "What else? 'Cause I'm broke!"

239

"What were the causes of the Great Crash of 1929?" the social studies teacher asked the class.
"I'm not too sure," answered one student who had obviously not been paying attention, "but it was probably pilot error."

Cell

240

"I want to congratulate you," the science teacher told the student. "You got an A plus on this test on the cell. Usually, you get F's and D's; how do you account for this change?"

"Well," said the student, "my brother told me that if I didn't change my behavior, I'd end up in a cell, and since I don't intend to change, I wanted to see what it was gonna be like."

241

Two teachers got to fighting, and it became such a scuffle that they were both arrested and taken to the local jail.

When one of the two, a science teacher, was placed in confinement, he immediately complained that it was raining and the roof was leaking.

"After all," insisted the irate educator, "if you're going to arrest me for battery, the least you could do is place me in a dry cell!"

Cent (See also: Money)

242

"Did you hear about the poor skunk?" asked a student. "He didn't have a scent to his name!"

243

"Suppose I have a dollar," said the math teacher, "and I buy a candy bar for five cents and a comic book for ten cents. What do I have left?"

"Your fantasies," answered one student, "'cause you sure ain't living in today's economy!"

Chain

244

"Mister," the little boy said to the store clerk, "where do you keep the leashes for pets?"

"Sorry, Son," replied the man with a smile, "but we don't carry leashes."

"And why not?" the boy said indignantly. "My teacher told me this was a chain store!"

245

"Why do they keep moving that chain?" asked the exchange student at his first football game.

"They are trying to see who got a down," explained his host.

"They don't need a chain for that!" exclaimed the visitor. "They wanna know who got-a down, all they got to do is look! Those guys is laying all over the field!"

Charge
(See also: Credit/Credit Cards)

246

"So, you finally paid off your charge account," the teacher said to her colleague. "You must feel wonderful!"

"Not really," answered her friend. "It took me so long to pay it off, that now I'm tired of what I bought in the first place!"

247

Said the coach, "I want you to get in there and charge that line! Charge that line!"

"Sure thing, coach," said the burly player. "Do I charge them one at a time or give them a group rate?"

Chart

248

The kindergarten tot strode into a department store one day and asked a clerk where the candy department was.

"See for yourself," the clerk said pointing to a chart on which was listed a directory of the store.

"They were right," said the youngster in amazement. "If you can't read, you ain't going nowhere!"

249

"I know you chart the grades of your students," said a parent to the teacher. "I bet Junior's looks like climbing Mt. Everest!"

"Actually," remarked the educator, "it's more like skiing a long and winding trail down the other side!"

Cheating

250

"How can you say that I cheated by copying my story from a magazine?" asked the student.

"Let me put it this way," said the teacher, "not many student authors put a phrase in the middle of their stories such as '. . . continued in next month's issue'!"

251

"I'm worried about Harry; he didn't study for the English tests," one student told another.

"How do you know that he didn't study?"

"Because I got an F on the test, and I copied every answer HE wrote!"

Chemistry

252

A chemistry student named Moore,
Was discovered quite dead on the floor;
What he'd drunk, don't you know,
Was not old H_2O
But a glass of H_2SO_4!

253

A student walked down the hall of school and eyes turned everywhere. Her hair stood up in wild tufts of orange, green, lavender, and other colors that defied description. Several fellow students gawked openly.

"Member of a rock band?" one student queried.

"No," answered a nearby teacher, "member of a group whose chemistry experiment exploded!"

254

Two chemistry teachers were having lunch.

"Please pass the sugar," said one.

"The what?"

"The sugar . . . "

"What?"

"Please pass the $C_{12}H_{22}O_{11}$ . . ."

"Why didn't you say so in the first place!"

Children

255

"Children provide the light in your life," the lecturer said.

"Of course," whispered one parent in the audience, "you can never get them to turn off the lights when they leave the room!"

256

"I like children a lot better than I like older people," remarked the teacher.

"Oh," said his colleague, "and why is that?"

"In all my years of teaching, not one child has ever bored me with photos of his grandparents!"

257

One mother discovered the only way to keep her two-year-old's clothing absolutely clean. She keeps the clothing in a drawer and lets the kid run around in his underwear!

258

"My child is seven," said one mother to another, "and he has nothing but questions!"

"Wait until he's seventeen," said her friend, "and he'll have all the answers!"

259

"Charlene!" said Father, "How dare you kick your little brother in the stomach!"

"I wouldn't have done it, Daddy," sobbed the repentant Charlene, "if he hadn't turned around so quick!"

260

When I got married, I knew that family life would be a wonderful adventure filled with bright and happy days, lovable kids, and a Mom and Dad who never argued and always had enough money to afford all the little extras of life . . .

. . . then we had children!

Children and Relatives

261

Five-year-old Junior took a screwdriver and proceeded to carve the word "CAT" into the surface of the brand new teakwood dining room table.

"Oh, how wonderful," said his grandparents as they looked on, "he can spell!!!"

262

"Honey," said Uncle Paul to his niece, "why did you throw water at Aunt Gina and me like that? We're all wet!"

"Because," said the child, "I heard Daddy tell Mommy that you two were the biggest spongers in the world, and I wanted to see you swell up!"

Children and School

263

"That Bobby Smith is the worst-behaved kid in the school," said the principal at the PTA meeting. "Where are his parents?"

"Over there," answered a teacher, "the ones wearing the Halloween masks . . . "

264

Said the principal to the student body: "I want you to know that you can bring in your parents at any time. We are here, in school, for you, *in loco parentis.*"

Whispered one student: "I can't. They are gone, on vacation, for themselves, *by loco-motive*!"

Choices

265

"Isn't Billy wonderful?" said the little girl as she picked herself up from the floor and brushed herself off.

"But he just pushed you down!" remarked a classmate.

"Yes," she answered starry-eyed, "and of all the kids in class, he picked me!"

266

"When you enter the business world," said the teacher to the class, "you may choose to work hard and succeed, or you may choose to not work and fail . . . "

"Personally," whispered one student to another, "I'm going to choose a job where my father owns the business!"

Christmas

267

"And what," asked the teacher, "does your father say once the Christmas tree has been put up?"

"He says," answered the child, "if that dog sniffs the tree ONE MORE TIME . . . "

268

"I never seem to have enough money at Christmas time," complained one teacher.

"Why don't you join a Christmas Club," suggested another.

"I thought of it, but you know how I hate going to meetings."

269

Feeling certain that the beard and make-up would fool the children, the uncle of one of the kindergarten students played Santa Claus at the Christmas party. Even when his own nephew got on his lap, the man was confident the child had not recognized him.

"And is there anything else you want for Christmas?" said the erstwhile Santa when the lad had finished his list.

"Just one thing," the boy added. "When you see my Dad, Uncle Bernie, make sure you tell HIM!"

Citizenship

270

Following the ceremony, the naturalized citizen all but ran home.

"My wife! My wife!" he cried as he burst through the door of their apartment. "Finally, I am an American, just like you!"

"How wonderful! I've been waiting so long," said his wife as she tossed a dish towel at him. "Now, after you wash and dry the dishes, come into the living room, because there's some vacuuming to be done!"

271

"I am afraid," said the teacher to the unruly child, "that I am going to have to inform your parents of your poor citizenship."

"Give me a break," said the student. "How could I vote? I didn't even know you was holding an election!"

Classroom

272

"Young man," the teacher said to the student, "I'll have you know that I have spent seven years in this classroom!"

"Wow!" responded the child, "I bet you got to go to the bathroom pretty bad by now!"

273

"What's the biggest classroom you've ever been in?" the child wondered.

Answered the teacher, "The one I entered when I stepped through my high school diploma."

Cleanliness

274

"We must straighten up this room," said the teacher.

"You know," a student remarked to a friend, "until she mentioned it, I wasn't aware that the floor was slanted."

275

Asked the teacher, "Who can tell me what cleanliness is next to?"

Answered one child, "Impossible!"

Clergy

276

"Did you enjoy the service?" the preacher asked the visitor to the church.

"Oh, yes," the visitor replied. "Wherever I go in this world, it's always pleasant to see a familiar faith."

277

After service, the minister walked up to one of the deacons.

"How would you characterize the response when my sermon was over?" asked the clergyman.

Answered the deacon, "The great awakening!"

Clothing

278

The kindergarten child was having difficulty pulling on her boots, and the teacher went to help.

"The reason you're having trouble," the teacher told the child, "is that you're trying to put the boots on the wrong feet."

"No, I'm not!" protested the small student. "These are my boots; and these are MY feet!"

279

"Do children outgrow clothing quickly?" the new mother asked.

"Do they ever!" replied a veteran parent. "Yesterday, my son put on his brand-new pants, and by the time he'd buttoned the waist, the cuffs were an inch too short!"

280

"Henry does have a lot of stylish clothes," a teacher remarked about a well-dressed colleague.

"They do say that 'clothes make the man,'" commented another.

"In Henry's case," continued the first, "they also make a substantial unpaid balance on his credit card!"

Coach

281

The principal received a panicked phone call from a senior in the school that his car had broken down; he couldn't find anyone at home; would the principal please help.

In the middle of a torrential downpour, the principal arrived and was quickly soaked to the skin as he looked under the hood and corrected the difficulty.

"It was just a loose connection," said the dripping educator. "You can go now."

"This means a lot to me," said the student. "I was taking the coach home; he's asleep in the back seat, and I sure wouldn't want him to be disturbed!"

282

"I have faced life and death; prosperity and poverty; pleasure and pain; the highest mountain peaks and the lowest valleys," she said.

"Were you fighting in the armed service?" he asked.

"What armed service?" she replied. "I'm talking about coaching the school's field hockey team during the championship game!"

Coffee

283

The principal stumbled into the office, grabbed her mail from the secretary's desk, and just stood there, staring into space, with an expression of pain and bewilderment on her face.

"A personal tragedy?" a teacher asked the secretary.

"I'll say," was the reply. "She just found out that the coffee machine is broken and can't be repaired until this afternoon!"

284

The teacher was known for never being without a cup of coffee. Therefore, when it became known that his doctor had advised him to cut down considerably, everyone watched with anticipation.

"You're allowed only ONE cup during the school day?" marveled a friend.

"That's right," said the teacher. "Here, help me unpack this two-quart Pyrex beaker . . . "

College

285

"So, you have a boy in college. What do you think he'll be when he gets out?"

"The way he's going," replied the parent, "about 35 to 40."

286

"Yes," said one young man, "I fondly remember the days I spent in college . . . they were a Tuesday and a Wednesday, I believe."

287

"You have two children in college; has it really improved their intelligence?"

"I'll say! You should see the innovative ways they have developed of writing home for money!"

Computers

288

"I'm a little worried about that master computer the school system just installed. It keeps sending out the same message over and over . . . "

"What message is that?"

"*Cogito Ergo Sum!*"

289

I won't say that the computers we're using in school are old, but each one of them came with an abacus as a back-up!

290

"I think we're putting too much of a demand on our computers."

"What makes you say that?"

"The repair people just ran a diagnostic, and the machines have ulcers!"

Conferences

291

Mamchak's Law of Educational Conferences: Any given conference resolves down to the level of the least emotionally stable person in the group.

292

"Let me see," mumbled the teacher as she checked out the contents of the paper bag before her, "cassette recorder, telephone number of my lawyer, ammonia capsules, box of Kleenex . . . "

"What is she doing?" asked a colleague.

"Getting ready for a parental conference . . . "

293

Teacher's note to a rambunctious student:

"Dear Murray,

You are cordially invited to a conference to be held this afternoon between your mother and me. Of course, you don't have to come if you don't want to, but if you intend on ever getting through a school day without detention at the end of it or eating another meal at home, I suggest that you attend!"

Conscience

294

A conscience is a bothersome thing. It lets us know when we've done wrong and will not let us rest until we've set things right; it steers us from streets that are dark and slippery and suggests paths that might be harder but certainly have an abundance of light; it will not let us sleep away the night unless we have put the day to rest.

Yes, a conscience is a bothersome thing. No wonder so many people try to kill it early on.

295

"I was going to tell you that I lost my homework," said the student, "but my conscience won't let me lie. I didn't do it."

"William," the teacher stated gently, "because I admire your conscience, I'm not going to punish you!"

"Wow!" the child exclaimed, "while we're both admiring my conscience, then, could we discuss the unknown culprit who put a tack on your chair and soaped up your car windows?"

Conservation

296

"What is meant by conservation of energy?" asked the teacher.

Answered the student, "When my Father makes ME take out the garbage!"

297

"We should all practice good conservation methods," said the teacher. "We should never cut down a tree without planting a tree."

"Sir," remarked a student, "I wish you would remember that principle when it comes to failing this student . . . "

Convention

298

Is it true that at the Convention of Teachers of Mathematics, the banquet was served on multiplication tables?

299

Recently, our school system held a convention of all educators who have always agreed with the actions of the Board of Education.
    It was held in the janitor's broom closet.

Cooking
(See also: Cafeteria; Home Ec)

300

Old proverb often quoted by my grandmother: God sends the food, but the Devil sends the cooks!

301

"You look as if you're enjoying that book."
    "I am! It has beatings and whippings and a lot of stirring material."
    "Really! What's the title?"
    "100 Ways to Prepare Eggs."

Cost of Living

302

"Two can live as cheaply as one," the prospective bride told her father.
    "Granted," said her parent, "but only if one doesn't eat!"

303

I used to worry about the cost of living, but then I got a credit card. Now, I get a real charge out of it!

Courage

304

"My uncle was a man who stood up for his convictions," stated a student in social studies class.

"Really?"

"Absolutely! The bailiff said, 'All rise!' and the judge sentenced him to a year at hard labor."

305

"I'm so brave," said the student, "that I don't know the meaning of the word FEAR!"

"Oh, yeah!" roared a student at least a foot and a half taller.

"Of course," continued the first, "I do know the meaning of the word STUPID . . . "

306

"Who can give me an example of 'historic courage'?" asked the teacher.

"I can," answered a student. "The day I went into the social studies class without my project!"

Court

307

"Son," intoned the Juvenile Court judge, "you've been found guilty twice before. Would you at least say that you were sorry for what you've done?"

"Oh, no, Your Honor," said the youthful offender. "My teacher told me that nobody should apologize for their convictions!"

308

"I've been reading this book about the Old West," said the student, "and it tells about this judge they discovered taking bribes for his verdicts in court."

"Really?" the teacher commented. "Did they suspend him?"

"I'll say! They hung him from a tree!"

"I thought you told me that your mother could not come to school yesterday because she had to go to court," said the teacher, "yet when I called her this morning, she said she was out exercising yesterday afternoon!"

"Well," replied the student, "when I said 'court' I assumed you would understand that I meant 'tennis' and not 'legal'!"

Courtesy

310

"Yes, that Roberts boy is a bit troublesome, but he's so courteous and polite. Why, look at this note he wrote me; it begins, 'Dear Sir . . . '"

"Look again," said a colleague, "he spelled 'Sir,' C-U-R!"

311

Mother was late coming home at dinner time, and she arrived to find her brood seated and eating.

"Couldn't you have waited for me?" she asked. "Is there no courtesy left?"

"I doubt it, Mom," said one youngster. "We pretty near ate everything on the table."

Coward

312

"Who in here is a coward?" yelled the school bully.

"I am," replied one small boy, whom the bully then proceeded to swing at with all his might. The little lad sidestepped, however, and caught the bully with a punch that sent him sprawling.

"Hey!" said the bully as he covered his black eye, "I thought you were a coward!"

"Coward?" the little boy blinked. "I thought you said HOWARD!!!"

313

Sign in a Teachers' Lounge: "In Front of a Classroom, There Can Be No Cowards!"

SIMON & SCHUSTER

Credit Card Payment Authorization Form

DEAR CUSTOMER:

FOR YOUR CONVENIENCE, WE ACCEPT VISA, MASTERCARD, AND
AMERICAN EXPRESS. PLEASE INDICATE METHOD OF PAYMENT BELOW:

VISA/MASTERCARD

AMERICAN EXPRESS

INVOICE # ....

AMOUNT $ ....   SIGNATURE _____

EXP. DATE
MONTH   YEAR

PLEASE RETURN THIS FORM, WITH YOUR INVOICE
OR STATEMENT, IN THE ENVELOPE PROVIDED.   THANK YOU.

DATE _____

8.1/2487A

Credit/Credit Card

314

"Son," said the frustrated father, "you've graduated from college, and you're still living at home, and that's all right, but you have to stop asking me for money! This is it! No more money from me, got it?"

"Sure, Dad," replied his son. "In that case, could I use your credit card tonight?"

315

"Come on, Mom," said the daughter. "When you were starting out at the bottom, didn't anybody give you credit?"

"Yes," said the girl's mother, "when I was at the bottom several companies gave me credit, and it helped me dig myself into an even deeper hole!"

Criticism

316

It is an easy task to escape the criticism of mankind. All you have to do is never say anything; never do anything; and, above all, never be anything.

317

"I'm sorry to tell you, Sir," said the guidance counselor to the parent, "but the aptitude tests your son took show that he is literally qualified to do absolutely NOTHING in life."

"Excellent!" replied the boy's father. "He'll become a social critic!"

318

"What do I do if somebody asks me about something I absolutely know nothing about?"

"Do what everyone else does."

"Which is?"

"When you know nothing—criticize!"

Crossword

319

The obviously irate teacher marched into the principal's office and demanded, "Do you like word puzzles?"

"Yes," said the startled administrator, "I do!"

"Good!" roared the teacher, "because I have several cross words for you!"

320

The teacher who passed away was an ardent crossword enthusiast. One of his colleagues asked, "Where is he going to be buried?"

"You know how he was," answered a fellow teacher. "Probably six down and two across!"

Crying (See also: Sorrow)

321

"Mrs. Sierra," the first-grader asked her teacher, "why are you so sad?"

"Oh, I'm all right, Sweetheart," answered the teacher. "It's just that I'm having a little trouble paying all my bills."

The little girl winked knowingly.

"Try crying!" the child said. "It works for me every time!"

322

"Buddy," said the teacher who discovered the distraught youngster, "why are you crying like this?"

"Oh, I'm OK," said the child as he straightened up and wiped clear his eyes. "It's just that I failed the math test because I didn't study, and I'm practicing for tonight, when I have to show the paper to my father!"

Culture

323

During the visit to the opera, mother and father carefully explained everything that happened and even helped little Michelle follow along in the libretto.

"Which did you like best," the parents asked later that night, "the arias or the libretto or the choral work?"

"Naw!" said the little girl, "what I really liked was when that guy who screamed a lot stuck the fat lady with the sword!"

324

Then there was the bacteria who lived in the science lab. He was extremely concerned about the growth of culture.

325

"When we got there," the girl told her mother, "we were served paté on squares of toast. Paté! I'd call that culture!"

"Phooey!" commented her little brother, "I'd call it liverwurst!"

Current Affairs (See also: Press, The)

326

"You don't understand," moaned the teacher. "When I said we were going to study current affairs, I did NOT mean that we were going to concentrate solely on the lives of Hollywood stars!"

327

"You see," the social studies teacher told the class, "studying current affairs by having you bring in clippings from the newspaper is a very good way of letting you know about what's going on in the world."

Whispered one student, "It's also a good way of letting you know what's going on in the living room when Mom or Dad find that half the front page has been cut out before they got a chance to read it!"

Curriculum

328

"Do you have a good curriculum?" the visitor to the school asked a student.

"I'll say!" replied the child. "Last year, they won almost every game!"

329

"Our curriculum," the principal told the parents who had come to register their child, "reflects the needs of the average citizen in today's society."

"You mean," they said, "that you actually have a course on avoiding the collection companies?"

330

"What do you mean, our curriculum needs updating?" stated one educator. "Our curriculum is totally up to date!"

"OK, OK!" said the other teacher on the committee, "Let's just get rid of the course on Techniques of Jousting . . . "

D

Dairy

331

During the field trip to the dairy farm, one child stood looking at the cows, obviously fascinated.

"Anything you'd like to know?" inquired the friendly dairyman.

"Yeah," said the child, "since they ain't labeled, how do you know which one of them things gives chocolate milk?"

332

"And this," said the farmer pointing to a large, churning vat, "is cottage cheese."

"What did he say?" asked one youngster on the tour.

Answered another child, "He said it's the plaster stuff they make cheesy little houses out of!"

333

As the children on the tour had milk and cookies, the dairy farmer was complaining to the teacher.

"The price of milk is so low," he said, "that it's hardly worth milking the cows. I'm really thinking of quitting."

Then a smile lighted his face.

"Say," he said to the teacher, "I don't suppose that you could teach those cows to do something BESIDES give milk?"

Dances/Dancing

334

"I have only two things holding me back from being a really great dancer," said the student.

"What's that?" asked a friend.

Said the disgruntled youth, "One is my right foot, and the other is my left!"

335

"I think I liked it better in my day," remarked an older teacher at the school dance. "At least we knew who our date was. These kids can dance all night and never see the person they came with!"

Danger

336

"I think our teacher must really love danger," said one student.

"Why do you say that?"

"She eats cafeteria food every day!"

337

"I live in constant danger," said the teacher. "Have you seen my take-home pay after deductions?"

338

"There is one comfort in all this," said the teacher to her friend as they stood in line at the bank. "With what I've managed to save, I'm in no danger of anyone trying to take it away from me!"

Dare

339

"I dare you to hit me!" prodded the bully. "I dare you!"

Whereupon the taunted youth flattened the other.

The bully looked up from the ground and said, "Don't you think you're a little too old to be provoked that easily?"

340

"Hey, Billy," called the student, "dare me to put a tack on the teacher's chair! Go ahead, dare me to do it!"

"Why do you want me to do that?"

"'Cause," answered the first child, "I really want to, but I don't think I should unless I have SOMEBODY to blame it on!"

Dating

341

"What's my blind date like?" the girl asked her friend.

"Let me put it this way," was the response. "Leave your glasses at home, and he'll look almost normal!"

342

"Harry's dating record," said one student, "is a lot like the books of classical poetry in our school library—UNCIRCULATED!"

343

"He dumped you after one date," said the student to her friend, "and you're not furious with him?"

"Well," answered the friend, "it's just that he told me that our date was so fantastic, that he couldn't take a chance on spoiling the memory by asking me out on another . . . "

344

A group of teenaged boys were caught talking about dating during math class.

"What does 'dating' have to do with math?" asked the teacher.

"Well," said one boy, "if you want to figure out the curves, you'd better know the right angles!"

Daughters

345

There is no daughter, anywhere, who does not marry a man who is totally inferior to her in breeding, demeanor, and mental ability—ask any father!

346

"Oh, and what does your daughter do?" asked a business colleague.
Answered the parent, "Her hair . . . "

347

Having a teenaged daughter is wonderful; just don't go into her room unless you've had a recent booster shot for tetanus.

Dawn

348

"Look, there's the sun!" said Father, who had insisted that his young child waken early to view the dawn.
"Wow," said his offspring, "You didn't tell me it came on slow; I thought you just switched it on!"

349

The two brothers stood overlooking the ocean at dawn.
As the first crimson light broke from the horizon, the older boy intoned, "Rise, O Sun; rise up from the sea!"
"Wow!" said his younger brother pointing to the orange fireball, "Will you teach me how to do THAT?"

Death

350

"What a beautiful home!" remarked the guest. "Do you intend to live in it forever?"
"Oh, no," replied the host, "only until I die."

"Who was it who said, 'You can't take it with you'?"
"It had to be either the IRS or the guy who sells coffins!"

352

"When he died," the teacher asked her friend, "did he leave a great deal?"
The other teacher looked at her friend in bewilderment and said, "Everything he had!"

Deception

353

"It was Sir Walter Scott," explained the teacher, "who wrote, 'Oh, what a tangled web we weave, when first we practice to deceive.'"
"Yes," responded one student, "but didn't you also teach us that 'practice makes perfect'?"

354

The teacher called Timmy's home, and it was obviously the boy who answered the phone. The teacher asked to speak to the lad's mother.
"She . . . er . . . she ain't home!" stammered the boy.
"Timmy," said the teacher, "are you sure your mother isn't there?"
"No! Really! Honest! Er . . . she's gone!"
At that, a woman's voice sounded from the background, "Timmy, who's that on the phone?"
"Fooled you, didn't I?" snapped the boy. "That wasn't her either! Now, would you like to hear me do an imitation of my father?"

Dedication

355

Every day for the last two weeks, the child had been sent to the principal's office for trying to place a tack on the teacher's chair.
"That's some kid!" remarked the principal.
"You don't mean you approve of that kind of behavior?"
"Of course not!" answered the administrator, "but you really do have to admire this student's dedication to a cause!"

The school was dismissed early, and most of the students disappeared in a flash—all except one boy who remained at his desk, quietly straightening up, as the others poured from the room.

"Staying after the others have gone, just to clean your desk," remarked the teacher. "I'd call that dedication!"

"Waiting until all the other kids have gone home," returned the student. "I'd call that ripping your pants and not wanting anyone to see you!"

Degrees

357

Then there was the graduate student who thought that he was hot stuff, just because he had gone up a couple degrees!

358

The two men began arguing on the street, and it soon began to escalate. Finally, one man stepped back and open-handedly slapped the other.

Said the man, "Take that, Sir! Ph.D.; Harvard; '93!"

Whereupon the other fellow proceeded to lay him out with full-fisted fury!

"And you take that!" said the one still standing. "Right uppercut; South Side Chicago; since I was a kid!"

359

"Really, Madam," stated the conceited counselor, "I know what's best for your child. I have a Ph.D.!"

"Oh, yeah!" returned the mother, "Well, I just happened to get my M.O.M. along with my M.A., and you don't know beans about kids!"

Dentist

360

"I learned to be a dentist in the army."

"Dentistry in the army? I suppose you were a member of the drill team . . ."

"The parent who organized the school fund-raising dinner, is he a dentist?"

"Why, yes, how did you know?"

"He's charging $200 a plate and wants to know if you want an upper or a lower . . . "

362

"These are the worst teeth I've seen in a long time," the school dentist told the student.

"Oh, yeah!" replied the child. "You should see my Dad's. His are so bad, he had to take them out at night and put them in a glass of water!"

Depression
(See also: Blues)

363

"Come on," said the encouraging colleague, "don't be depressed. After all, you haven't reached bottom yet!"

"Of course not," answered the other teacher. "But I'll get there if I continue climbing upward!"

364

Are we living in a depression? Let me put it this way, I couldn't make ends meet if I were a Siamese twin!

365

"Some place on this planet," said the teacher, "there is a button, which, if pushed, could start World War III and unleash a nuclear holocaust on the world!"

"Then people are a lot like that button," commented one student. "The world is always a better place to live in when you're not depressed!"

Desk

366

"Is that school system financially depressed?"

"I'll say! It's so bad off, the teacher's desk consists of two orange crates and an ironing board!"

367

"Johnson!" roared the teacher. "The inside of your desk is jammed with candy wrappers, old test papers, and chewed bubble gum! What do you have to say for yourself?"

"It's really your fault, Sir," replied the youth. "If you hadn't been so strict about throwing junk on the floor, this never would have happened!"

368

Did you know that in the Dairy College, all the desks come with three-legged stools?

Detention

369

Then there was the kid who served so much detention that he didn't graduate—he retired!

370

The teacher forgot that he had assigned a student detention for that afternoon, and at the end of the school day, he went home. Around suppertime, he suddenly remembered, and on an impulse that just would not go away, he returned to the school, got the night watchman to let him in, and went to his room.

There in the dark sat the student whom he had assigned detention.

"Gosh," said the child with a sigh, "I've served detention with other teachers, but you are REALLY tough!"

371

There was a kid in our school who was so bad, that in order to assign him detention, the teachers had to take a number!

Deterrent

372

The principal arrived to find the walls of the school covered with soap suds. The bubbles were dripping from every surface. Immediately, the administrator called the custodian.

"What is the meaning of this?" asked the principal. "Didn't I tell you just yesterday that we had to find a deterrent for all the writing on the walls?"

"Deterrent?" stated the custodian blankly. "I thought you said DETERGENT!"

373

"You have amazing discipline in your class," a younger teacher told an elder colleague. "How do you attain it?"

"Simple," said the educator. "If a kid is REALLY acting out and giving me a hard time, then just before recess I call him up to my desk and in the loudest possible voice, I thank him for suggesting tonight's homework and for volunteering to come to my house on Saturday to polish my car.

"It's the best deterrent I've ever discovered!"

Diet/Dieting

374

"The second day you're on a diet is always easier than the first," remarked one teacher.

"Of course," countered another, "by the second day, you've abandoned the whole thing and are eating whatever you like again!"

375

"Has the diet helped you lose weight?"

"Oh, yes! I used to gain a pound a week. Now, I only gain ten ounces!"

376

One teacher lauded the diet plan where you have a specially constructed "milk shake" for breakfast and lunch and suggested to a colleague that he try it.

"No success," the teacher reported. "I got the powder and made the milk shakes, and they tasted fine. I even had one after my breakfast, one after my lunch, one with my dinner, and two or three over the course of the evening, and I STILL gained weight!"

Digging
(See also: Excavations)

377

"If you think I'm thin," the boy told the teacher, "you should see my brother."

"He's thinner than you?"

"Let me put it this way," said the lad, "my brother once lay down in the middle of an open field and three dogs tried to bury him!"

378

"The guy who sold me the horse said that it was a race horse," the teacher told his friend, "but I'm not so sure."

"Why is that?"

"Every time I ride him, he keeps looking around, as if he can't figure out where the plow is!"

Diploma

379

"Remember," said the graduation speaker, "that with this diploma comes the future; with this diploma, the future is yours."

At which, one student whispered to another, "Is she threatening us?"

380

"This is a photo of my son-in-law, 'Diploma' Jones," said the teacher.

"What an unusual name."

"Actually, his name is Harold. I just call him 'Diploma' because my daughter got him at college . . . "

"I have my diploma now!" exalted the graduate. "I'm free! No more having to be in class every minute; no more threats from the teachers; no more people telling me what to do!"

"Son," the boy's mother interrupted, "there was a call for you from the factory. They said to report at nine on Monday morning, make certain you bring your tools, and be on time or you'll be docked an hour's wage!"

Diplomacy

382

Diplomacy is the saying of the worst possible things in the best possible way!

383

"He missed his calling by being a teacher," said one educator.
"Why is that?"
"Because, he just convinced his wife that diamond jewelry detracts from the natural sparkle of her teeth. . . . That guy should have been a diplomat!"

384

"What do we call someone," asked the teacher, "who lies down on the job?"

"Someone who lies, down on the job???" mused one youth. "I know, a DIPLOMAT!"

Discipline

385

Achieving good discipline is like being a groundskeeper at a football stadium—you have to draw the line somewhere.

386

"Son," said the father to the boy he was about to punish, "this is going to hurt me just as much as it hurts you . . . "

"In that case, Dad," commented the lad, "make sure you take it easy on me; you know how I hate to see you suffer!"

387

A student was being interviewed by the guidance counselor, who asked, "Do you have any trouble with discipline?"

"Oh, no!" said the pupil. "I can handle discipline just fine."

Then the student added in a whisper, "It's controlling the behavior that brings ON the discipline—that's my problem!"

Discussion

388

Two students were rolling on the ground, pummeling each other and raising a cloud of dust, when a teacher walked by, saw the commotion, and took both offenders to the principal's office.

"Wow!" said one child to the other combatant, "things are pretty bad when you can't even have a private discussion without some teacher interfering!"

389

"You won't let me use my book during a test," fumed the student to the teacher, "you won't excuse me from doing homework; you won't let me daydream out the window during class. Look, if we can't discuss the basic issues, how are we ever going to resolve my report card grades?"

Divorce

390

"Do you realize that one out of two marriages ends in divorce?" asked the sociology professor.

"Yeah," sighed a disgruntled student, "and that's only because the other couple is too busy fighting to file papers!"

391

"Name one benefit that belongs to married people alone," asked the teacher.

Answered the student, "Divorce!"

Doctor

392

"Suppose you went to a doctor with a case of loss of memory," mused one student, "would the doctor make you pay BEFORE the treatment?"

393

"When my doctor told me that I had to do more exercise," explained the teacher, "I asked for a second opinion."

"What happened?"

"He made me come back the next day, and he told me again!"

394

Does it seem rather contradictory that doctors will tell you to avoid all stress just BEFORE they hand you their bill?

395

"Son," said the school doctor as he looked at the student's back, "you have a case of the measles!"

"Look again, Doc!" said the boy. "I sit in front of a very immature student with a red ball-point pen!"

Double Negative

396

Is it true that using a double negative is a No-No?

397

"I don't want to take no test!" exclaimed the student.

"'I don't want to take ANY test,'" corrected the teacher.

"Well," replied the student, "if neither of us wants to take the blasted thing, we ain't got no reason to fight!"

Drink/Drinking

398

The little girl took an empty bottle and filled it with a mixture of lemonade, pickle juice, and Tabasco sauce.

"Why did you do that?" asked her friend.

"My teacher is coming over to talk to Mom this afternoon," said the student, "and you know how mothers always offer a guest something to drink . . . "

399

The teacher came upon a sobbing first-grader who was sitting and holding a full can of soft drink.

"What's the matter?"

"Teacher told us about all the problems that drinking can cause, but I can't figure out how to get this soda inside me WITHOUT drinking it!"

Driver's Education

400

Said the student to the driver's ed teacher, "I'm sorry I lost control of the car, and you had to take over."

"That's all right," sighed the teacher, "I rather enjoyed driving on the correct side of the road for a while."

401

"Mom!" said the student, "Today in driver's ed, the teacher said that I was like lightning!"

"You didn't drive fast, did you?"

"Better than that! I hit a tree!"

402

Student to driver's ed teacher: "Sure, he had the right of way, but I'm left-handed!"

Drop-out

403

"How sad that he dropped out of school," commented a teacher. "He just couldn't see the handwriting on the wall, eh?"

"Oh, he could see it," answered the other. "The problem was that he couldn't read it!"

404

"That student is so weird," commented one teacher, "that I'm afraid he may become a drop-out."

"I don't think there's any danger of that," remarked his colleague. "First, he has to drop IN!"

Drugs

405

"Shhhh!" said one tyke as he and a friend passed the bathroom door, "I heard Mom tell Dad that there are sleeping pills in there, and I don't want to wake them up!"

406

"This common drug," continued the teacher, "begins with an 'A' and your parents probably take it to get rid of their headaches. Who can tell me?"

"Gosh," whispered one child to another, "I didn't know 'Vacation' started with an 'A'."

Dull

407

"In all my years as a principal," the educator continued, "I have never known a dull moment!"

"Of course not," whispered a teacher in the audience, "the dull moments were reserved for those of us who had to listen to him!"

408

Then there was the teacher who was so dull, light wouldn't reflect off his bald head!

409

"Is he a dull speaker?" one teacher asked as the lecturer climbed to the stage.

"Let me put it this way, his speeches are donated to the Society for the Preservation of the Quickly Forgotten!"

Duties (See also: Responsibilities)

410

The new teacher came into the classroom to find it an absolute mess. She singled out one lad and called him to her desk.

"What are your duties around here?" she asked.

"For the most part," he answered, " . . . avoided!"

411

"You have a right to be taught," said the teacher, "but you have the corresponding duty to learn. Now, what does that mean for us in this class?"

Answered one student, "A lot of lectures on responsibilities, huh?"

412

"You mean everybody in class is going to pass the course except me?" stated the student.

"That's right."

"Then you gotta pass me! You got a duty to keep up appearances, and you wouldn't want a failure on YOUR record, would you?"

Eagle

413

The coach was trying hard to inspire the team for the second half.

"Like our mascot, the eagle," said the coach, "we will soar high, because we own the sky; we own the sky!"

"Maybe we own the sky," commented one weary player, "but the other team owns the field, and right now they're crushing us into it, bit by bit!"

414

Mother to child: "I don't care how much you cry, I cannot go out and get you a mummified eagle's talon at 2 A.M. of the night before your science project is due!"

Ear/Earring

415

"Tell me," said the long-winded guest, "have you ever had your ears pierced?"

"No," remarked the tired host, "but I'm having them bored . . . "

"Thank you all!" said the art teacher when her class threw her a surprise birthday party. "This was as surprising as hearing Vincent Van Gogh summoned to the office because he's left something in lost and found!"

Eccentric/Eccentricity

417

"You know," remarked one teacher, "I have observed that most teachers who make education their career tend to grow a bit eccentric."

"Really?" said his colleague as he walked three times around his chair, stamped his left foot twice, and sat down. "I hadn't noticed."

418

"Why does Ms. Johnson talk so much?" the child asked her mother about one of her teachers.

"It's just eccentricity," answered the mother.

The next afternoon the child came running into the house.

"It is not eccentricity!" she informed her mother. "I switched off the eccentricity in the room, and Ms. Johnson still kept talking like she was gonna run out of words!"

419

After wearing black ties for four years, the principal showed up with a red and yellow striped model.

"I knew it!" exclaimed the school secretary. "It's just a matter of time before the eccentricity starts!"

Ecology

420

"What can I do to save our trees?" the ecologist asked the class.

"I know," answered one student. "Shoot every beaver you see!"

"Moms just don't understand science," bemoaned one student.

"Why do you say that?"

"Because my Mom refuses to believe that my room has an ecosystem of its own, and THAT'S why there's something growing in one of the corners!"

Economics/The Economy

422

"I have made a solemn vow," the teacher stated, "that from now on, I am going to live within my income . . . even if I have to borrow a couple thousand to do it!"

423

"How many does it take," asked the teacher, "to make a million?"

"Only one," answered the small student, "but he or she has to work VERY hard!"

424

If MONEY can't buy happiness;
Then I suggest a switch,
I'll gladly take the chance to be
Some guy who's sad and rich!

425

"Do you understand the Law of Supply and Demand?" asked the teacher.

"Sure," said the class bully. "I demand that you supply me with a passing grade or my father will beat you up!"

426

Administrations come and go;
Some dull; some bright to see;
And in the middle of it all
Sits our economy;
Each party speaks in glowing terms
Of plans and growth and buffers;
Which means, hold on to your wallets, folks;
We're REALLY going to suffer!

Education

427

Education is really a simple matter; just determine to learn more tomorrow than you did today, and you'll do fine!

428

Two chameleons were sitting on a limb that overlooked the window of a house. Inside the house, a woman pressed a button on a spray can, and fourteen flies fell dead to the floor.

"And that," stated the elder lizard, "is what an education will do for you!"

429

Education and ignorance always go hand in hand; the more we learn, the more we find out how truly ignorant we are!

430

If education gets any more expensive, there are going to be a lot of people who will be majoring in ignorance!

431

In education, we must believe that every individual has a spark of intelligence; a spark of enthusiasm; a spark of wonder. Our job as educators is to be ignition specialists!

432

Trying to acquire an education on your own is like trying to teach your children to be thrifty by getting them a credit card!

Effort

433

Said the visitor to the child in school: "Could you direct me to the principal's office?"

Answered the child: "Yes, I could . . . but I don't want to make the effort!"

"He says he's found a foolproof way to never fail . . . "
"He has; he never tries to succeed!"

The teacher discovered the student cheating. He had written answers on the bottom of his shoe, on his hand, on his pants, and on several slips of paper hidden throughout the room.

"OK," said the student, "so I flunk the test, but when you recall this incident, please remember the massive effort I put into it!"

Elder

Then there was the student who had been kept back so often, the system considered him an "elder" of the school!

"You must respect your elders," a mother told her first-grader.
"What's an 'elder?'" asked the small student.
"Anyone who's older than you . . . "
"That's impossible!" stormed the child. "NOBODY can respect an eighth-grader!"

Eloquence

The restaurant was packed, but when the foursome entered, one of their number went up to the head waiter, shook hands with him, and asked if there might not be a table for them. To everyone's surprise, they were led to a place immediately.

"I really think," said one of the party to the person who had spoken, "that it was the eloquence in your speech that got us here!"

"True," the other answered, "and the twenty bucks in the handshake didn't hurt any either!"

The graduation march began to play and the graduates began to move down the aisle, followed closely by a train of circus elephants who shook the auditorium.

"No! No!" cried the principal from the stage, "I said I wanted you to walk in with ELOQUENCE!"

Emotion

440

"Johnson!" exploded the teacher as he grew red in the face, "you didn't have your homework; you failed the quiz; you put gum in Lou Ann's hair; and now you throw a spitball at a classmate! What do you think I should do!?!"

"Actually," replied Johnson, "I'd get into some job that was a little less emotionally demanding . . . "

441

"When you look at her," said the director of the school play, "you should look at her with love. If you can't do that, think of something that means love to you, and picture that in order to get the proper emotion."

There was a long pause, and the director said, "Do you have your image for love yet?"

"Any minute," said the teen-aged actor, "I'm trying to decide if it should have pepperoni or just extra cheese . . . "

Engagement (See also: Marriage; Wedding)

442

There's one good thing about a long engagement; it makes the marriage seem shorter.

443

The teacher showed the class her engagement ring.

"This diamond," she told them, "will last forever."

Commented one youth, "Which will be two days short of the last installment payment!"

444

"Well," said the best friend at the engagement party, "I know two people who are overjoyed about this engagement!"

Said the prospective groom, "You've met her parents?"

England

445

Just remember that he who laughs last . . . is probably an Englishman.

446

Then there was the teacher from England who sat at his desk for the first six weeks of school and never said a word—he was waiting for someone to properly introduce him to the class.

447

Our England is a garden,
And such gardens are not made
By singing, "Oh, How Beautiful,"
And sitting in the shade."

—Rudyard Kipling

English

448

"Some day, English will be the universal language!"

Said the English teacher: "You haven't met my fifth-period class, have you?"

449

Composition submitted to an English teacher:

"This year I learned to not never use no double negatives. capitalize what you write. sentence fragments. spel things rite, and to always proof-read you writing."

Student at teacher's desk: "I'm thinking of taking a foreign language."

Teacher looking up from student's composition: "How about English?"

"Do you think English is a challenging language?"

"Challenging? It beats the stuffing out of four of five of my classes!"

English as a Second Language (ESL)

452

The dog was in hot pursuit of the kitten. Just as the dog was ready to chomp down, the mother cat appeared, reared up, and in a loud voice said, "BAD DOG!"

The dog screeched to a halt, turned quickly and ran off.

"Now," said the Mama cat, "Now do you see the value of English as a second language?"

453

"Look at this note!" exclaimed the teacher.

"I don't understand," said the principal, "this note calls you every name in the book, and yet you seem happy about it?"

"Look at it," the teacher continued. "The kid who wrote this is an ESL student, and all the words are spelled correctly!!!"

Entertain/Entertainment

454

"Is it true that children nowadays don't want to learn; they just want to be entertained?"

"Not at all," replied the teacher. "Give me a moment to take off the rubber nose and the makeup, and I'll explain."

455

On the return to school after the field trip to watch the play, the teacher began to skillfully question the class. As the students began their recall, it became evident that they had gained a great deal from their experience. Finally, one child stood and placed her hands on her hips.

"You teachers are so sneaky!" she exclaimed, "Here we were, learning all this stuff, and YOU had us fooled into believing that we were being entertained!"

456

"The teacher said we were going down to an assembly to be entertained."
"Oh?" "She lied!"

Envy

457

"So, Johnson got the chair of the department, eh? Tell me, aren't you just the least bit envious?"

"Not at all! The school will continue as normal . . . just as soon as I let the air out of all four of his tires!"

458

"They say that Professor Jones has never known envy. To what do you attribute that?"

"To his ego; he simply refuses to believe that there is anybody who is BETTER than he is!"

Erase/Erasure

459

"Look at this composition!" stated the teacher. "It's covered from top to bottom with erasures! I won't accept this!"

"Aw, come one!" pleaded the student. "Please take it. When my father got all finished doing it for me, I couldn't let you see it with all those mistakes!"

460

Mother to two children who are staring out the window at a very rainy day. "You don't understand; this is life! I can't erase it and draw in the sun!"

Estate

461

The teacher didn't leave much money when he died, but he did leave his niece his collection of 753 clocks. That was one estate it took her a long time to wind up!

462

"Do you think your estate will be complicated?" asked the lawyer.
"Hardly! My children get the money and my ex-spouse gets the bills!"

Ethics

463

"Give me your homework paper!" roared Bobby, and he took it from the quivering student and copied it.

Just then, another boy chanced by, ripped the paper from Bobby's desk, and started copying it himself.

"That's the trouble with this world," sobbed Bobby, "there are no ethics left any more!"

464

"You mean he's only one point below passing, and you're giving him an F? Is that ethical?"

"The kid didn't do homework all marking period! You will please note that there are times for ethics and times for retribution!"

Events, Special

465

"How did it go in school today?"

"Well, the teacher said we were going down to the auditorium for a special event, but it looked like just a bunch of kids singing to me . . . "

The children were taken to the auditorium and seated, waiting for the play to begin. All at once, one of the supports broke and the massive stage curtain began to fall, ripping as it went. This caught a bar of lights, and they crashed, knocking over the scenery, which fell into the orchestra pit, crushing the base drum!

"Wow!" remarked one child who had just witnessed the devastation, "When Ms. Jones says we're going to a special event, SHE MEANS 'SPECIAL'!"

Examination (See also: Tests)

467

"Tommy, this note from school says that you failed your dental examination."

"Honest, Mom, I didn't even know I was taking the course!"

468

"Before I give you the first page of this make-up examination," stated the teacher, "I must ask if you have ever seen it before?"

"Absolutely not!" attested the youth. "And I didn't make that mark you'll find on page five, either!"

469

The student received the examination paper, took one look, and began to cry.

"I . . . I . . . " the child stammered, "I c-c-can't understand even the first q-q-question!"

"No wonder," said the teacher looking at the paper, "I gave you the French final by mistake . . . "

470

"This examination," explained the school psychiatrist, "consists of having students try to force square blocks into round holes. They can't do it, of course, but it sure does teach them what they're up against in life!"

471

"I don't think I should get the grade you gave me on this exam!"
"Neither do I, but the school has nothing lower to offer!"

472

On the exam paper, the student wrote, "God and I took this test!"
On the paper, the teacher wrote, "God gets an A+; you get an F! One guess who needs to study more!"

473

"Yes, I know I didn't tell you that writing your name on the paper would be on the test, but believe me, it's standard procedure!"

Excuses

474

"Frankly, I do find it a bit difficult to accept that you couldn't do your homework last night because you had to have brain surgery . . . "

475

"You're gonna be proud of me today, Mr. Jones," said the student. "I am not going to give you an excuse for not handing in my homework!"
"Wonderful!" remarked the teacher.
"Of course," mumbled the student under his breath, "I'm not going to hand in any homework, either!"

476

The teacher had faced a long line of students who had nothing but excuses instead of homework. Therefore, when he reached a student who was new to the class the day before, and before the boy could say a thing, the teacher snapped, "And what's your excuse?"
"M-M-My parents took a second honeymoon," the flustered lad stammered, "and then I was born . . . "

Exhibition

477

"I do admire your audacity, Henry," said the teacher, "but somehow I don't think that your little brother, smeared with honey and staked out over an ant hill, would make a proper exhibition for our class fair."

478

"Excuse me for interrupting your class, but in your science fair, you placed the exhibition on live lava flow next to the exhibition on the polar ice cap, and unless you do something fast, we're expecting a tidal wave in the gymnasium in five minutes!"

Experience

479

"I tell you, the school of life and experience is the best teacher!"
"Agreed! But have you seen the tuition you have to pay?"

480

Experience is one of the few things in life that is always valuable, cannot be given to you by someone else, and is NEVER free!

481

The experiences in one's life only achieve value in retrospect—at the time we're going through them, they are usually the pits!

Experiment

482

"Let's perform an experiment," said the teacher. "All those who plan on passing this course, please hold up your homework!"

483

"Now where," muttered the science teacher, "is that experiment on bacterial growth?"

"I believe," commented a student holding his stomach, "that they served it for lunch!"

484

"Sir," asked a student, "are bee bites always fatal?"

"No," answered the teacher. "They can be if the victim is allergic, but most of the time they are a harmless annoyance. Why do you ask?"

"When you were a kid," answered the pupil, "did you ever drop your science experiment on the way to class?"

485

The principal and the visitor entered the home ec room while it was vacant.

"Look," said the principal. "Here's a bowl of chocolate pudding. How about a snack?"

And, as they licked their lips, a student stuck her head in the door and asked, "Have either of you seen my science experiment on primeval ooze?"

Expert

486

The teacher told the Board of Education, "The reason your fuel bills are so high is that the windows need caulking."

The Board then went out and hired a firm to do an analysis of heat loss. Fifty-two thousand dollars later, their recommendation was to caulk the windows.

"That's what I told you months ago!" exclaimed the teacher.

"Ah," answered the Board president, "but you are one of ours, and therefore not an expert!"

487

"If you want tropical fish to really flourish, you must feed them on the larvae of the tsetse fly . . . "

"But, where do I get the larvae of the tsetse fly?"

"How would I know? I'm an expert on fish, not flies!"

"Better take me now," the lecturer told the principal of the school. "Next month I receive my Ph.D., and once I'm an expert, my lecture fee will triple!"

Express

489

"We will begin this course by calculating the velocity and orbital variations of the planet Mercury," said the teacher.

"I thought I was in the wrong class!" said one student as he consulted his schedule. "I knew I signed up for the local, and here I am on the express!"

490

"What is an express?" asked the teacher.

Answered one small student, "A device that prints only one letter of the alphabet?"

Extra-Curricular Activity

491

Did you hear about the student who had so many extra-curricular activities that her guidance counselor advised her to cut down? Right now, she's trying to decide which academic subject to drop!

492

"Yes," said the teacher, "I'm the coach, I direct the school play, I run the chess club, and I'm head of the debating team."

"What about teaching?"

"Ah, now you're talking about MY extra-curricular activity!"

Extravagance

493

An extravagance is something YOU buy for yourself that somebody else thinks you don't need!

"I think your budget requests are a bit extravagant," said the principal. "Since you are teaching Eastern cultures, I can see why you would need a map of the area, but the request for an unlimited expense account at Chong's Imperial Gardens Restaurant is out of the question!"

Eye Liner

495

"What makes you think I did my homework now instead of at home?" the young lady asked the teacher.

"Rarely," answered the teacher, "do students who do the homework at home do it in eye-liner on the back of a brown paper bag!"

496

"No," said the school nurse to the student, "you are not going blind. The reason you can't see the blackboard is that you have so much eye liner on, the weight of it is forcing your eyelids shut!"

Eyes

497

"You know that hospital where they do all those corneal operations? Well, they're giving it a new name."

"Really, what are they calling it?"

"A Site for Sore Eyes!"

498

"Your aim in life," said the teacher, "is to be like an optometrist—a person of vision!"

499

Said the manager of the cafeteria, "Be careful, those potatoes might have bugs in them!"

"OK," said the worker, "I'll keep my eyes peeled!"

500

"The phrase," said the teacher, "is that the person's eyes look like pools—pools."

"Oh, I thought they said 'schools'!"

"Why would they call her eyes 'schools'?"

"They have pupils, don't they?"

Faculty

501

"My grandfather was a school principal, I think," said the student, "but he wasn't very good, because he couldn't find the teachers in the school . . . "

"Maria, are you making this up?"

"No, Ma'am! My mother told me that just before Grandpa died, he lost all his faculties!"

502

"Now," the social studies teacher said, "who can tell me what I call a group of men and women who have the power to determine whether you are guilty or not guilty and in some cases, whether you live or die?"

Answered one trembling youth, "The faculty of this school!"

503

Then there was the speaker who mixed up the words "faculty" and "facility" and told an astonished audience of educators that the trouble with the school was that the "faculty" suffered from dry rot and would improve greatly with caulking, scraping, and a new coat of paint!

Faculty Meeting

504

"There's only one other place where I have felt the excitement, the pace, and the enthusiasm of one of our faculty meetings."

"Oh, and where is that?"

"In a mortuary!"

505

"Did you schedule a faculty meeting for Thursday afternoon?" the secretary asked the principal.

"Yes, I did. How do you know?"

"Because, it's only Tuesday, and I already have fourteen requests from teachers to leave early on Thursday afternoon because they have a headache!"

506

In each teacher's mailbox, the principal placed a sheet of paper that read: "In order to develop a positive attitude about faculty meetings in this school, I would _____."

The principal received a 100 percent return. Each one read . . .

" . . . cancel them!"

Failure

507

Parent on the phone to a teacher: "Well, yes, I did see the Fs on his papers, but he assured me they stood for 'Fantastic'!"

508

"Remember this," the teacher told the class. "If you do poorly, I do poorly; if you fail, I fail!"

"Sure," commented one student, "but if you tell my mother, YOU don't get sent to YOUR room!"

509

Student to teacher while looking at graded test paper: "Does it ever bother you, late at night, that you might be setting my feet on the road to failure?"

Faith

510

"I believe that you have studied," said the teacher as she passed out the test papers. "I believe that you have done your best; I believe that you will all do well on this test . . ."

"Ma'am," said one student who stared blankly at the paper, "have you ever heard of a crisis of faith?"

511

"Why does your school run so efficiently?" asked the visitor.

"I can tell you in one word—Faith!" the teacher answered. "Without Faith, no one would have any idea what was going on; without Faith, the school would come to a standstill . . ."

"My, what a wonderful spiritual resolve you all have!"

"What resolve? I'm talking about Faith McCarthy, our SCHOOL SECRETARY!"

Falsehood (See Lies and Liars)

Family

512

"'Beauty is truth; truth beauty,'" quoted the English teacher.

Whispered one student, "This guy has never seen my family album!"

513

"Say," said the teacher whose first child had just been born, "have I ever shown you pictures of my family?"

"No, you haven't," answered a colleague, "and I want you to know that I am truly thankful for that!"

514

"Look," said one educator, holding up a popular news magazine, "this entire issue is on deficit spending!"

"An article about my family! How can I get copies?"

"So they had their family tree done, eh?"

"Yes, I guess they figured that since the branches were so bent, they'd see if there was anything to boast about in the roots!"

Farmers/Farming

516

"I don't think farming is so hard," said one youngster. "My uncle took up farming and he retired a rich man after only one year."

"You can't possibly make a success of a farm in one year," stated the teacher. "How could that be?"

"He was digging a hole and he struck oil!"

517

The farmer agreed to address a class at the local school.

"Tell us," asked the teacher, "what do you have to be, as a person, to make a success of farming nowadays?"

Answered the farmer, "Independently wealthy . . . "

Fashions

518

"Is it true that male teachers tend to wear the same clothes over and over?"

"Do you see Johnson over there?" returned a fellow observer. "He's worn that suit so long, it's back in style!"

519

"What do you think about these tight jeans that people are wearing nowadays?"

"I do wish they'd develop some hindsight!"

Fate

520

"My darling," said the boy to the girl late one night on her front porch, "don't you know what this feeling is? It's fate, and we can't fight it!"

"Don't you know what this sound is?" came a voice from just inside the door. "It's her father, and he CAN fight you!"

521

"Do you think there's such a thing as 'Fate'?" asked one educator.

"If there wasn't," answered the other, "there would be mass panic. We'd have nothing to blame our failures on but ourselves!"

Father (See also: Family; Mother)

522

"So, what did your kids give you for Father's Day?"

"All the bills they ran up for Mother's Day!"

523

"Did your son do anything special for you on Father's Day?"

"He certainly did; he let me use the car!"

524

"My family gave me breakfast in bed on Father's Day."

"How wonderful! How did they do it?"

"Easy, they rolled the day bed into the kitchen!"

525

"So, Mrs. Jones, it appears that Billy has some very serious learning and behavioral problems."

"Tell me," sighed Billy's mother, "have you ever met his father's side of the family?"

526

"Yes," said the father to his friend, "last night I told my kids about the value of money in today's economy."

"Did it do any good?"

"I'll say! Now they want their allowances in gold!"

527

"Dad," asked the teenaged daughter, "can you help me with my social studies paper? Was Alexander Graham Bell ever married?"

"I'm not sure," Dad answered, "but if he was, I know he was never a father."

"How do you know that?"

"Well, think about it. If he had a teenager in his home, do you think he would have invented the telephone?!"

Fear

528

"Ma'am," asked one student, "is it true that a person shouldn't be penalized because he or she has a handicap?"

"Absolutely!"

"Ma'am," continued the student, "have you ever heard of homework-a-phobia?"

529

"How do you manage to keep such an orderly class?"

"Love and respect have a lot to do with it," answered the teacher.

All at once, she spotted a student about to throw a spitball, snapped her fingers once, and the would-be troublemaker dropped the object and tried to bury himself in his desk.

Continued the teacher, "And a little fear doesn't hurt, either!"

Feedback

530

"You are about to hear a concert by our school band," the principal told the assembled students.

Just then there was a long, ear-splitting squeal of feedback from the speakers.

"Ah," commented one member of the audience, "they've been practicing!"

531

One student who was running for the Student Council gave a speech on the playground that was greeted with assorted fruits and tomatoes from student lunches being thrown at him with particular accuracy.

As he was being cleaned off in the nurse's office, one teacher asked how he thought his speech went over.

"Actually," said the pupil, "I'm rather pleased. How often does a speech get feedback that is THAT well defined?"

Festival (See also: Holidays)

532

Principal to student: "Yes, I know we hold celebrations for many reasons, but I don't think a festival in honor of your passing the math test is appropriate . . . "

533

"Is that school district having financial difficulties?"

"Why do you ask?"

"Look at that sign. It says they're holding a SCHOOL-FEST. Didn't they have enough money for the last four letters?"

534

The children were dressed in their costumes ready for the festival to begin.

"Remember," said the teacher, "this festival is a joyous time!"

"Oh, yeah?" answered one student. "Did you ever have to walk to school dressed as a tree past about a million dogs?"

Fighting/Fights

535

"The fight that took place after the football game was just like a crossword puzzle," wrote the student in the school newspaper. "Some were vertical, and some were horizontal!"

"Why, in Heaven's name, did you stand there and fight the biggest kid in class?" asked the school nurse as she applied the antiseptic.

"I took one look at him," said the lad, "and I was too scared to run away!"

537

"Ma'am! Two kids are fighting, and one of them wants you to come right away!"

"Which one is that?"

"The one on the bottom!"

538

"See," explained the student, "Billy wanted me to fight him, so I said I would, but first I'd like to buy him an ice cream cone. So, we went down to the corner store, and I bought him a triple-decker cone!"

"And because of that, you became friends," mused the teacher. "How wonderful!"

"Of course not," continued the pupil. "When all Billy's attention was on the ice cream cone, I jumped him from behind and twisted his arm until he gave up!"

Fire Drills

539

"Today," the teacher told the first-grade class, "we are going to have a fire drill!"

"Wow!" said one tot to another, "I knew they got oil by drilling, but I didn't think they got fire the same way!"

540

The teacher wanted his students to know that if they just studied for the test, all would go well.

"What is it," he asked, "that will give you great relief when you come to a hard question on the test?"

Answered one student, "A fire drill, so we can ask someone else the answer!"

"And why do we have fire drills at least twice a month?" asked the teacher.

Answered one acute observer, "So the principal can get to use his stopwatch?"

Fish/Fishing

542

The two teachers were passing a lake on their way to school.

"Harry," said one, "what do I teach?"

"Communication skills," answered the colleague.

"Right," said the first. "So let's stop and drop the fish a line!"

543

"Are you going fishing today?" asked the wife.

"I was planning on bringing home our supper," smiled the husband, "just like usual."

"In that case, I'll have some hamburgers thawed and ready to cook!"

544

"The fish had to be at least two feet long," bragged Father, "but, being the true sportsman I am, I threw it back!"

"Dad," asked his son, "are you talking about the one the man in the next boat used for bait?"

545

The teacher looked at the paper and remarked, "There's something fishy here!"

"I can't help it," commented the student, "ever since I wore this shirt when I went fishing with Dad, I can't get the smell out!"

Flag

546

Teacher to student in class: "All right, Johnson, you can stop waving that white flag, I'll be with you as soon as I can!"

"Look," said the teacher, "when I told you to flag down Billy Smith, I didn't mean for you to tie him up in 'Old Glory' and hoist him up the flagpole!"

Flattery

548

"Remember this," the teacher told the novice teacher, "when it comes to our students, we can get a great deal out of them with a flattering word and a boot in the rear end . . . especially if you leave out the flattering word!"

549

"Gosh, Mr. Johnson, you really look neat today! What a great jacket! What a fantastic tie!"

"Billy," said the teacher, "are you using flattery?"

"Sir, I'm failing your subject! I'll use anything!"

550

"Johnson," said the teacher, "I should be very angry at you, falling asleep like that during my lecture!"

"Actually," maintained the student, "you should be quite flattered. Think of how much I trust you in order to relax to that degree!"

Float

551

"Therefore," lectured the teacher, "by pumping hot air into the old wreck, the ship rose to the surface."

"Hey," whispered one student, "if hot air will do that, I'll bet he must be the champion floater of all time!"

552

"I don't care if the students have voted for it," said the principal, "we are NOT going to enter a float in the community parade that depicts ME being hung by a group of angry students!"

Flowers

553

"Who can give me one of the great questions of life?"
    "I can!"
    "What is it?"
    "Suppose a florist goes into the hospital, what do you send him?"

554

"Can I have some of those silent flowers?"
    "Silent flowers?"
    "You know, the MUMS!"

555

"Ms. Jones," said the student, "you remind me of a flower . . . "
    "Why, thank you!"
    Continued the student under his breath, " . . . a snapdragon!"

556

"Yes," said the teacher, "I once bought a house plant. I got an 'impatience.'"
    "What happened?"
    "It got tired of waiting and died!"

Focus

557

"And this is a picture of my last year's class," said the teacher.
    "But, this is out of focus . . . "
    "Please, that's the only way I can stand remembering them!"

558

The teacher adjusted his glasses and said, "Please, I must have time to focus on your paper."
    Commented the student, "If you'd clean those lenses once in a while, you'd get the right focus a whole lot easier!"

Fog

559

"'Fog comes on little cat feet,'" quoted the teacher, "Carl Sandburg!"
    "'Fog messes up rush hour,'" countered a student, "*Morning Tribune*!"

560

"We can't go out on the field and play baseball," said the teacher, "it's much too foggy."
    "Aw, come on, let us out. If the other team can't see us, it may be the only chance we have!"

561

"My goodness," said the principal as he stepped outside the school, "I can hardly see my own hand. When did this fog come up?"
    "That's not fog," answered her companion. "It's just the cafeteria getting an early start on lunch!"

Football

562

Was our last game rough? Let me put it this way—by the end of the first half, there were two broken arms, three concussions, and five missing teeth . . . and that was just the guys who were selling hot dogs!

563

Then there was the student athlete who gave his all to "Block that kick!" The only problem was how to remove the ball from his mouth.

564

They say that football gets you into great physical shape. Well, I'm not so sure of that. After all, last weekend I watched at least four games, and I'm still fat and short of breath!

565

Some people say that football is too violent, and maybe they're right. You should see the battles that rage in our living room when I want to watch a game!

"There is no truth to the rumor that football players are all brawn and no brains!" said the coach. "I'll have you know that my players are straight-A students!"

"Right!" exclaimed one member of the team. "And next semester, they're gonna teach us the letter B!"

567

"The question," mused the school principal, "is whether we can come up with an Alumni Association of which the football team may be proud?"

568

"Why so glum?" one fan asked another at the Saturday morning school football game.

"My favorite uncle died this past week," was the answer. "He was very close to me, more like a brother or a father than an uncle. It really broke me up."

"That's why you're so sad, huh?"

"Sure, and if our team doesn't hurry up and finish this game, I'm going to miss Uncle Bob's funeral that started an hour ago!"

Foreign Language

569

"Who can tell me," asked the French teacher, "what is meant by the term *faux pas*?"

"Well," answered one student, "my Aunt Helen had a statue of Julius Caesar that got tossed around during shipping. My family was over at her place one day when the minister was also visiting. My father went out to the hall with my aunt, but we were in the living room and could hear them talking. At that point, my father, in a loud voice, said, 'Helen, your bust is a disgrace; you'll have to have it cleaned and patched up before it's fit to look at!'

"That was a *faux pas*!"

570

"Did you have a nice drive with Daddy?" mother asked the six year old.

"Yep," was the reply, "all except when the tire blew out and Daddy talked in some foreign language I didn't understand!"

"When I get to Middle School and have to take a foreign language," said the fifth grader, "I'm going to take Spanish."

"That's fine," said mother. "Is there any particular reason why you chose that language?"

"Today in school," explained the lad, "we saw a movie about Spain, and there were kids who were younger than me, and they were speaking Spanish, so I figure it has to be real easy to learn!"

Formal

572

"Oh, no!" exclaimed the teenager, "I just got an invitation to Mindy's party, and it's formal!"

"A formal party at this age?" mused mother. "What does that mean?"

"That means," sighed the teenager, "that everybody has to wear a clean shirt AND shoes!"

573

The argument ensued as to whether the teenaged daughter was old enough to wear a strapless gown to the formal dance. Finally, her seven-year-old brother spoke up.

"Let her put it on," he said, "and if it stays up; she's old enough!"

Foundation

574

"Elementary school is the foundation of all your learning," the principal told the assembly.

Commented one youth, "That's why my grades are in the cellar!"

575

"Before you can go any further in your studies," the guidance counselor told the student, "you must make sure that you have a very firm foundation."

"What did the counselor tell you?" Mother asked later.

"He said," commented the student, "that I have to get a girdle!"

"Today's lecture," said the college professor, "is called 'The Proper Foundation.'"

"Drat!" exclaimed one student. "I so wanted to learn about eye liner!"

Frantic (See also: Anxiety)

577

"Mr. Jones didn't look at all well yesterday," said the student. "I hope he stays home if he's not feeling well. He really should stay home if he's ill!"

"Will you stop that!" mother responded, "Why are you so frantic about Mr. Jones' health?"

"Because if he's NOT out, the three of us are going to be having a conference after school today that I forgot to tell you about yesterday!"

578

"I realize," said mother, "that your project is due in about an hour, and I understand that you're getting frantic, but there is no way I can arrange an overnight trip to Paris for your entire class, even if you DID tell them that I can do anything!"

Fraternity

579

Dear Mom and Dad,

I love college, and I love my fraternity. The fraternity, however, cannot hope to take the place of home. I know how busy you both are, but I've been here three days, and I do miss hearing from you. So, if you could just let me know you're there by placing your name at the bottom of a blank check . . .

580

Dear Mom and Dad,

You were so right; I have learned a great deal by joining a fraternity here on campus. I have learned how to live with others; I have learned how to share what I have; and, as soon as I learn how to make up those classes I learned to cut, my suspension will be lifted!

Friends

581

Said the skeptical student, "Always remember that a friend in need . . . is someone whose phone calls you want to avoid!"

582

"Tommy Smith stinks!" roared the little boy. "He's ugly; he's rotten; and he's the worst kid in school!"

"Billy!" chided his mother, "How dare you say nasty things like that about someone!"

"It's OK, Mom," counseled Billy, "Tommy and I are best friends!"

583

The next time all your enemies start getting you down, just resolve to treat your friends a little kinder the next time you see them!

584

"A new kid came into class today," said the child. "The first thing I did was to go up to him and tell him that I could beat him up with one hand; then he spit in my eye, and we were rolling around on the floor, and the teacher took us both to the principal's office and we gotta stay after school for a week . . . "

"Goodness," sighed the mother, "What a horrible child he must be!"

"Naw!" answered the lad. "He's coming over tonight; we're gonna be great friends!"

585

The teenager picked up the phone and spoke for the next two hours with the caller about all those matters that so seriously affect the lives of youth.

Finally, the person on the other end of the line said, "Well, it's getting late. I'll see you in school tomorrow, OK, Sherri?"

"Sherri?" said the other, "My name isn't Sherri!"

"Oh, I'm so sorry," said the person who called. "I have the wrong number!"

Fringe Benefits

586

The kindergarten teacher had a long and tiresome day, and now, as she struggled to get the last child into a snowsuit and boots, her headache began to assume migraine proportions!

When she had finished, the child motioned the teacher to bend down. When she did, the tiny student kissed the teacher on the cheek, whispered, "I love you!" and ran swiftly from the room.

"Let's face it," said the teacher, her headache forgotten, "it's the fringe benefits that keep us going!"

587

"Mr. Jones," said a student who had lingered after class, "today, when we got to a subject you didn't know, you admitted it and said you'd have to look it up. How come you admitted you didn't know something?"

"You have to understand," answered the teacher. "Learning with your students is one of the greatest fringe benefits of teaching!"

Frustration

588

"The results of this test are horrible," said Mr. Smith. "I'm so frustrated with you, I don't know what to do!"

"Get your hair done!" shouted one student. "That's what my Mom does whenever she's on the outs with the old man!"

589

It was Parents Visitation Night, and a line of parents waited to be let into the school building. Suddenly, one man appeared and tried to cut in at the head of the line. The crowd grew angry at this intrusion and manhandled him to the rear. Again the man tried to move up, and again he was roughly shoved to the back. Finally, in frustration, he climbed onto the roof of his car.

"Hey!" he shouted, "don't you recognize me? I'm the janitor; I got to unlock those doors if you want to get in!"

Fumble (See also: Football)

590

"I know what you've been taught at home," the coach told the Pee-Wee Football Team of seven year olds, "but when the other team drops the ball, PLEASE don't pick it up and give it back to them!"

591

"Son," said Dad to his distraught son, "I know you fumbled the ball on the goal line, and the other team recovered and ran 97 yards for a touchdown, but I don't want you to be too upset. Just remember that if you're like most alumni, twenty years from now YOU will have made the recovery, run into the end zone, and saved the day for Alma Mater!"

Funeral

592

The elderly teacher was obviously on his last legs. His breathing was erratic and he looked horrible. All at once his long-term friend came into the room, whispered in his ear, and the man visibly brightened and began to rally.

"Good grief, man!" said the doctor, "what did you say to him?"

"I just told him," answered the friend, "what his funeral would cost him if he died!"

593

"Yes," intoned the minister at the funeral, "Tom Smith was a wonderful man, always kind and patient; always loving and tender; always generous and giving . . . "

"Junior," whispered Mrs. Smith, "go see if that's your father in the box!"

594

"Do you think he believed in life after death?" asked one mourner at the funeral.

"Oh, yes," answered another. "You know how some people have phones installed in their tombs in case they come back?"

"Did he do that?"

"Even better! Not only does he have a phone in his tomb, he has an answering service so he won't miss any messages while he's gone!"

Fussy

595

My teenaged son is very, very fussy about what he eats—it has to be food, or he won't put it in his mouth!

596

The brand-new teacher was getting ready for the first day of class. In the teacher's lounge she sprayed her textbooks with antiseptic, gargled with a strong mouthwash, and swallowed a handful of vitamins.

"I'm very fussy about my health," the novice teacher explained.

"Let's follow her," whispered a veteran teacher to a colleague. "I want to be there when the first kid sneezes all over her!"

597

The new principal was speaking to the cafeteria manager.

"I'm very particular and fussy about my food," said the administrator, "I won't eat just anything. That's why I look forward to my daily lunches in your establishment."

"If that's the case," said one student who was passing by, "you can also look forward to dropping about fifty pounds over the school year!"

Future

598

"How I look forward to the future," said the speaker, "when children will be taught by a computer, without the need of a human teacher! Any questions?"

"Mister," asked one student listener, "can a computer hug you and tell you it's gonna be all right?"

599

"Yes, I know I said that the future belongs to those who can take it, but that did NOT apply to the apple sitting on my desk!"

600

"Who can tell me what the term 'Future Shock' means?"

"That's the day, sometime next month, when my father gets the bill for the credit-card purchases I made yesterday!"

Galaxy

601

"Just imagine," said the teacher, "what it will be like when we can travel through the galaxy, traveling from Earth to Alpha Centuri!"

"Yeah," said one student, "with an hour layover on Jupiter while they try to find your luggage!"

602

"Yes," lectured the teacher, "the galaxy is expanding outward at tremendous speed. Every second there are stars and planets that are traveling farther and farther away from Earth!"

"Gosh," sighed one student, "they must know something that we don't!"

Garden/Gardening

603

"Thank goodness for crab grass!" said one educator.

"Surely you can't be serious," returned a colleague. "Have you seen what crab grass does to a lawn?"

"Listen," commented the first, "if it weren't for crab grass, I'd have no lawn at all!"

604

I'm a terrible gardener. Last week, I thought I would surprise my spouse, so I got some silk flowers and planted them in the garden. They died!

605

He's such a poor gardener, he couldn't keep a rock garden alive!

606

"Your Honor," said the wife in Divorce Court, "it's his garden! He spends every minute of his spare time in that garden. He never has any time for the children or me, because he's always working on that garden!"

"Really," answered the husband, "I can't see why I should be penalized just for trying to improve my lot!"

Gasoline

607

"Come on!" said the young lady, "going out for a drive and then 'running out of gas,' is as old as the hills. Boys don't do that any more, do they?"

"Oh, no?" said her wiser companion. "Why do you think I carry this container of gasoline in my handbag?"

608

"I know you don't want to go to the classical music concert," said the mother, "but it will do you good. I don't care what you say, you're going!"

Two hours later, a phone call came from the school nurse that Junior was not feeling well and should be taken home.

"He's faking!" said his mother. "He just doesn't want to go to the concert!"

"Oh, he's not faking," returned the nurse. "He got pretty sick when the gasoline backed up as he was siphoning it out of the school's field-trip bus!"

Gender

609

"Equality of gender doesn't mean that men and women can't be polite to one another," said the teacher. "Just the other day, for example, I saw a man hold the door open for his wife."

"Sure," whispered one girl, "he probably had to, because she was carrying all the bundles!"

610

"Who can use a masculine, feminine, and neuter pronoun in the same sentence?" asked the English teacher.

"I know one we use around my house all the time," answered one boy. "'Take this bill,' SHE said, 'and give IT to HIM!'"

Generation Gap

611

The family was gathered and they were talking about stars of the stage and screen.

"I'm thinking about someone," said mother, "but I can't get his first name. You know, the 'Rogers' fellow."

Said the son, "Kenny!"

Said the father, "Roy!"

Said the grandfather, "Will!"

612

"Listen," extolled the father to his son, "when I was your age, I thought nothing of working sixty to seventy hours a week!"

"No disagreement, Dad," said the son, "I don't think a heck of a lot of that either!"

613

Junior was running late, and he got to the stop just as the school bus pulled away. He came running home to tell his mother, who prepared to drive him to school.

"When I was your age," commented Grandpa, who was visiting for the week, "we didn't have fancy school buses!"

"Please, Mom," said Junior, "I don't care if we are late, I want to hear the part again where Grandpa crawled for six miles over broken glass just to get an education!"

Genius

614

"So you see folks," concluded the teacher, "by staying home 'ill' and intercepting every note I sent, Billy has totally avoided every homework assignment as well as every test and quiz for the entire marking period!"

"Good grief!" exclaimed the parent. "The kid is more of a genius than even I imagined!"

615

"Thomas Edison once remarked that 'genius' was one percent inspiration and 99 percent perspiration!" said the teacher.

"I think that's true," responded the student.

"Good, now just remember that the next time somebody tells you that you're acting 'cool'!"

Gentleman/Gentlemen
(See also: Lady/Ladies)

616

From a student's test paper: "A gentleman is somebody who doesn't work and comes from England . . . "

617

On their tour of the Stock Market, the teacher pointed to an elderly, well-dressed man and said, "That is a very distinguished gentleman. His picture is constantly in *The Wall Street Journal*, and he is worth a great deal of money!"

"Big deal!" responded one of the students. "My brother has his picture on the wall of the Post Office, and he's worth ten thousand to whoever turns him in!"

"Remember," chided Mother, "when you get to Maria's birthday party, I want you to act like a perfect little gentleman. Do you know what that means?"

"Sure," said the little boy, "I get to sit in the living room and read the newspaper while Maria does the cleaning up!"

Geography

619

"Name a state that borders on Oklahoma," asked the teacher.

"New Jersey," answered the student.

"Just yesterday," remarked the teacher, "I told the class that New Jersey was over 1500 miles away from Oklahoma!"

"How about that!" said the wide-eyed student. "It moved overnight!"

620

"So one source of income for this small country is the export of a particular type of fertilizer called 'guano.'"

"What's 'Guano'?"

The teacher explained that it was the droppings of birds and bats.

"Wow!" commented one youngster, "That really is a GROSS national product!"

Gesture

621

The child's part in the play was to enter, make a grand gesture to the right, and state, "The enemy approaches, Sire!"

On the night of the play, the nervous youngster entered, said his line, and made his gesture to the LEFT, whereupon the 'enemy' soldiers entered the stage from the opposite direction the boy was pointing.

There was a second's pause, and the distraught actor proclaimed in a loud voice, "How about that, Sire! Them dirty rats snuck up behind us!!!"

"I've noticed that Mr. Johnson has a particular gesture that he uses a great deal," commented one teacher about a colleague. "Whenever he gives the class a task to do, he sits at his desk and scratches his right ear, as if he were lost in thought about his students."

"How observant of you," returned another teacher, "but had you looked a little closer, you'd have noticed that the gesture wasn't contemplation; he's turning down his hearing aid!"

Gift

623

"Rachel," said the teacher, "I want to thank you for this fine gift, but I really found it difficult to accept a box of five multicolored kittens, just because your mother said they have to be gone by nightfall!"

624

"Raymond," said the teacher, "this is a brand new CD player! This is much too expensive for me to accept as a gift!"

"Please take it," moaned the youth. "If I were you, I wouldn't change my report card grade for a box of chocolate chip cookies!"

625

"Look at all those gifts your class gave you," commented one teacher to another during the holiday season. "You can tell they picked them out all by themselves. Aren't they precious!"

"Oh, yes," commented the recipient. "I can hardly wait to exchange them!"

Gifted Child

626

Two students were talking outside the school building when a limousine drove up. The chauffeur opened the door, and a boy stepped out dressed in the finest and most modern clothes imaginable. The chauffeur then got the boy's books and proceeded to carry them into school, walking a few paces behind the student.

"Now, that," commented one of the observers, "is a truly gifted child!"

627

"Do all parents perceive their children as gifted?" asked one observer.

"Let me put it this way," answered the educator, "in our school we only have three tracks—Gifted, Truly Gifted, and If-You-Don't-Think-They're-Gifted-Just-Ask-Mom-and-Dad!"

628

The teacher wrote a sentence on the board and asked, "Who can tell me something about this sentence?"

One child began, "I is . . . "

"Karin," the teacher interrupted, "a gifted student like you using a construction like 'I is . . . '? You know perfectly well that it's 'I am . . . '"

"As you wish," said the gifted child. "'I' am the first word in that sentence!"

Girls

629

"I always get good grades in home ec," said the student. "I figure that if I learn how to cook, I can always find a boy who will know how to eat!"

630

"Mom and Dad," said the preadolescent daughter, "I want to become a mother; I want to become a mother right now. May I, please?"

Mother and Father sat in open-mouthed wonder, until one of them finally blurted out, "B-B-But, Honey, y-y-you're too y-y-young!"

"I am not!" protested the child. "Sally Johnson has a kitten and she's a year younger than me!"

631

"Mommy," said the girl, "can you get me that pink handbag over there?"

Since this was the first time that the child had expressed an interest in items of a feminine nature, mother was glad to oblige.

"Now," mother continued, "how about a dress to go with that handbag?"

"Naw! But when I load this handbag with rocks and swing it by those long straps, Billy Johnson is going to be sorry! So, thanks, Mom!"

632

"Mom!" said the girl, "You gotta do something about Billy Johnson!"

"Why? What did he do?"

"When we went through the revolving door down at the department store, he got in after me and kept pushing the door so fast, I couldn't get out!"

"Is that all . . . "

"Mom, you don't understand! Now he's telling everyone that we were going around together!"

Girls and Boys

633

It was a case of opposites attracting. He was a poor boy, and she was a girl with a small fortune!

634

After a health class in which the subject of rabies was discussed, the boy and girl were fighting in the hallway.

"I hope your dog bites you and gives you rabies!" exclaimed the boy. "What would you do then?"

"The first thing," shouted back the girl, "would be to bite you!"

635

"I think you're the ugliest boy on earth!" said the girl.

"Well," returned the boy, "I think you look like a cover girl!"

"Really?" said the girl, softening visibly.

"Yeah," continued the boy, "every time I see your face, I want to cover it!"

636

"That Billy Johnson sure burns me up!" said the girl to her friend.

"But, Billy is just sitting over there reading. He's not paying any attention to you whatsoever . . . "

"Exactly! That's what burns me up!"

Glass

637

"I remember," said one reminiscing educator, "when milk came in glass bottles!"

"That's nothing," returned another, recalling his youth on a farm, "I remember when it used to come in cows!"

638

"Generally," the science teacher told the class, "glass is being replaced in windows by plastic, because while plastic is very durable, glass is quite fragile."

At that point, a softball, driven by an athlete on the playing field outside, crashed through a back window of the classroom!

"Wow, Mrs. Johnson!" exclaimed one wide-eyed youth, "You give the best demonstrations of any science teacher in the school!"

Glee

639

"In a short while," said the teacher, "we will be going down to the auditorium to see the local college glee club."

"Great!" whispered one student to a friend. "I always wanted to see what a 'glee' looked like!"

640

"Tomorrow," explained the teacher, "this class will have its annual holiday party, and I know we will all be filled with glee!"

"What's 'glee'?" whispered one student.

"The cookies and candy we bring from home, of course," answered another student. "Didn't you hear her say we was gonna be filled with it!"

Glutton

641

"One should never eat between meals," commented the lecturer.

Commented one teenager, "The answer to that is to keep eating all the time, so you eliminate 'between meals.'"

"We had a house guest over the weekend, and in two days, he drank five quarts of milk, ate three chickens, about two dozen hamburgers, perhaps ten pounds of potatoes, and completely and totally cleared out our pantry!"

"Good grief! Was he a glutton?"

"No!" A teenager!"

Government

643

"Why do politicians usually get promotions in government service?" asked the social studies teacher.

"Because," answered one wise student, "hot air rises!"

644

"Excuse me! When was this structure built?"

"I don't know."

"Well, how much did it cost?"

"I don't know."

"Then, who built it?"

"I don't know."

"Government worker, huh?"

645

"There are so many ways in which mankind can meet destruction," intoned the teacher. "There is fire and pestilence and war and natural disaster . . . "

Commented one student, "Sounds to me like normal government operations!"

Governor

646

Smith and Jones were running against each other for governor. One day, candidate Jones showed up at a local school and asked for an assembly to be called.

"If I am elected," Jones told the children, "I will raise taxes, spend more money, take away all benefits, and make it all but impossible to live in this state!"

"That's terrible!" the students roared.

"Just tell your parents where you heard it!" said Jones. "My name is Smith! S-M-I-T-H!!!"

647

The governor visited the elementary school and was talking with the principal when a fifth-grader happened by.

"This is the governor of our state!" commented the principal to the student.

"What do you do?" the unimpressed child asked the politician.

"Oh," the governor commented modestly, "I don't do very much . . . "

"Two of you with the same job!" exclaimed the fifth-grader. "No wonder this state and the schools are in such bad shape!"

Grades/Grading

648

The president of the agricultural college asked one of the professors what his grading system was. The teacher answered that it was about five percent to allow for proper drain-off.

649

"I've made a resolution," said the teenager to his mother, "that from now on I am going to be straightforward and honest; every question gets an outright answer; no equivocation. Go ahead; ask me a question! Go on!"

"OK, how are your grades in school?"

"Lovely weather we've been having lately, isn't it?"

Graduate School (See also: Degrees)

650

"So, you have a son and daughter in graduate school! What are they majoring in?"

"Check cashing . . . "

651

"When your son gets out of graduate school, what will he be prepared to do?"

"At the rate he's going—apply for Medicare!"

652

"When your children got out of graduate school, they had an M.A. and a Ph.D. and two assistant fellowships. What did you get?"

"Me? I got a B.R.O.K.E. and a bankruptcy!"

Graduation

653

"Mrs. Jones," said the student, "I really like you, so I feel it's my duty to warn you to change my final mark so I can graduate from eighth grade."

"Warn me?" quizzed the teacher. "Are you threatening me?"

"Oh, no, Ma'am!" said the child. "It's not me, but last night I heard my father tell my mother that if I didn't graduate, somebody wasn't going to be able to sit down for a week!"

654

"Son, you'll never know how proud I am to be at your college commencement. By the way, you're a college graduate now; what does 'commencement' mean?"

"Well, Dad, 'commencement' means 'to begin.'"

"Good, Son! In that case, commence to get a job or I'm tossing you out of the house!"

Grammar

655

The English teacher was hiking in the mountains when he came upon an isolated mountain family who invited him to stay for the noonday meal.

During the repast, the eldest son remarked, "Please pass me them there peas!"

"How horrid!" remarked the English teacher. "Your lack of proper grammar is disgusting!"

Whereupon the lad pulled out a Bowie knife, stuck it into the table, and glared at the teacher.

"Hey," said the educator, "while I pass you these here peas, how about giving me some of them there potatoes!"

656

The English teacher stopped the two boys who were fighting and took them to a place where they could be handled.

"I want you two to write out what happened, and I want it in perfect English!"

"What case do I use?"

"What do you mean?" asked the teacher.

"Do I write it in first person as in MY story or in third person as in HIS story? There is a difference, you know!"

Grants

657

"You just got a research grant from the government? What's it for?"

"Research on how to get research grants from the government!"

658

"Jean, now that you have your degree, what do you think you'll do?"

"Well, Dad," she answered, "right now, I think I'll make the rounds and look for a grant."

"That's not a good idea," Dad cautioned. "Not many people lose a fifty; try looking for some Washingtons and here and there a Lincoln!"

Graph (See also: Charts, Reports)

659

In math class, a student came up to the teacher and asked if she could have several sheets of paper. The teacher gladly obliged.

"I am very pleased to see that you want to practice the graphs we have been studying in class."

The child smiled and returned to her desk.

"I didn't have the heart to tell her," she whispered to a friend, "that the best thing about graph paper is that you can play tic-tac-toe without having to draw the lines every time!"

660

"You want me to ask your Uncle Bill to come to school to demonstrate how to do a graph?" said father. "Your uncle is a politician; he doesn't know the first thing about math!"

"But I heard you tell Mom that Uncle Bill knew more about graphs than anyone."

"Not 'graph'! I said GRAFT!"

Grave (See also: Death; Funeral; Sorrow)

661

The two friends had argued for years. This was the pinnacle of battles!

"I promise you," said one, "that I will live long enough to walk across your grave!"

"How wonderful!" returned the other. "I've just given orders for a burial at sea!"

662

Two gravediggers were hard at work and talking.

"Do you think the dead ever come back?"

"Naw! Not in this world!"

"Well, let's dig down a couple of extra feet. My old English teacher is being buried here, and I don't want to take any chances!"

Gravity

663

One of the students in the science class was pulling a joke on his friend, and he had arranged for a lemon meringue pie to fall on the victim as he came through the door. Unfortunately, the teacher entered the room first, and he stood there covered with pie filling and fuming with anger.

"Sir," said the perpetrator, "I do wish you would take into consideration the fact that we have just proven, with scientific accuracy, the existence of gravity!"

664

The teacher came across a student who sat with a gigantic frown across her young face.

"Come, now, young lady," said the teacher. "There is no reason for gravity!"

"Of course there is," returned the pupil. "Without it, we'd all float away!"

Grease

665

" . . . and, of course," continued the science teacher, "grease is an excellent lubricator as well."

"That's got to be true," commented one student. "Whenever I eat the cafeteria food, it goes right through me!"

666

"Will old Miser Johnson let us play in his back field?" asked one youngster.

"I asked him," answered another, "and he said we could play there if I greased his palm."

"What did you do?"

"Well," said the lad, "I couldn't find a palm tree anywhere on his property, so I just smeared lard all over the big elm!"

Great Britain (See: England)

Grief (See also: Death; Funeral; Sorrow)

667

A student and a teacher were crossing a city street on the way to school when the student slipped and the textbook he had been carrying fell into a street drain and was lost in the muck below. The boy sat on the curb and began to cry.

"Come, come," said the teacher, "there is no need for such grief; we can always get you another textbook."

"Sure," sniffled the youngster, "but it's gonna take me another three hours to make up a set of crib sheets for your exam like those that were inside!"

668

"I understand," said the teacher to the principal, "that part of the new curriculum will be a course on how to handle grief, and I'd like to apply to teach it."

"Thank you for your interest," commented the administrator, "but you should know that I'm going to find it difficult to recommend someone who bursts into tears when the oatmeal cookies in the cafeteria aren't done on time!"

Guards

669

The teacher had taken a trip to London, and went, of course, to Buckingham Palace.

"Excuse me," the teacher said to a passerby, "if I stand here, will I be able to see the guards changing?"

"Oh, no, Dearie," explained the Londoner, "they got private rooms for that!"

670

"I have heard that some of you believe that I don't trust this class," said the teacher, "so today, when I pass out your test papers, I'm going to walk right out that door. That should show you what I think of you.

"There will be nobody here but you, your pencil, and the test paper . . .

"Unless, of course, you count the three security guards I've hired to patrol the room in my absence!"

Guidance

671

A distraught student walked into the guidance office.

"Can somebody tell me," he said with a sigh, "why am I here?"

A guidance counselor heard the lad, took him into an office, and spent the next two hours explaining life and the worth of the individual human being.

"Now, do you understand?" finished the counselor.

"Sure," said the student, "but I was supposed to pick up my brother's homework from the math teacher, and I was told to report to this office instead, so I still want to know, 'Why am I here?'"

672

During the change of classes, the teacher noticed one young man who was walking down the hallway backwards. While everyone else walked in one direction, he faced the opposite way and was back-pedaling as swiftly as possible.

"Young man!" called the teacher, "what you need is guidance!"

"No, Ma'am!" returned the pupil, "what I need is a new pair of pants that didn't just split up the back!"

Guilt

673

"So, you were working on the sets for the school play, and you knocked over a can of gold paint, and it fell all over the teacher? What did she do?"

"Nothing, she just stood there, looking gilt-y!"

674

"I . . . I'm sorry that I didn't study for your test," said the student.

"But," the teacher replied, "the test isn't until tomorrow . . ."

"I know, but I want to get rid of the guilt now, so I can get a good night's sleep!"

Gum

675

"Sir," asked a student, "how effective are you on enforcing the NO GUM rules in this class?"

"Young lady," answered the teacher, "the last student who chewed gum in this class graduated over three years ago!"

140

"Then you'd better call him back and tell him to bring scissors, because I just got a wad of it caught in my hair!"

676

"You'd better not chew gum in Ms. Jones' class!" warned one student. "She's an expert on gum! She'll get you!"

"Come on! How good could she be?"

Whereupon Ms. Jones entered the room, sniffed the air, and said, "Juicy Fruit, two sticks, purchased this morning at the corner grocery store, third row, second seat—Johnson, see me at once!"

Gym

677

"And how is school, Dear," Grandmother asked her granddaughter.

"Fine, Grandma," said the young lady, "I'm taking gym!"

"That's good, Dear," replied Grandma. "Just make sure you check out his family!"

678

The gym class was assembled when the doors burst open and another pupil entered the area.

"I will not have students coming late!" intoned the gym teacher. "Do three laps around the gym!"

The youth proceeded on his task, and the P.E. teacher got the class started on the activity of the day. He then began to pace the student who was circling the gym.

"I don't like to give these punishments," he said, "but I cannot have people coming late to class!"

"I understand, Sir," the running lad puffed, "but I'm not in your class. I was sent from the office with a message that I'll gladly give you if we can just stop running long enough for me to catch my breath!"

H

Habits

679

"Why so glum?" one teacher asked another.

"I've just come back from seeing my accountant," the other replied, "and my net income doesn't match up with my gross habits!"

680

"Habits are extremely hard to break," said one teacher to another. "When I was young, for example, I held down three jobs in order to get through college. Now that I'm older, I still hold down three jobs!"

"But, you have your degrees. You don't need to put yourself through college again."

"Who said anything about me?" replied the teacher. "I'm talking about getting MY kids through school!"

681

During the trip to the courthouse, the class watched as a trial was conducted.

One person was brought up on charges of having robbed three banks after having embezzled half a million dollars from the company for which he worked.

"But, Your Honor," pleaded the defense attorney, "my client doesn't smoke, doesn't drink, and gives regularly to charity!"

"You see," whispered the teacher to the class, "just because you're a criminal doesn't mean that you have to have bad habits!"

Hair

682

"But, Dad!" argued the teenager, "I have to go out and find myself!"

"Get your hair cut once a year," said the Father, "and you'll find out that there you are!"

683

It was a romantic anniversary for the teacher and his wife.

"Do you remember," he said, "when we were courting, and you used to run your fingers through my hair?"

"Oh, yes," his wife replied. "Get it down from the shelf, and I'll do it right now!"

Halls

684

A visiting parent asked the principal, "How did you get such lovely white hair?"

"Simple," answered the educator, "I stood in the hall during the change of class!"

685

The teacher opened a knapsack and placed in it two cans of soda, three sandwiches, several magazines, a novel, and a few candy bars. Hefting the pack on his back, he headed for the door and left the room.

"Field trip?" inquired an observer.

Answered another, "Hall duty!"

Ham

686

Let me show you how it should be acted," said the teacher, who then proceeded to perform the Shakespearean scene with much emoting and hand-waving.

When he hadfinished, he bowed to the class and said, "Now, what did you think of that?"

"I think," whispered one student, "that if we only had some cheese and a loaf of bread, we could start our own cafeteria!"

687

"Who can tell me where breakfast foods come from?"

"I know one! Ham and eggs come from a chicken!"

"Oh, no, dear. A breakfast with ham comes from a pig."

"Aw, come on, teacher! When was the last time you saw a pig lay an egg?"

Hamlet

688

"So, in Colonial times, everybody loved Shakespeare, and they all pretended to be characters from Shakespeare, and they went all over dressed like these characters . . . "

"Just a minute!" interrupted the teacher. "That's totally inaccurate! Where are you getting your facts?"

"From the history book," answered the student. "It says here that Paul Revere spread the alarm to all the 'hamlets' in the county!"

689

"What do you think he emphasized in his performance as 'Hamlet'?"

"The first syllable of the name!"

690

"Shakespeare's father was a butcher, and they also had a small farm," the English teacher said. "What does that suggest to you?"

"They had 'Ham-lets' for breakfast?"

Handy

691

The elderly teacher was walking down the street when he was beset by two youths who tried to rob him. Just as they were starting to push him

144

around, a young lady stepped forward, knocked one of the assailants a good ten feet away, and got a wrist lock on the other until he dropped the teacher's wallet and had both subdued as the police pulled up.

"You certainly are handy with self-defense," the elderly teacher said. "U.S. Army Special Forces?"

"No," she smiled. "Only girl; six brothers!"

692

The couple were visiting when their friend remarked that the lamp on the desk had broken and would have to be replaced.

"Nonsense," said the husband, "I'll fix it right now!"

"Is he handy like this at home," the friend asked the wife.

"I'll say," the wife replied as the lights flickered. "He's so handy at home, we haven't had electricity for the past ten days!"

Hanukkah

693

"Did you like your Hanukkah gifts?" Mom and Dad asked their teenaged daughter.

"Oh, yes," she replied. "I hardly know which one to exchange first."

694

"Really," said the teacher to a colleague, "I think Hanukkah and Christmas have a lot in common. In both there are candles and songs and the family together and presents, and one other factor that is common to both . . . "

"You mean love?" asked the companion.

"No, I was thinking of the horrendous bills that arrive a month later!"

Happiness

695

"I was quite happy as a teacher for some time."

"Then what happened?"

"The teacher preparation days ended, school opened, and the kids came in!"

"Sir, do you think that happiness depends on how much money you have?"

"While money is a necessity of life," returned the teacher, "it cannot buy everything, and certainly not happiness!"

"I'm so glad you feel like that, because I heard my father say that he ain't gonna pay you for the tutoring you done!"

Hardship

697

The couple celebrated their seventy-fifth wedding anniversary, and, naturally, they were asked how they stayed together that long.

"We were married a year," said the wife, "and we were convinced that we had made a bad mistake. We took a look at how much it would cost to get a divorce, and then we looked at how much we had and found that hardship had eaten up all our resources!

"We decided the only thing we could do was to learn to live with one another, and that's what we've been doing for the last seventy-four years!"

698

"My staying overnight won't impose a hardship on you, will it?" asked Aunt Minnie.

"Of course not," returned the wife. "You'll have to sleep with Billy, but his bed-wetting problem is mostly under control."

"Er . . . on second thought, I believe I have reservations at the hotel."

Whispered the wife to her husband, "Works every time!"

Haste

699

"If you keep jumping at conclusions like that," said the teacher, "you are going to be the first person here to get nowhere in great haste!"

700

"Come, come, children!" prompted the teacher. "Let us make haste!"

"You know," said one small student as the class moved along at a brisk pace, "I wish she'd find the recipe for that 'haste' thing so we could stop running up and down these hallways looking for it!"

Hate

701

Mother and a neighbor were talking outside when her son came walking home from school.

"I hate school!" mumbled the youth. "I hate my teachers! I hate the other kids! I hate homework! I hate books!"

"Hey," said mother to the neighbor, "as long as he's happy!"

702

In lieu of a poor showing on a test, the football player had been assigned a research paper on Shakespearean sonnets. Now he sat in the library surrounded by books.

"Shakespeare!" he moaned. "Shakespeare is driving me insane!"

"Take it easy," said a fellow player on the team. "Just point out this Shakespeare kid to me, and I'll make certain he doesn't bother you any more!"

Headache

703

The teacher was feeling out of sorts, so she shared it with the class.

"Do you all know what a headache is?" she asked.

"Not exactly," answered one youngster, "but whatever it is, my brother is one, because that's what my Dad keeps calling him!"

704

"Now," said the speaker after an hour and forty-five minutes, "I have filled you with new ideas; I have presented you with new thoughts; I have given you something for your mind!"

"Yes," murmured one bored student, "and it's called a headache!"

Health

705

"I tell you," said one student to another, "I am really worried about the English teacher's health."

"But," replied the other, "the English teacher's health is perfect. In fact, that's one teacher who's never absent!"

"Exactly!" That's why I'm worried!"

706

"What would be one way to keep people healthy?"

"Tell them not to get sick!"

707

"Remember, an apple a day keeps the doctor away!"

"Yes, and a clove of garlic will do the same thing for everyone else!"

Health and the Family

708

"Mom, my head hurts and I feel like I'm gonna be sick. Can I stay home from school today?"

"Yes, you certainly may."

"Gee, thanks, Mom! I'm sure I'll be healthy in just a little while."

"I'm sure you will, too. You didn't look at the calendar. It's Saturday!"

709

Father took his son to the doctor.

"Remember," Father coached the lad, "keep telling him how poor we are; you'll get cured faster!"

710

The boy played ball until supper time, ate a full meal, talked on the phone for two hours, watched TV, and finally rolled over on the floor and intoned, "Gosh, I feel real bad! I think I'd better stay home tomorrow!"

"English," asked Mother, "or math?"

"Math . . . "

"Come on," said Mother, "I'll help you study for the test!"

Heat

711

"I swear," said the exhausted teacher, "if it gets any hotter in here, I'm going to have to stop teaching . . . "
Shouted one student, "Close the windows! Close the windows!"

712

The student had transferred from a modern, air-conditioned city school to an open-air model in the country at a time when the temperature was in the nineties.
The first afternoon there, the student met the principal in the hallway.
"Sir," said the pupil, "take my advice; borrow the money, pay the electric bill, and turn on the blasted air-conditioner!"

713

"It is essential," stated the school business administrator, "that we air-condition the school; you have no idea of the havoc and destruction that may be caused by high heat and humidity!"
"You know," said a parent afterward, "it's nice of you to be so concerned about the children."
"What children?" said the school official. "I was thinking about the computers!"

Helicopter

714

The principal had to attend a conference upstate and was about to take her first helicopter ride.
"I admit I'm a little nervous," the principal told the vice-principal who had accompanied her to the heliport. "These things don't crash very often, do they?"
"Oh, no!" assured the vice-principal. "Just once!"

715

Talk about high security! The last school I taught in had such tight security, the students were flown in by helicopter to avoid the mine fields!

Hem

716

"What do you think about the hemline of a dress?" the girls asked their English teacher.

"I think the hem of the dress should be like a good composition," she answered; "long enough to cover the subject, but short enough to keep it interesting!"

717

The student, who had obviously eaten a very powerful lunch, kept pressing closer and closer to the teacher. Finally, the teacher threw up her hands!

"Sewing 101!" she shouted.

"What?" said the surprised student.

"Sewing 101," continued the teacher, "taught me that if you keep hemming me in, I'll be wearing you very tightly in no time at all!"

Heritage

718

At the International Food Festival held at the school, the teacher noticed one boy who went to almost every booth. One moment he was eating Italian food, then German, then African, then Chinese."

"Pardon me, young man," said the curious teacher, "but exactly what is your heritage?"

Answered the lad, "Hungry teenager!"

719

"We should all be proud of our individual heritage and what has been passed down to us," said the teacher, who then asked several students to say a few words about their ethnic heritage. All was going well, until the teacher came to one pupil who sat in sullen contemplation.

"Aren't you proud of your heritage?" asked the teacher.

"Oh, sure," answered the student. "Both my grandfather and my Uncle Willie were expelled from school, so right now I'm wondering what I'm doing here!"

History

720

On a class tour of an historic ship, the guide stopped beside a plaque attached to the deck.

"And it was here," said the guide pointing to the plaque, "that the gallant captain fell!"

"No wonder," mumbled one of the schoolchildren, "I almost tripped over the blasted thing myself!"

721

Her grandchild was studying World War II, so Grandma was recalling for her what she had been doing that day in 1941 when Pearl Harbor was attacked.

"Actually," recalled Grandma, "we who lived through it knew that we were listening to history!"

"Yeah," commented her grandchild, "did you also know that we who would be born later would have to write compositions about it?"

722

"I don't get it," said the child after an historic tour of Revolutionary War inns. "If George Washington slept all the places they said he did, how did he ever have any time left to fight the British?"

723

"I got a question," stated one member of the class.

"Go ahead," said the social studies teacher.

"Washington, Lincoln, Martin Luther King, Columbus—how come they were all born on holidays?"

724

"So Ponce de León spent a great deal of his life searching for the fountain of youth," explained the social studies teacher.

"He shouldn't have looked so hard," commented one youngster. "My mother keeps it in a jar in the medicine cabinet and puts it on her face every night!"

725

"Do you know the essence of history," asked the teacher.

"Sure," said the student, "if it happened any time before today, we write about it!"

Hobbies

726

"I used to have a hobby," the student said, "but my mother made me give it up."

"Too expensive?" asked the teacher.

"No, she just didn't like me keeping those fish heads under my bed . . . "

727

"Long ago, the doctor told me I should start a hobby in order to reduce stress," said one teacher.

"What did you take up?" asked a colleague.

"Worrying!"

728

"Good grief!" exclaimed the teacher as the student's book fell to the ground and at least ten crib sheets for past and future exams fell out.

"Before you ask anything," said the student, "please tell me you believe that I'm not too young to have been starting a hobby!"

Holidays

729

"Tell me, little boy, what holidays do you like best?"

"All those that give us off from school!"

730

"Tell me, little girl, which holiday do you like least?"

"The Fourth of July!"

"Goodness! Why do you dislike that holiday?"

"'Cause it comes when we're not in school, so we can't get out, because we are already!"

Principal to small boy standing in the school office: "You don't understand! I can't declare the next week a school holiday just because you passed your English exam!"

Home Economics

732

"You gotta do something about that home ec class," stated the student to her mother. "The teacher is using food for cruel and unusual punishment!"

"Do you mean," questioned the mother, "that she doesn't allow you to eat what you cook?"

"Just the opposite!" returned her daughter. "She MAKES us eat what we cook; that's where the cruel and unusual punishment comes in!"

733

"Taste this, Ms. Pacaro," said the home ec student to her teacher, "this recipe has been handed down from generation to generation in our family."

"Of course it has," said the teacher as she sampled the concoction and mumbled to herself. "No one has been willing to take the blame!"

Homework

734

"Why don't you have your homework?"

"Er . . . my mother broke her leg before I got home from school, and I had to take care of her . . . "

"I saw your mother at the mall last night, and she was walking normally. What do you have to say to that!"

"Wow! Ain't modern medicine wonderful?"

735

"Son, do you believe in life after death?"

"Oh, yes, Sir, I do."

"That's good, because you know how you couldn't do your home-work last night because your grandfather died? Well, he's down in the office wanting to take you out of class, and I just didn't want that to come as too much of a shock!"

736

Homework is the bane of the school bored!

737

"Henry," said the teacher, "did you do this homework yourself?"

"Yes, I did," answered the student. "Why do you ask?"

"Because it is very unusual to have a student write that the first thing we should do is ' . . . impeach those blood-suckers in Washington, so an honest businessman like me can get a decent tax break!!!'"

738

"And why don't you have your homework?"

"I did it! Honest! But, it floated up from the table and flew right out the window!"

"Sure! And exactly how did that happen?"

"Would you believe it, my parents were one payment late, and that heartless company turned off the gravity in our house!"

Honesty

739

"It is reported that Honest Abe Lincoln once walked ten miles to return five cents to a customer who had overpaid. Now, what does that teach you?"

"That money went a lot further in those days!"

740

There is one great advantage to being honest; you never have to remember what you said!

741

"Why do you think honesty is the best policy?"

"Because so few people are willing to pay the premiums on it!"

Honor

742

"I am a person of honor!" said the speaker. "Honor runs in my family! I am a slave to honor! My motto is, 'Honor Above All'!!!"

"Tell me honestly," said one student to another, "doesn't he make you want to reach to see if your wallet is still there?"

743

"Did you do this paper yourself?"

"Yes, I did."

" . . . without any help?"

"Absolutely! All by myself!"

" . . . on you honor?"

"Could you rephrase that question?"

744

"So, you think that students should be honorable?"

"Yes, I do!"

"Are you honorable?"

"I sure am! Take homework, for example; I NEVER copy from more than one person at a time!"

Hospital

745

"Goodness, are hospitals getting overcrowded!" said the teacher who had just returned from medical leave.

"Really," asked a colleague, "was it six to a room?"

"No," answered the first, "to a bed!"

746

"What took you so long to return to school?" asked a colleague. "We had word that you were out of the hospital in ten days."

"I was," answered the recovered teacher. "In ten days, my heart had improved so much, they sent me home. Unfortunately, before I left the hospital, they showed me the bill, and my relapse took another three weeks!"

747

If you are ill, they put you in a hospital, and the hospital cures your body. Then they send you the bill, and you have to see a psychiatrist to keep from going insane.

748

"What did they do to your Mommy in the hospital?" one child asked another.

"I don't know," answered the first tot, "but she did a lot of sewing while she was in there . . ."

"Sewing? How do you know that?"

"Because I heard her tell Daddy that every time she turned over, somebody was slipping her a needle!"

749

"I think a hospital is a learning center," stated one student.

"You mean because it teaches you about coping with illness . . ."

"No, I mean that with the hospital gowns they give you, everytime somebody walks away from you, you get a real education!"

Hotel

750

The two educators arrived late in the convention city, and the only rooms they could get were in a rather run-down and seedy hotel.

"Do you think they at least changed the sheets?" asked one.

"Certainly," said the other, "from the room across the hall to here; from here to the room across the hall . . ."

751

The last trip we went on for the school board, they insisted on saving money by putting us up in one of those economy hotels. The lodgings were so small, you couldn't get claustrophobic; there was no room to fit it in!

House

752

"Mr. Jones," asked the student, "is it true that you live in a boarding house?"

"For the time being," said the teacher.

"Then I want out of this class! My mother told me that I should never listen to roomers!"

753

A truth that is known by every home owner: You never own a house; the house owns you!

754

"So, your husband did all the electrical wiring on your house all by himself?"

"Yes, just before it burned to the ground!"

Humanity
(See also: Mankind)

755

"What is one of humanity's major drawbacks?"

"People!"

756

"Now," said the speaker, "I am going to tell you what's wrong with humanity!!!"

"Don't you think," whispered one student, "that he should be part of it before he criticizes it?"

757

If vegetarians eat vegetables, what do humanitarians eat?

Humor

758

The principal stopped the two teachers in the hall and told them a joke she had heard recently. One of the two particularly laughed and laughed, proclaiming it the best joke he had ever heard.

"Listen," said the calmer of the two when the principal had left, "I told you that same joke yesterday, and you barely smiled!"

"Ah, yes," said his companion, "but that joke was being told by a colleague and this one by my principal!"

759

If life is a factory, then humor is the lubricant that keeps the gears turning!

760

The teacher had to leave early, and it was announced that a student from the upper grades would take over. Consequently, one class member had coated the chair of the teacher's desk with honey and put glue on the desk's surface.

At that point the principal of the school walked in and announced, "Because Mr. Smith had to leave early, I will be your teacher for the rest of the day. Now, what would you like to discuss?"

Said one student, "The necessity of a sense of humor in all of life's situations?"

Husband

761

"I really want to get involved in my child's education," said the mother over the phone to her child's teacher. "I want to be part of it; to be a partner with you; to be there when needed!"

"Wonderful!" said the teacher. "When can we meet?"

Said the mother, "My husband will be in to see you on Thursday!"

762

"My husband got on this do-it-yourself kick," said the wife. "Now, the minute anything breaks down, there he is with his tool kit!"

"That must save you a good deal of money."

"Not really," replied the wife, "it costs a small fortune to have those service people in to repair the things he's fixed!"

763

"I am a man of few words," said the teacher. "Do you know what that means?"

"Sure," answered the student, "that means you're a husband!"

Hygiene

764

The little tyke came into school covered with dirt from head to toe. The principal took one look at him and exclaimed, "Hygiene! Hygiene!"

"No," said the child, "my name's Paul, but 'Hi!' to you, too!"

765

"Look at you!" exclaimed the teacher. "Here we are in a class on hygiene, and that hand of yours is filthy. Why, I'll give you a dollar if you can show me another hand in the room that is dirtier than this one!"

The child immediately drew his other hand from his pocket and held it up.

"Here it is!" he shouted. "Now, where's my buck?"

Hyperactive

766

"How hyperactive is he?"

"Yesterday, I yelled at him five times, he knocked every book off the shelf, pulled the pigtails of three girls in class, and the janitor had to be called in four times to clean up the messes!"

"What a day that must have been!"

"Day? That's what happened in the ten minutes before school started!"

767

"Yes, Sally used to be hyperactive," mother told the kindergarten teacher, "but she's much better now."

"Glad to hear it; is there anything else I should know?"

"No, just make certain her leash is buckled tightly, and you'll be fine!"

Hypnosis

768

"In hypnosis," one student explained to another, "you just go to sleep with your eyes open."

"I get it!" said the other. "Just like English class!"

769

"Is it true that under hypnosis, they can only make you do things that you would normally do when you're awake?"

"That's right."

"Remind me never to get hypnotized!"

Hypochondria

770

"I must tell you," said the school doctor to the principal, "that you are quite healthy. Your only trouble is that you're a hypochondriac!"

"Oh, no!" said the educator. "Now I need a psychiatrist. I knew I was sick!!!"

771

"Oh, boy! Wow! This is great!" exclaimed the teacher as he was being wheeled into the hospital emergency room.

"Please, Sir," said the nurse. "I don't believe you realize that you're having a heart attack . . . "

"Sure, I realize that," he stated, "but I just can't help thinking about when I return to school, and what I'll say to that math teacher who keeps calling me a hypochondriac!"

772

Inscription for the tombstone of a hypochondriac: "Now do you believe me?"

Hypocrisy

773

A boy was sitting on his front porch, sadly contemplating another school day, when another youngster sauntered by, also on his way to school, whistling merrily and with a huge smile on his face.

"Where are you going?" asked the sad boy.

"To school!" smiled the other.

Mumbled the first lad, "Hypocrite!"

774

"This is the stupidest agenda I have ever seen!" said one teacher just as the principal, who had called the meeting, stepped into the room.

Without missing a beat, the educator continued, "And that's what anyone would say who did not know what an expert our principal is in conducting meetings!"

775

Then there was the person who was extremely good looking, no matter which of the two faces he had on!

Ice

776

Two teachers were walking into school one frosty winter morning when one of them grabbed the other by the sleeve and pulled to the right.

"Careful!" said that teacher. "There's a patch of ice straight ahead, and you might slip."

"Thank you! My goodness, how perceptive of you; I can barely see it."

"That's OK," said the first teacher, "my ice-sight is 20/20!"

777

"My sister said that her lemonade was warm, and I brought her some ice, and that's how come I got in trouble."

"That doesn't sound like something you'd get punished for."

"It is when you deliver it by pulling out her waistband and dumping the ice down her pants!"

Ideas

778

An idea is very much like a child; naturally, the best one is the one to which WE have given birth and raised and nurtured.

779

"Last night, just before I fell asleep, I had the greatest idea I ever had!"

"Wonderful! Share it with me!"

"I can't! When I woke up this morning, all I remembered of it was that it was great!"

780

"We need fresh ideas around here," said the principal as he pinned up a sign that read, "Take That Idea and Do It Now!"

That afternoon the gym teacher ran off with the school secretary!

Idiom

781

"When you use slang expressions like that," said the teacher to the student, "I fail to understand your idiom."

"Ms. Johnson was really hard on me today," the same student later told his brother.

"What did she do?"

"She said she couldn't understand me, because I was an idiot!"

782

"I been a-waitin' the boy's test marks to see!" said the elderly gentleman.

"My," remarked the teacher, "what an interesting idiom!"

"Yep, interesting he be, but he also be my grandson, so you be watchin' what you call him!"

Idiot

783

"God made the idiot. He did this for practice. When He had perfected the art, He made the School Board."

—Samuel Clemens (Mark Twain)

784

The boy stood up on the playground and addressed another child.

"What did you call me?" he roared.

The other boy stepped forward, a full foot taller and about fifty pounds heavier. He glared down at the smaller boy and hissed, "I said you were an idiot! So what?"

"Oh," gulped the boy as he stared upward at the massive shape before him, "I just wanted to thank you for such an accurate diagnosis!"

785

"Hey!" shouted the boy's older sister, "did you just call Billy Smith an idiot?"

"Yeah! You know what he . . . "

"Enough! Not only is it not polite to call anyone names such as 'idiot,' but such terms are prejudicial and at the very least can seriously damage a relationship . . . "

"I . . . I'll tell Billy that I'm sorry . . . "

"Good!" said the boy's sister, "and don't do it again, you little moron!"

Idol

786

"So, how's your new teacher?"

"The kids all think of him as an idol."

"They do?"

"Yeah, permanently scowling and made out of stone!"

787

"That teacher is crazy!"

"Why do you say that?"

"She told me that I got bad grades because I was an idle student."

"So?"

"I looked up 'idol' and she's insane! Do you know of ANYBODY who would ever worship ME?"

Ignorance

788

"Honest, Sir," said the student to the principal, "I didn't know it was against the rules to skateboard down the hallway."

"Son, haven't you ever heard that ignorance is no excuse?"

"But it has to be!" pleaded the lad. "How else can you explain me?"

789

He was grossly ignorant, which meant that he said the same stupid thing at least 144 times!

790

The wise person is the one who begins to search for a definition of ignorance by looking in the mirror . . .

791

"I'm sorry, young man, but I do not think that you can claim your father's ignorance as a valid reason for not doing your math homework last night!"

792

"Come, come!" said the teacher to her colleague, "you shouldn't get so upset; every student is ignorant unless he or she is taught."

"It's not his ignorance that upsets me," returned her friend, "it's that he is SO positive of all those things he knows nothing about!"

Illness

793

"The doctor examined me and told me I was perfectly healthy," the man said to his friend. "He told me I was nothing but a hypochondriac!"

"What did you do?"

"I told him I wanted a second opinion . . . "

"And . . . "

"He said I was paranoid, too!"

794

"Ma'am, do you think it's right to punish a kid just because someone in the family got ill?" asked the student.

"Of course not," stated the teacher.

"Then will you please talk to my mother," continued the lad. "I'm being punished just because my brother got sick after I forced him to eat those worms!"

795

Then there was the student who tried to get out of school by swallowing a doorknob and claiming that it turned his stomach!

Image

796

The two young boys made their way to school dressed neatly and cleanly. Halfway to their destination, one boy stopped, lay down and rolled in the dirt, ripped his pants, ran his fingers through his hair, and pulled out his shirt tails.

"Now we can go to school," he said. "After all, IMAGE is everything!"

797

The adolescent donned a pair of jeans run through with holes; put on a purple, yellow, and green shirt that was a mass of wrinkles; tied on sneakers with the toes all but disintegrated; and, finally, placed a baseball cap on his head backwards.

"Ah!" he said as he looked in a full-length mirror, "dressed for success!"

Imagination

798

"Mom," said the girl, "I want to do my homework now, but my hands are shaking. On the way home from school just now, this great big dog started chasing me, and I just got to our fence in time, and he was barking and snarling! I was so scared!"

"You poor dear," said the mother. "Come on, we'll put your favorite video on and I'll get you a glass of milk and a slice of cake."

As she sank into the sofa before the TV, she remarked to her older brother, "You were right! Imagination is an extremely powerful tool!"

799

"I know you don't like doing the homework," the teacher explained to one pupil, "but just imagine the good it will do you in later years."

"That's fine for the future," returned the student, "but as for the present, couldn't you just imagine that I had it to hand in?"

Immigration

800

For any nation, IMMIGRATION is the sincerest form of flattery.

801

"We all have heritages in different countries," the math teacher said to the class. "Indeed, America has been called a nation of immigrants!"

"You see" whispered one student, "I told you he was speaking a foreign language!"

Impersonal

802

"George," said the teacher to the student, "I care about you; I want you to succeed, George; you see, George, that's why I'm so hard on you . . . "

"Sir . . . "

"Yes, George, what is it?"

"My name is Harry!"

803

"We are getting too impersonal around here," said the principal to the faculty. "You should make every effort to memorize the names of each and every one of your students!"

"Here! Here!" exclaimed one teacher.

Said the principal, "And I want to thank what's-his-name for that support!"

Impossible

804

Teachers do the impossible every day; they take minds that are set rock hard and turn them into fertile soil for the seeds of learning.

805

The difficult is what we can accomplish by tomorrow; the impossible is that which may take half a marking period!

806

"Your child," the teacher told the parents, "is rather like a waterfall that flows upward . . . "

"But," returned one parent, "a waterfall that flows upward is impossible."

Said the teacher, "Exactly!"

807

"Remember," the teacher told the class at the end of the school day, "nothing is impossible if you just concentrate on it!"

"I hate to prove him wrong," commented one student as they left the class, "but I don't think this 'F' on my test is going to change into an 'A+' by the time I get home no matter how much I think about it!"

Inch

808

The out-of-shape teacher had been talked into a race with the school's track star. Before the teacher was five yards down the track, the youth had practically covered the entire distance. Then the student avoided the finish line and lapped the track once more, passing the teacher a second time. Finally, the exhausted teacher collapsed just an inch before the finish line and never did complete the run.

"I'm rather proud of myself," said the teacher later. "After all, considering my age and condition, I only lost by an inch!"

809

"Look at that!" said a teacher to her colleague. "Young Jones grew two inches over the summer!"

"How can you tell so exactly? Do you pick an imaginary spot on the wall to measure against?"

"Easier than that," answered the teacher. "Just estimate the number of inches between pants' cuffs and shoe tops!"

Inclement

810

The principal was in the main office when a teacher walked in dripping wet from head to toe.

"Inclement weather?" asked the principal.

"Class with water pistols!" answered the teacher.

811

"Local schools will be closed today, because the weather is inclement," said the voice on the radio.

"I'm sure glad school's closed, Mom," said one boy as he looked out the window, "but it ain't in Clement, wherever that is; it's snowing like crazy right here!"

812

"Tomorrow," said the principal to the faculty, "will be open-house day, and I have asked every parent in the community to visit the school and your classrooms. Now, what are we going to do to prepare for this?"

Whispered one teacher, "Pray for inclement weather!"

Indebted

813

"Finally," said the retiree at the conclusion of her speech, "I am indebted to my colleagues . . . "

"I'll say," whispered one member of the audience, "She still owes me that five dollars she borrowed back in 1973!"

814

"How could I retire," said the teacher in his retirement speech," without paying homage to the concept of personal indebtedness that has kept me going in teaching for these many years!"

Industrial Arts

815

"Mr. Johnson," said the industrial arts student, "my project is finished; I followed all the plans; I used the best wood; I sanded it twice, and I gave it three coats of varnish! So, Mr. Johnson . . . "
"Yes."
"What did I make?"

816

"What was the last thing said to you when you showed me your project?" the industrial arts teacher asked the student.
"You said it was usual to end the project by varnishing everything!"
"But I was pointing to the project! Not the band saws, sanders, and drill presses!"

817

"When I was taking Industrial Arts almost thirty years ago," said the English teacher, "I made something that is still around today."
"What is it?" asked a student.
"A reputation for being totally incompetent with any kind of tool whatsoever!"

Ineligible

818

"Give me one good reason why my son is ineligible for the team." the parent demanded of the coach.

"All right," the coach said, "he's unreliable, his grades are terrible, and he has no athletic talent whatsoever!"

"Hey," said the parent, "I asked for only ONE!"

819

The student handed in the report the day AFTER it was due. The teacher handed it back to the pupil.

"This paper," the teacher said, "is ineligible."

"No, it's not!" replied the youth. "That's why I typed it!"

820

It was the first football game the English teacher had ever attended. A few minutes into the event, a penalty was called against the home team.

"Why are we being penalized?" the English teacher asked.

"There was an ineligible receiver downfield," answered her companion.

"I tell you," she commented, "I have half these boys in class, and if we start arguing about eligibility, they might as well call the game right now!"

Infection

821

"Ms. Johnson," said the tiny kindergarten student, her eyes filled with tears, "could you give me a hug? I'm kinda sad!"

"Oh, Sweetie, of course!" replied Ms. Johnson who held the child, kissed her, and sat the little girl on her lap.

"Now, Sweetie, tell me what's the matter?"

"I gotta go to the doctor this afternoon," sniffed the child as she burrowed closer. "Mama thinks I have the mumps AND the measles!"

822

The teacher was in bed with the flu when a friend came by.

"How do you figure you caught it?" asked the friend.

"Every kid in my class had it," the teacher replied. "You might say that this is a token of their infection!"

Ingenious

823

The teacher was explaining the lesson to the class when a large fly got into the room and began to buzz around the educator's head.

"Whenever this happens," the teacher admitted, "I can never decide whether to simply ignore the fly or stop until the fly goes away."

At which point, a student in the front seat took a book and smashed the fly flat!

"Ingenious!" said the teacher. "Why didn't I think of that!"

824

"I must congratulate you on the smooth flow of traffic in your school," the visitor told the principal. "How did you ever accomplish it?"

"Well," replied the principal, "the key to easy passage in the halls was the north stairwell. It had to be used for DOWN traffic only."

"How did you manage that?"

"I put up a sign that said, 'UP ONLY, UNDER NO CONDITIONS MAY ANY STUDENT OR FACULTY MEMBER GO DOWN THESE STAIRS!!!'"

Initiation

825

The president of a college fraternity was being interviewed by the campus newspaper.

"What do you think of the new college policy against initiations and hazing?"

"I'm all for it," the frat leader answered. "Initiations are barbaric and certainly have no place in our campus life. Now, if you'll excuse me, by now the pledges will have finished shining my shoes and ironing my shirts, and I want to make certain they hang them properly, so they don't wrinkle!"

826

At the fraternity initiation, one lad stood covered in whipped cream and panting from having to run around the frat house ten times. As he breathed heavily, he noticed another pledge who stood calmly, not a hair out of place and without a single drop of perspiration on his brow.

The calm young man noticed the stare and said, "I'm exempt from initiation."

"Oh," panted the other pledge, "bad heart?"

"No," sighed the first, "rich father!"

Innovation

827

"Let me explain," said the teacher. "When I told you that if you were going to learn, you had to be innovative, I did not mean writing the answers to the test questions on the toes of your sneakers!"

828

The teacher went to look up something in the unabridged dictionary she kept in her room, only to find the book missing. She searched and finally found that it had been taken by a student who was sitting on it in order to reach the keyboard of a school computer.

"Are you going to punish him for taking the book?" asked another student.

"I haven't decided whether to punish him," said the teacher, "or compliment him on an innovative use of an educational resource!"

Insanity

829

INSANITY: One of those new horizons your students open up to you.

830

INSANITY: One of those things parents catch from their kids.

831

INSANITY: The prevailing condition in the (2nd; 7th; 9th; etc.) grade!

832

INSANITY: Working against insurmountable odds to accomplish the impossible with individuals who, to a large extent, will fight you every step of the way in order that they may have a chance of succeeding and forgetting all about you in the process; a synonym for this type of insanity is "dedicated teacher."

Insincerity

833

"Gosh, Ms. Johnson, you certainly look attractive today!" commented the student.

"Rhonda," asked the teacher, "do you really mean that?"

"No," came the reply, "but I'm failing your course!"

834

"Mrs. Jones," said the student, "I realize that in the past I have failed to do my homework; not paid attention in class; and, in general, been a distraction to you and others, but I want you to know that I'm turning over a new leaf. From here on in, I'm going to work and succeed."

"Marvin," asked the teacher, "are you sincere in wanting to change?"

"Heck, no!" answered the student, "but I'm sincere in not wanting the whipping my Daddy was gonna give me if I didn't say what I just did!"

835

"Good morning," said the teacher to the small student, "how are you today?"

"Okay," replied the child, who then felt silent.

"Aren't you going to ask me how I am?"

"No."

"Why not?"

"Because," answered the student, "I don't really give two cents how you are!"

Institution

836

"Mom," said the boy, "I'm real worried! Today, our teacher said that the school was an institution of learning!"

"Your teacher is right," returned mother, "the school is an institution of learning. Why does that worry you?"

"Institution," answered the lad, "is a word they also use for asylums and prisons! I tell you, this has sure made me think!"

837

"Jones! You are not allowed to blow that trumpet in the middle of the hallway while class is in session!"

"Why not, Ma'am? Just the other day, you said that this school was an insti-TOOT-ion!"

838

"Did you say that Mr. Jones is an institution around this place?"

"Yes, I did."

"I know what you mean. He is starting to fall apart around the edges, isn't he?"

Integrity

839

"What we need in this school is integrity!" proclaimed one teacher.

"How dare you say that!" returned the principal. "We've always had a representative racial balance in this school!"

840

The teacher read the paper and realized that he had seen the same theme the previous semester handed in by another student.

"I am afraid, Sir, that someone I know has lost his integrity," said the teacher.

"Oh," returned the youth, "tell him to look in the lost and found in the gym. They got everything there!"

Intelligence

841

"Actually," said one parent to another, "my son is so intelligent that school work bores him, and that is why he does so poorly in his grades . . . "

"Good grief!" returned the other. "I have a son who cuts school entirely. He must be a genius!"

842

"Do you think," asked the parent, "that given Maria's intelligence, she should go to Harvard or to some technical institution like M.I.T.?"

"Actually," answered the teacher, "I think she should get out of kindergarten first!"

843

"Very well," said the teacher, "perhaps you do have a perfectly fine reason for not having your report today; a reason that will keep me from recording your grade as 'F'; go ahead and try."

"Before I do that," said the unhappy student, "let me ask you this: How intelligent are you?"

844

"In a moment," said the teacher who was addressing the Parents' Day assembly, "I am going to introduce our principal, a person of great learning and unsurpassed intelligence!"

One student leaned over to another and said, "When did we get a new principal?"

Interception (See also: Football)

845

The teacher was walking on the school grounds when from out of nowhere a tomato came sailing toward his head. A student was passing by, and he reached out a hand and grabbed the juicy object in mid-flight.

"Young man," said the teacher, "I want to thank you for that fine interception. You kept me from getting quite dirty."

"Don't thank me," returned the youth, "I'm on the team, and I did that out of pure reflex. I don't like you any more than anyone else in your class!"

846

"What an event to pick for your first football game!" said the host to his overseas visitor. "Johnson just made his fifth interception of the game!"

"I find it difficult to understand the way you reward dishonesty!"

"Reward dishonesty? What do you mean?"

"This Johnson fellow," said the visitor, "look how they cheer him, and all because he steals the balls five times!"

Introductions

847

I'd like to introduce you to a person who got the job by lots and lots of hard work. After all, you have no idea how tiring begging and crying can be!

848

I've known our speaker for a very long time. How long? Well, let's just say that I was around when he got his first order of school supplies. I remember that coal scuttle and the stack of dunce caps!

849

Now, here's a fellow whose accomplishments speak for themselves, and even though they don't say much, I'm sure he will!

850

I'd like to introduce you to a marvelous speaker who is well loved and renowned for his wit and sagacity. Unfortunately, we couldn't find anyone like that, so instead, I'd like to present . . .

Invention

851

"I just invented a device that will keep the school 100 percent safe from all break-ins and theft!"

"Great! Let me see it!"

"I can't! Some vandals broke into my lab and stole it!"

852

"Who can name an invention that has caused unrest and trouble in the world?'

"I can," said one girl. "BOYS!!!"

"I heard that someone went and invented a mechanical cook."

"I believe it! Our school has been serving mechanical foods for years!"

IQ (Intelligence Quotient)

854

"I remember as a child that I had very small feet, but I outgrew them."

"I can do better than that, everybody considered me quite brilliant as a child, but I grew out of my IQ!"

855

Then there was the parent who claimed that her son was doing poorly in school because of heredity. She maintained that the lad's IQ was the sum total of ALL the IQs on his father's side of the family!

856

"How could a person with your IQ run up such a huge credit card debt?"

"I knew of more things to buy?"

857

We must be a brilliant nation. In all your years of teaching, have you ever met a parent with a child whose IQ is BELOW average?

IRS (See also: Taxes)

858

"Who can tell me where I will find the sentence, 'It is better to give than to receive'?"

"The IRS Tax Preparation Manual!"

859

Are we in hard economic shape? Let me put it this way, the IRS has just decided to sell gift certificates!

860

Well, I finally settled with the IRS. Now I'm up to date and current . . . through the year 1979!

Issues

861

Stated the teacher, "Today, we are going to learn about modern issues."

Commented one student, "What's to learn? You pull one out; another pops up!"

862

Somebody said that we must be aware of the issues facing us. The ones facing us aren't the ones I'm worried about. It's those that sneak up behind you that will give you the most trouble!

863

"What are you and my parents going to talk about at the conference this afternoon?" asked the student.

Answered the teacher, "Oh, certain educational issues . . ."

"Great!" said the pupil, "As long as you don't talk about how I'm doing in school!"

Itch

864

The teacher sat at her desk and began to wonder if she were allergic to something in the room. Her skin was one massive itch that she couldn't seem to ignore. She was seriously considering going to the school nurse when one little fellow raised his hand.

"Ms. Jones," he stated, "could you help me look for my ant farm? I was playing with them at your desk, and now they're all gone!"

865

"I tried dating that new kid," one girl told another, "and he's nothing but a big nuisance; just a big bother!"

"Well, why did you date him; I told you he was a real itch!"

"Itch?" said the astonished young lady. "I thought you said he was RICH!"

866

The teacher spotted one of her students crying. She called the girl to her and held the child's hand in hers.

"I'm sorry you're sad," said the teacher, pressing the child's hands to her own cheek. "Won't you tell me what's wrong?"

"Well," sniffed the child, "yesterday I got poison ivy all over my fingers, and now they really itch!"

Ivy

867

"Why do so many of the older buildings on college campuses have ivy all over them?"

"Probably because the walls are falling down, they don't have the money to fix them, and they still want to keep up appearances!"

868

"Yes," said the teacher, "I have quite a lot of experience with ivy."

"English?" asked a colleague.

"No," came the reply, "poison!"

869

"Some of the best days of my life," the teacher explained to some students, "were spent in the halls of ivy!"

"I'm not saying anything against you," commented one student, "but if I were you, I wouldn't brag about it and take a chance of my wife finding out about that 'Ivy' woman!"

J

Jacks

870

The children were on the playground when the toughest kid in school sauntered by with a huge car jack on his shoulder. With great noise and a cloud of dust, he threw it to the ground.

"Now," he snarled, "who wants to play jacks MY way?"

871

"Why don't you play jacks with Timmy?" Mother asked Father.

"Look," Father replied, "I have more dexterity and speed and coordination than our son, and I don't want to embarrass him, nor do I want to 'let' him win. However, if you insist, I will play a game of jacks with him."

Some time later, Mother asked, "How did it go?"

"As I predicted," said Father, "I won the first game . . . and he won the next 37 games. Now let's change the subject!"

872

"Honey," asked a parent in a booth at the school bazaar, "I'd like to buy one of your brownies, but why are you trying to balance the money on top of that set of jacks?"

"I don't understand it either," answered the child. "All I know is that I heard the principal talking to my teacher, and she said that with all the parents coming, we had best jack up the price of everything!"

Jail

873

"Remember the famous poem by Richard Lovelace," quoted the English teacher, "that 'Stone walls do not a prison make,/Nor iron bars a cage . . . '"

"Sure," whispered one student, "but they do make a school where it's mighty hard to play hookey!"

874

"Jones!" bellowed the guard at the local jail, "were you trying to escape just now by walking out among the visitors?"

"Oh, no, Officer!" stated the prisoner. "You see, my old teacher just visited me; we got to reminiscing; and for a moment, I thought this was a school "Open House'!"

875

"You're home early," said the teacher's wife. "I thought you were going to the local jail to teach a course in the 'Philosophy of Morality.'"

"I was," returned the teacher, "but we had to cancel it; somebody stole the books!"

876

During the tour of county facilities, the teacher was asked if she would like to "try out" a jail cell. With many a giggle from the students, the educator was "locked in." Just then, a student who had lagged behind caught up with the group and took in the scene.

"I knew it!" he exclaimed. "Sooner or later she was bound to be jailed for giving us killer homework!"

Jam

877

Ask any child: JAM is fun food . . . particularly when smeared in you baby brother's hair!

878

The student brought the teacher some homemade jam, which the teacher proceeded to eat with great relish. Between spoonfuls, the educator asked, "Did you make this jam?"

"No, Ma'am," answered the student, "my mother made it, but I was the one who got most of the bugs out of the fruit!"

879

I think people use the expression "In a jam," because such situations are so sweet going in and so sticky once you're there!

Janitor

880

"How's the new janitor working out in your school?"

"Just fine! This janitor is a real reformer."

"Reformer? What do you mean?"

"Ever since he's come, it's been one sweeping reform after another!"

881

"And remember," the principal told the new teacher, "if you need to know anything about this school, there is a source to whom you can turn for the correct answer every time."

"You mean that I can always come to you, Ma'am."

"Of course not!" answered the principal. "I was talking about the school janitor!"

882

When I first started teaching over three decades ago, I asked an older educator what was the first rule of good teaching.

She looked around her spotless room with all her supplies put neatly away and said, "Make friends with the janitor!"

883

The teacher came late and uninformed to the meeting where the superintendent of schools was to be introduced. The principal had already begun.

"We have with us today a person of integrity and vision," she intoned, "whose knowledge and quick thinking are all but legendary . . . "

"What's she talking about?" said the educator. "I don't see Harry the janitor anywhere!"

Jaw

884

"Do you believe the Bible story about Samson killing more than 200 people with the jawbone of an ass?"

"Why not? At school, the English teacher has been doing the same thing for years!"

885

"Johnson!" exclaimed the teacher. "You're chewing gum! That's not allowed! Is there any reason why I should not assign you detention?"

"Yes, Sir!" answered the youth. "I'm on the forensic team; the coach says you need a strong jaw to win those debates, and I can't see why I should be punished just because I'm in training!"

886

"So, you say your brother is a big eater, huh?"

"I'll say! They even made a movie about him; it's called 'Jaws'!"

Jazz

887

The avant-garde music critic from a local newspaper was visiting the school when he stopped in the hallway.

"Wow! Just listen to that!" he exclaimed. "That's modern and progressive jazz at its best! You school is to be congratulated for its far-thinking attitudes toward music!"

At which point a student emerged from the band room.

"OK," he said, "we've finished tuning our instruments; we can begin any time you're ready!"

888

"We spent our vacation visiting relatives in Florida who live in Key West," the student told the music teacher.

"Did you bring your instrument and practice that jazz piece we've been working on?" asked the educator.

"I sure did!"

"Very good! At least there will have been one time when you played the whole thing in one Key!"

889

Our school was so progressive when it came to music that our jazz quartet had six students in it!

Jet

890

The teacher visited his friend in the hospital.

"I was on this big jet," the patient explained. "I was sitting there, and I began to think that if the jet ever crashed, I'd be killed, so I made my decision, got up, and walked off the plane!"

"So?"

"Well, it happened to be taking off at the time . . . "

891

The businessperson was seated on the jumbo jet, waiting for takeoff when she noticed an elderly man next to her who was obviously praying.

"Excuse me, Sir," she said gently, "are you a clergyman?"

"No," he answered, "I am a retired teacher, but I just found out that our pilot is the clumsiest kid I ever had in eighth grade!"

892

"Our guest today," explained the teacher to the class, "is a renowned expert in jet planes and jet engines. Before we begin, do any of you have any technical questions for our expert?"

"Yeah," said one student, "if you're such an expert on jets, how come you keep losing our family luggage each time we get on one?"

893

"Suppose," asked the teacher, "that you took a jet to Paris; then took a jet to Rome, and then took a jet three hundred miles north. Where would you be?"

Answered one student, "In some other family who could afford all those plane fares!"

"My grandfather was flying in planes when Lindbergh flew the Atlantic!" boasted one student.

"Oh, yeah!" returned another, "Well, MY grandfather was so good, he was flying jet planes when all they had were propellers!"

Jetty

895

"How did you spend the summer, Mr. Johnson?" asked a student.

"I spent a good deal of time on a small jetty."

"You did?" returned the student. "When we visited my uncle in Canada, we rode on a little planey, too!"

896

"Don't you love the sea?" asked the naturalist. "It is so good to go fishing along the coast line! You get out at the end of a jetty, and there's nothing but you and the sea and the fish and the rubber tires and the industrial waste!"

Job

897

It isn't a very difficult job; in fact, just the other day, one of the employees fainted from underwork!

898

My teenaged son just quit his job; he found out that they actually expected him to work!

899

When I was going to school, I had a summer job in a farm market. They didn't pay me any money, but I had an excellent celery!

900

"Dad," said the young lad, "is it right for a company to fire someone just because he takes a coffee break?"

"No, Son," answered the father, "I think most places now give their employees a rest period."

"Good," said the son, "because after I took my ninth coffee break today, they fired me!"

901

"I had a job with my father this summer," said the student, "and I liked almost all of it."

"Oh," asked the teacher, "what parts of the job didn't you like?"

"The parts where I had to work!"

902

"I'm here," said the youth at the employment office, "because my father has convinced me that I need a job."

"Great! I hope you don't mind hard work and long hours!"

"On the other hand," murmured the lad, "you're doing a great job of convincing me that I don't need a job!"

Job Description

903

"These letters have been here over a week," said the principal. "Why don't you put stamps on them and mail them out?"

"I looked at my job description," answered the secretary, "and nowhere could I find 'stamp licking' as one of my duties!"

904

"Why don't you simply study for the test?" asked the teacher. "You would do well; I know it."

"I'd like to, Ma'am," said the student, "but the school has me down as an underachiever, and I just gotta live up to my job description!"

905

After a particularly trying day, the principal called the superintendent of schools.

"Do you think you could change a part of my job description?" the principal asked.

"What part?"

"The part," answered the administrator, "that says, 'Gets dumped on by all the parents and teachers in the school!'"

906

"Johnny!" roared the teacher, "why must you make a joke out of everything?"

"Hey!" answered the student, "I'm the class clown; look up my job description!"

Jogging

907

"I tell you," said one educator to another as they stood and stretched one early morning on the school's track, "there's only one thing about jogging that I don't like."

"Oh? What's that?"

"The part that comes between putting on these expensive jogging shoes and taking them off!"

908

"I used to jog, but I gave it up."

"Oh? How long had you jogged before you quit?"

"About twenty-five yards . . ."

909

"I don't think you'd enjoy jogging with me; I jog very, very slowly."

"Come, now! How slowly could you jog?"

"Let me put it this way, when I stop jogging, the first thing I do is shake off the pigeons!"

910

"I love jogging!" said the teacher.

"You do."

"Oh, yes! I can sit in the park and watch others jogging for hours!"

Joke (See also: Humor)

911

The principal was being honored because of the high academic record of his school. He was asked how he had achieved such a distinction.

"Every day," he said, "I used to begin and end the school day by telling a joke over the intercom."

"And that got the students to study?"

"No, but the head of the student body did appear in my office with a promise from every kid in the school to raise his or her grades if only I STOPPED telling those jokes!"

912

"Any drawbacks to becoming a principal?"

"Just one. Now, whenever I tell a joke and somebody laughs, I can never tell if that's because it's a good joke or the person wants to get on my good side!"

913

"Did you hear the joke about the English teacher and the football player?"

"Yes, I did!"

"Well, let me tell you anyhow; I'd love to hear it again!"

914

In the teacher's lounge, one educator told a long, involved and extremely boring joke. When he was finished, his audience, a fellow teacher, got up and left the room without a comment.

"I'm worried about him," mumbled the joke teller. "He's either lost his hearing, or he has no sense of humor!"

Journalism

915

"If I become a journalist," said the boy to his English teacher, "I can live on words!"

"Indeed you can," answered the teacher. "Many a journalist has had to eat his!"

"How about doing a story on a kid cutting off his finger in home ec?" suggested the student to the school newspaper adviser. "Or how about the principal running off with the gym teacher? Or the cafeteria adding unknown ingredients to the students' food!"

"Now, just a minute!" said the adviser. "None of those things is true! Where did you ever get your idea of journalism?"

"Hey!" said the child, "I read the newspapers by the checkout counter in the supermarket!"

"Now, let me see if I have this right; if I disagree with the editorial then it's slanderous, but if you agree with what it says, then it's an outstanding example of American journalism at its best!"

Journey
(See also: Trips)

"There was a time in my life when, wherever I went, I went first class!" said one teacher.

"How do you go now?"

Snarled the first, "With children!"

As the two students entered the classroom, they noticed a sign above the door that read, "The Journey to Knowledge Begins Here!"

"He forgot to mention," whispered one, "that so does the journey to the principal's office!"

"Why is motivation so important in learning?"

"Because of something every locomotive engineer knows; you can't begin the journey unless you have first stoked the fire!"

Joy

921

"If you try," said the teacher to the class, "you can find joy in every situation."

"Yeah!" whispered one student. "The red 'F' on this test and my father's face when he sees it will be a perfect match. Oh, joy!"

922

"Let me ask you this;" said the teacher to the student, "would money really help you to find joy?"

"Maybe not," answered the student, "but I could go out looking for it in a Ferrari!"

923

The teacher stumbled into the house and sagged into an easy chair. Her hair was a mess, her sweater was torn in several places, and there was fresh paint all over her skirt. As she pushed the shoes from obviously sore feet, she addressed her husband.

"Tell me again," she sighed in an exhausted voice, "about the joys of teaching!"

Judgment

924

"And how," the teacher asked the class, "does a jury decide which side will win the case?"

"They see," answered one impressionable youth, "which side has the nicest lawyer?"

925

Have you ever noticed that when people make a mistake, they will claim poor memory but never poor judgment?

926

Don't make SNAP judgments; wait until you can button it up!

927

"Excuse me," one student asked another, "but what is meant by the term 'Judgment Day'?"

"In here," answered the second, "it's every day the old man gives a quiz!"

928

"This melon is not ripe," said the home ec teacher. "My judgment is never wrong!"

"Maybe not," whispered one student to another, "but her eyesight sure is. She's sniffing a basketball!"

Juggle/Juggling

929

Last summer I visited a side-show performer who could juggle ten balls in the air at one time. After the show, I sought him out and asked him how he did it.

"This is just my summer job," the man said. "Regularly, I'm a teacher, and after juggling five classes a day of thirty kids per class, this is a piece of cake!"

930

"Suppose a person weighing 100 lbs and carrying three watermelons, each weighing ten pounds, wants to cross a bridge that can stand 120 pounds before collapsing; how can it be done?"

"I know!" said one student. "If he juggled the watermelons, one would be in the air at all times, so he would never weigh more than 120 pounds!"

"Excellent!" commented the teacher. "Are their any other solutions?"

"Oh, yes," answered one young lady. "Forget about crossing the bridge; eat the watermelons on the spot, and then launch a full-scale investigation into the politicians who allowed a bridge to be built that could carry only 120 pounds!"

931

"Ma'am," said the student, "is juggling a crime?"

"Of course not," answered the teacher, "it's just a form of entertainment."

"Then how come my uncle is going to jail for juggling the books?"

Jumping

932

"I think your brother has a good chance at the high-jump medal," said the coach. "We both have to try to provide the motivation!"

A day later, when the class was gathered on the field, there was a loud shout and the young man in question ran down the track, jumped in the air, and easily cleared a tremendous height!

"How did you get him to jump like that?" asked the coach.

Replied the jumper's brother, "Sir, you have no idea of the motivational power there is in a tray of ice cubes dumped into one's gym shorts, do you?"

933

"Rope jumping is really good for your health!"

"I don't know. I tried class skipping for years, and didn't do me any good!"

934

"That Johnson child is really bright," said the teacher. "Why, he's always jumping up with the answer!"

"I had him last year," commented the colleague, "and he wouldn't be half so bright if he weren't sitting in front of his brother, who likes to play with really sharp pencils!"

June

935

Quoted the teacher, "'What is so rare as a day in June . . . '"

Answered one student, "A day in June when the kids AREN'T thinking about summer vacation!"

936

"I just love that Rodgers & Hammerstein song, 'June Is Bustin' Out All Over'!" said the teacher.

"In that case," commented a student, "wait until the final bell of the school year, and you'll see some 'bustin' out' in June for sure!"

"I think June is an unfair month!" proclaimed the student.

"Why do you say that?"

"Because, just the time when it gets warm enough to enjoy playing hookey, the school up and closes and takes all the fun out of it!"

Jungle

938

"What are we going to do?" said Baby Tiger to Mama Tiger in the jungle. "Here comes a hunter, and he has five rifles, three special sighting scopes, and devices to allow him to see in the dark!"

"Hush!" answered Mama Tiger, and she taught her cub how to sneak up from behind and pounce.

The hunter was never heard of again.

All of which goes to prove that technology may be fine, but it will never be a substitute for a good basic education.

939

"Yes, Ma'am," said the student, "my Mom says she can arrange for the class to visit the office building where she works, but we gotta do a few things first. We have to get every kid a rifle, and high boots, and lots and lots of bug spray!"

"Just a moment. Did your mother tell you this?"

"No," answered the pupil, "but every time I ask her about her work, she says, 'It's a jungle out there!' So, I figure we'd better be ready for it!"

Junior

940

Before you start calling anyone "Junior!" it would pay to remember that a toothpick is, in reality, a "Junior Redwood!"

941

"Will someone tell me," the teacher asked the class of second graders, "what is a junior high school?"

"I don't know exactly," answered one exasperated tyke, "but I'll bet that when it talks to the regular high school, it says, 'Gosh, Dad, do you have to keep calling me "Junior" in public?'"

942

"Time for you to address the class rally," said the guidance counselor to the principal, who grabbed some notes from his desk and hurried to the auditorium.

"I salute the junior class!" he said. "The junior class has a bright future ahead of it. Indeed, the school will long remember this junior class!"

Smiling, the principal looked out at an amazing sea of stone cold faces.

"Check your notes!" whispered the guidance counselor. "You're at the senior class assembly!"

Junk

943

"Junk" is what other people keep in THEIR attics and basements, while you keep valuable antique materials in YOURS!

944

"What is all this junk in your desk?" exclaimed the teacher.

"Junk? Junk?" said the student. "Are you referring to my priceless used bubble gum collection?"

945

"What is all this junk in your desk?" exclaimed the teacher.

"Please have a little respect!" said the student. "That's EDUCATION-AL junk!"

946

"What is all this junk in your desk?" exclaimed the teacher.

"These," said the student, "are all the 'valuable' papers you told me not to throw away, because I-would-be-happy-I-had-them-one-day!"

Jury

947

" . . . and so, he went to trial before twelve of his peers."

"Twelve of his piers! I didn't know he owned waterfront property?"

948

Then there was the class clown who went before a student jury and was found not guilty by reason of inanity.

949

The teacher went to court on a small civil suit and came before a petit jury. Immediately, he turned to his attorney.

"Quick," he said, "drop the case right now!"

"But, why?" asked the lawyer.

"I just looked at the jury," said the educator, "and it has at least five of my ex-students on it. Let's just get out of here before I spend the next century in the county jail!"

Justice

950

Most people who cry for justice want that justice for others; when it comes to themselves, they would prefer mercy!

951

"Mr. Johnson," said the student, "on the report I handed in you didn't give me any grade. All you did was write the words, 'JUSTICE! JUSTICE!'"

"That's right," returned the teacher, "and that means 'Justice' (just-as) long as you hand in the report your brother did for me two years ago is 'Justice' (just-as) long as I'm going to keep giving it back!"

952

"Look there," said the child who was out for a ride with Grandma and Grandpa, "that sign says the person is a 'Justice of the Peace.'"

"That never made any sense to me," commented Grandma. "Your grandfather and I were married by one of those almost fifty years ago, and I haven't known a minute's peace ever since!"

Juvenile

953

They admitted a juvenile to the hospital recently. It seems the lad was doing some chores around the house and when he found out that he was actually working, the shock was too much for him!

954

Wrote the teacher, "Your son is acting very juvenile!"

Answered the parent, "He's in first grade; how would you expect him to act?"

955

A visitor to the neighborhood was walking along when he almost tripped over a bicycle that had been left in the middle of the sidewalk. He went up to the house.

"Excuse me!" he said when the door had been answered. "Do you have a juvenile living here?"

"Only my husband," came the reply. "Yes, that's his bike, and he likes to be called youthful rather than juvenile!"

956

Did you see the big spread in the newspaper yesterday? It seems there was actually a juvenile who turned down the CD player WITHOUT being asked!

Juvenile Delinquency

957

Then there was the group of juvenile delinquents who formed a rock band. You should hear their duet for switchblade and bicycle chain!

958

Then there was the group of juvenile delinquents who formed a rock band. Nothing new in that!

959

As one parent put it, juvenile delinquency is a disease of the mind caused by too little heat being applied early to the opposite end!

960

"Juvenile delinquency is different today than when we were youths," said one teacher.

"Of course it is!" answered a colleague. "With all the advances in technology nowadays, they are much better armed!"

Kangaroo

961

A kangaroo escaped from the zoo and hopped past the local school just as the janitor looked out the window.

"Joe," he commented to his assistant, "remind me to put in a requisition for bigger mouse traps!"

962

Mother had taken several neighborhood children to the zoo. Now they watched as a baby kangaroo stuck its head out of mother's pouch.

"What must that poor animal go through," said the human mother, "when it's bad weather and the kids have to play inside!"

963

The small child watched as the kangaroo came to a standstill and placed both front paws into its pouch.

"Look, Ma!" said the tyke. "It's wearing a snowsuit!"

Kennel

964

"So you had a summer job in a kennel. Did you do all right financially?"

"Well, you might say I cleaned up!"

"My father says the family business is going to the dogs," said the student.
"I'm so sorry," returned the teacher.
"No," explained the child, "that's good! We own a kennel!"

966

"I don't care what you think of your baby brother!" said Father. "You cannot give him a birthday present consisting of a gift certificate good for one week's stay at the 'Pooch and Purr' boarding kennels!"

Keys

967

"This school holds the key to your future," the teacher extolled, "and this class holds the key to knowledge . . . "
Just then a boy who had been excused earlier came dancing into the room.
"And I sure hope you hold the key to the boy's lavatory," he said, "because the janitor forgot to open it!"

968

Each child is a special key, just waiting to be turned in the right lock.

969

Several students were in the main office when the cafeteria manager came running in.
"I forgot my key," she said to the principal, "and if I don't use your master key right away, we won't be able to prepare lunch for the students!"
"Psst!" whispered one of the students to the principal. "I got five bucks if you forget where you put that key!"

Kibitz

970

The teacher was visited by his friend and colleague who proceeded to entertain the class with some idle chatter.

"Don't mind Mr. Jones," said the regular teacher. "He's a great kibitzer!"

"Wow!" shouted a student. "You lived on a collective farm in Israel?"

971

"When I was a kid," said Grandpa, "of a summer's night, we would sit on the front porch or go down to the playground and kibitz."

"We still do," commented his grandson, "only now it's called loitering, and you get asked to move on!"

Kickoff
(See also: Football)

972

"I hear the other team has a real great kicker," said a member of the team.

Then came the kickoff, and the opposing player kicked the ball over the walls of the stadium and a good four blocks down an adjacent street.

"He's not so much," said another player. "He can't even keep the ball on the playing field!"

973

The two captains were at the coin toss, just before kickoff.

"Heads I win; tails you lose!" said the opposing captain.

"No you don't!" stated the captain of the home team. "You probably got a double-headed coin there, so how about tails you win and heads I lose!"

974

The quarterback was asked in to the principal's office.

"We are going to have a kickoff dinner to raise money, and I want you at that banquet," said the principal.

"A kickoff dinner?"

"That's right."

"OK," said the student athlete, "but I don't think I can eat a whole football all by myself!"

Kidding

975

"Ms. Jones," said the student, "I'm sorry that I've caused so much trouble by kidding around all the time, but I won't be bothering you any longer. My dad lost his job, and it looks like we will lose our house, so I'll be moving away . . ."

"Oh, Dear," replied the teacher, "I'm so sorry."

Said the student, "Only kidding!!!"

976

Did you ever notice that when a practical joke is played ON you, it is immature, childish, and juvenile; while a practical joke played BY you is a tasteful example of kidding around.

977

"We have had it with you, Billy!" said the teacher sternly. "Your constant attempts to be the class clown and do nothing but joke around have become intolerable. Therefore, you must appear tomorrow night before the Board of Education with your parents."

"Oh, no!" gasped the mischievous student, "I . . . I . . . "

"And, Billy . . . "

"Y-Y-Yes . . . "

"Only kidding!"

Kidney

978

"Mrs. Jones is alive today, because she had a kidney transplant," the teacher told the class.

"Sure," answered one student, "but how about the kid who gave his knee? How's he doing?"

979

"What did you learn in school today?"

""We studied about the urinary tract. What's for dinner?"

"Kidney stew."

"Suddenly, I'm not hungry . . . "

Kids (See also: Children)

980

I like kids. After all, have you ever known a kid who pulled out photos of his parents and told you how well they were doing at work lately?

981

Your kids are really easy to raise. Just ask your neighbors!

982

"Do you want to be a kid all your life?" argued the father. "Don't you want to grow up to be special, like Lincoln?"

"Come on, Dad! Who wants to be like a car!"

983

You know, parents would never have any trouble with their children if it weren't for kids!

Kilt

984

"What was he wearing?"

"Who?"

"MacGregor."

"MacGregor? A kilt."

"MacGregor kilt! I didn't even know he was sick!"

985

The family decided to go to a Scottish Heritage Festival held at a local park. When they arrived, they were immediately greeted by the sight of a number of men, all dressed in kilts.

"Let's go!" said the child of the family. "There are bad people here!"

"What do you mean?"

"Just look! Somebody stole their pants, and now they have to wear their mothers' skirts!"

Kin (See also: Family; Relatives)

986

Did you ever notice that the moment you want to borrow money from your relatives, your rich kin turn into your poor can't!

987

"Name one of your kin," stated the teacher to the first grade class.
Answered one student, "I kin tie my own shoes!"

988

Long-lost Uncle Harry arrived one night after ten years absence. He was disheveled, unwashed, and his hair looked as if it had not been combed in weeks. Tentatively, he approached his seven-year-old nephew.
"I," he said, "am your very own kin!"
"Thank goodness," replied the child, "for a moment there, I thought we might be related!"

Kindergarten

989

"Before we start our Thanksgiving feast," said the kindergarten teacher, "who will tell me one thing for which he or she is thankful?"
Answered one small lad who hungrily eyed the table, "That I'm not a turkey!"

990

"Who can tell me," asked the kindergarten teacher, "the shape of the world?"
"According to my father," answered one girl, "rotten!"

991

"Please, help me," said the kindergarten child. "I can't put my boots on!"
So the teacher, tired as she was, spent the next five minutes pushing and pulling on the boots until they were finally on the child.
"There!" she puffed. "Your boots are on!"
"No, they're not!" returned the child. "These are somebody else's boots! I couldn't find mine, and THAT'S why I couldn't put them on!"

Kindness

992

"Here Ma'am," said the student, "let me hold open your car door while you get in."

"Thank you," said the teacher. "No act of kindness ever goes unrewarded."

"That's exactly what I'm hoping you'll remember," said the lad, "when you correct those tests we took today!"

993

The visitor to the school was knocked down by the onslaught of students during the change of class. One young man stepped forward, however, aided the visitor to her feet, and left.

Just then the principal arrived on the scene.

"What incredible kindness!" said the visitor.

"Yes," mused the principal, "but you'll have to forgive him; he's new to the school!"

994

Billy slammed open the door, knocked over a tower of blocks his baby sister had been building, pulled the cat's tail, and burst into the kitchen where he handed Mother a note from his teacher.

"Billy was so helpful in school today," she read. "How wonderful it must be to have such a kind and thoughtful child!"

King (See also: Royalty)

995

Asked one child, "When kings went out in bad weather, did they wear REIGN-coats?"

996

One student mounted a small knoll on the school grounds.

"I'm King of the Hill!" he shouted. "King of the Hill!"

Whereupon five other students rushed him and knocked him to the ground.

"Hey!" said the ex-king, "a simple petition would have done fine! You didn't have to mount a rebellion!"

997

"Listen," said one student to another, "you are so bad that if you were king, they'd have to call you, 'Your Royal Lowness!'"

Kiss

998

"Do Eskimos kiss with their noses?"
   "Yes, they do."
   "Wow! How do they get a nostril to pucker up?"

999

"Hey, Sweet Thing!" shouted the brash young man in the hallway of the school. "If I close my eyes and pucker up, will you give me what I need?"
   "Why, sure!" said the young lady.
   He did . . .
   . . . and she slapped him!

1000

"May I kiss your hand?"
   "Have you no higher aspirations?"

Kitchen (See also: Cafeteria; Cooking; Home Economics)

1001

Said the wife to her husband, "Let me explain something about our kitchen. You cannot defrost the oven!"

1002

My son started cooking the other day. Now we have a shelf in our kitchen with fireproof cookbooks!

1003

"If cooking is so arduous," proclaimed the husband, "can you tell me why my grandmother all but LIVED in the kitchen!"

"Of course," answered his wife, "she couldn't stand to be with your grandfather!"

Kites

1004

Said the teacher, "The proverb states, 'It is an ill wind that blows no one good!'"

Remarked the student, "They had kites in those days, too, huh?"

1005

"A kite won't fly correctly without a good tail," father instructed his children.

Half an hour later they were back with just the body of the kite.

"Where's the tail?" asked father.

"We ripped out pages from 'The Arabian Nights' book and pasted them all over it!" stated the children. "With all those tales, it's bound to get off the ground!"

1006

"Today," the teacher told the class, "I am going to tell you about the history of the kite!"

Remarked one student, "With all the hot air in this place, that subject should get off the ground!"

Kittens (See also: Cats)

1007

"Kittens have nine lives!" said one child to another. "That's why they're such good pets!"

"Oh, yeah," said the companion, "well my frog croaks every day and he's still going strong!"

1008

"I'm thinking of getting my child a pet," said the teacher. "What do you think is the price of a kitten?"

"Oh, about five bucks," answered a colleague whose cat had just had a litter, "payable to whoever takes them away!"

1009

The kindergarten child sat in her room where she had been sent by her mother.

"Three little kittens," she chanted, "lost their mittens; but I flushed mine down the toilet!"

Kits
(See also: Hobbies)

1010

"What did he do?" inquired the principal of the student before him.

"He's been selling the other students an 'anti-homework' kit," replied the teacher, "consisting of a pair of glasses painted black on the inside, so they could honestly swear to their parents and the teacher that they never saw the assignment on the board!"

1011

The student was cleaning out the closets in the science room, and he came across a kit to build a model of the heart, another kit for the lungs, and yet another for the stomach.

"Good grief!" the small lad exclaimed, "So that's how it's done! We come in kits!"

1012

"All right, class," asked the teacher, "name something you think should be in a survival kit."

"Obviously," said the richest kid in the class, "a charge card with an unlimited balance!"

Knee

1013

Did you hear about the rich man who had to stop hiking? He got Perrier on the knee.

1014

"Stop fighting with your brother! Love and affection will get his attention."
"So will a knee in the stomach, and it's a whole lot faster!"

1015

At a class outing to a nearby lake, a male teacher went for a swim. Two boys from his class observed him closely.
"You're right," said one of the lads, "his knees are knobby, just like my father's. It must be one of those 'grown up' things!"

Knife

1016

"My brother got stabbed with a knife!" young Billy shouted throughout the neighborhood. "My brother got stabbed with a knife!"
"How horrible!" commented a neighbor. "Is his brother all right?"
"He's fine," sighed Mother. "All we did was tell Billy that his brother got cut from the team!"

1017

"Son, this knife belonged to your great-grandfather, who gave it to your grandfather, who gave it to me. Now, I'm giving it to you. Do you have anything to say?"
"Dad . . . "
"Yes, Son."
"Don't you think it's time we stopped passing on all this macho symbolism?"

1018

A student may not understand why there is a rule about knives in school, but many a desk top has gotten the point!"

Knight (See also: Royalty)

1019

Mama Flea took one look at the downtrodden warrior before her and immediately grabbed Baby Flea's hand.

"Come away, Junior," she said. "I wouldn't send anyone out on a knight like this!"

1020

"Who can name a musical or a song about King Arthur and Lancelot?" asked the music teacher.

Answered one student, "How about, 'You and the Knight and the Music'?"

1021

"What do you make of this?" said one teacher, reading a scientific journal. "They just discovered some medieval armor in England that was for someone at least seven feet tall, and it was covered inside with fur!"

"Obvious," answered a colleague. "You know those British winters! It was probably made for one of those long, cold winter knights!"

Knitting

1022

A large, brawny athlete from the school's football team sat on a bench outside the school, reached into a knapsack, and took out some knitting. Soon, several young ladies were around him, giving advice and talking about how wonderful his hobby was.

"I'm really surprised that you would take up knitting," said the athlete's friend later, "instead of something sporty like fishing!"

"I don't knit," answered the lad. "I just take it out and sit there, and the girls come. Look, you fish your way, and I'll fish mine!"

1023

"So, your daughter took up knitting in school, eh? Well, I must say, that's the longest muffler I've ever seen. It must run twenty feet!"

"Thanks, but it's not a muffler; it's a sweater, and you're looking at the sleeves!"

"Oh, you poor dear! You spent the whole summer with a broken leg! Well, I hope the bones knitted properly."

"I don't think so, I couldn't even learn how to crochet!"

Knockout

1025

As the student boxer came to consciousness, the coach commented, "What I liked most was the way you kept blocking his knockout punches with your face . . . "

1026

"There have been six knockouts in my record," said the student boxer.

"You knocked out six people?" asked the coach.

"People?" returned the athlete. "I was talking about teeth. One of mine has been knocked out in each of my last six fights!"

1027

The English teacher was talking about some of the battle scenes in Shakespeare and was swinging a mace when it flew upward unexpectedly, hit him solidly in the forehead, and knocked him out—cold!"

"Excellent English teacher," commented one student; "but he really could use a course in medieval soldiering!"

Knots

1028

Question: What do you get when you cross a champion Scout knot tie-er with a home ec teacher?

Answer: A cook who specializes in pretzels!

1029

"Why did you call the art teacher insane?" asked the principal.

"I didn't," protested the pupil. "She was teaching us how to do macrame, and all I said was that she looked knots to me!"

1030

The Motto of the Macramé Teachers of America:
   "I WILL KNOT!"

Knowledge

1031

"This afternoon," the principal told the faculty, "I would like to tell you everything I know about education . . . "
   "Oh, good," whispered one teacher, "we're going to get out early!"

1032

After we have completed our formal education, then our quest for true knowledge may begin!

1033

One hour and fifteen minutes into the guest's speech, one of the educators present leaned over to a colleague.
   "He doesn't know anything!" the teacher whispered.
   "True," answered a colleague, "but you have to admit that he is extremely fluent at expressing his ignorance!"

1034

I wish that I had complete and total knowledge of every subject in the entire world—unfortunately, I'm not a teenager!

1035

The five year old curled up in Daddy's lap and whispered, "Will there ever be a time when I know as much as you?"
   "Oh, yes," answered father. "In fact, there will be a time when you'll know more than I could ever know. It's called adolescence!"

1036

Sign above a teacher's classroom door: Knowledge given away free every day. Please bring your own container!

1037

The teacher accidentally backed his car into a ditch. As he looked around, he saw one of his students standing nearby.

"Is there a garage around here?" he asked.

"I don't know," said the student.

"Well, where's the police station?"

"I don't know."

"Where can I find a telephone?"

"I don't know."

"You don't know very much," stated the frustrated teacher, "do you?"

Answered the child, "I know enough not to back into a ditch!"

1038

"One thing I must say about Johnson," said one educator of another. "In all the time I've known him, he has never allowed knowledge to stand in the way of his opinions!"

Kung Fu
(See also: Martial Arts)

1039

"We study Kung Fu here," said the teacher to the new student. "To become a Kung Fu master takes a lifetime of dedication, devotion, and hard, hard work."

"Gosh, sir," gulped the lad, "couldn't I just stay until I learn enough to beat up my big brother?"

1040

The small student who had had enough finally approached the school bully in the cafeteria.

"Arrrrgh!" roared the bully. "I know how to make you hurt!"

Whereupon the smaller student took a rock from his pocket and pulverized it with one blow of his bare fist.

"I know Kung Fu," he said softly.

"I don't care who your friends are," said the bully as he backed away, "but when the teacher sees that mess, she's gonna make you AND that Fu kid clean it up!"

1041

An elderly lady was walking down the street when she was beset by five young thugs.

Suddenly, the woman became a powerhouse of energy, tossing her attackers left and right until they ran away in fear and confusion.

"How did you do that?" asked one onlooker. "A lifetime of Kung Fu?"

"No," the senior citizen replied as she dusted herself off, "thirty-five years as a teacher on playground duty!"

Laboratory

1042

The new boy in school asked to go to the boy's room and received a pass to do so. Later that day, the teacher met the new boy in the hallway.

"I should have asked," said the teacher, "did you have any trouble finding the lavatory?"

"Oh, no," answered the boy. "I saw the sign on that door over there and went right in."

"But, that door is marked LABORATORY, not LAVATORY."

"Well!" stated the lad, "that certainly explains all the dirty looks I got!"

1043

"And, after all the experimenting and the chemicals and the involved processes," asked the science teacher, "what do you think comes out of the laboratories of this school?"

Answered one student, "The 'Daily Special' in the cafeteria?"

1044

"Aren't laboratory classes a big waste?" one student asked another.

"Most certainly not!" answered the other. "Why in the lab class I took last year, we made enough noxious odors to clear out the school three times!"

Labor Day

1045

The teacher and his wife were having their first child, and he got more and more nervous as the day approached. In fact, in the teacher's lounge one educator asked the name of the holiday in September and another answered, "It's Labor Day!" The nervous teacher yelled, "What, already!" and took a cab to the hospital!

1046

One mother had ten children in school at the same time. Now there was a person who knew the true meaning of "Labor Day!"

1047

"I'm writing an essay on Labor Day," announced the young lady of the house. "My only trouble is that I can't think of anybody who really labors hard.

"Oh, by the way, Mom," the girl continued, "after you clean my room and do my laundry, will you please make me a sandwich? I'm starved from all this thinking!"

Language

1048

English is a most peculiar tongue. What can you say of a language where you drive on a parkway and park in a driveway?

1049

The linguist was traveling through a part of the city that boasted many accents, most of which the professor could identify. One, however, puzzled him.

"I beg your pardon," said the language expert, "but what is your native tongue?"

"What is my tongue?" he answered. "It's $4.95 a pound at my delicatessen. Drop in sometime!"

1050

"Do you think Judy should take a second language?" asked mother.

"Absolutely not!" answered father. "I've seen the phone bill she can run up with one tongue; imagine what she could do with two!"

1051

The kitten stopped playing with the ball of yarn and stretched in the warm sun.

"Woof!" said the kitten, "Woof! Growl! Woof!"

"Don't you just love it," said Mama cat, "when your children learn to speak a foreign language?"

1052

I know of one gentleman who claims that all his financial difficulties stem from sign language. The store said, "Sign here," and he did!

Latin

1053

Latin is a dead tongue,
Dead as it can be;
First it killed the Romans,
And now it's killing me!

1054

"I feel about passing Latin," said one student, "rather like Caesar's commentary, '*Veni; vidi; vici*'—'I came; I saw; I conquered!'"

"I feel kind of like that," remarked another ex-Latin student. "Except mine is sort of like, 'I came; I smuggled in the translation; I passed!'"

1055

"I know I have a reputation for giving hard tests," said the Latin teacher to one of the students, "but I don't think you have to start each answer you give by writing, '*Qui moratori, te salutamus*!'"

(Note: "We who are about to die salute you!" was the salute of the Roman gladiator to the emperor in the arena before the fighting began.)

Laughter (See also: Humor)

1056

Laughter has always been the best medicine, and with the price of prescription drugs these days, it's also the most economical!

1057

A student began giggling in the back of the room, and the teacher asked the reason for the outburst.

"You always tell the best jokes," snickered the student.

"But, I haven't told a joke," said the teacher.

"I guess you wouldn't believe that I was practicing in case you did," replied the student, "would you?"

1058

"Well," said the assistant, "how did your speech before the faculty of the high school go?"

"Great!" answered the politician. "I told them my plans for education if I am elected, and they invited me back to speak to them again."

"They did?"

"Yes! In fact, the principal told me she had never heard the faculty laugh so much in the history of the school!"

Lavatory

1059

"Can I go to the boy's lavatory, Ma'am?" asked the boy.

"MAY I go to the boy's lavatory," corrected the teacher.

"It's OK with me," said the student, "but don't you think people will talk if we use the same one?"

1060

"I sent you to the lavatory over thirty minutes ago," stated the teacher to the student. "Where were you all this time?"

"Sorry," answered the pupil, "but the cafeteria served its famous 'Taco Surprise' for lunch, and the line at the lavatory was so long, I was waiting the whole time!"

1061

The English teacher was on hall duty and as he checked the boy's lavatory, he saw one of his students near a wall with a black marking pen in his hand.

"Jones!" snapped the teacher. "Are you writing graffiti on the lavatory walls?"

"No, Sir!" exclaimed the boy. "Your class so inspired me, that I was merely correcting the grammar!"

Law/Lawyers

1062

"How many laws do we have?" a student asked the social studies teacher.

"I don't know exactly," answered the teacher, "but certainly there are millions of laws to keep people from lying and cheating and stealing and hurting one another."

"Wow!" exclaimed the youngster. "Millions of laws, just to enforce the Ten Commandments!"

1063

"The twins' father is a lawyer," a teacher told her colleague. "You could tell that from what he named them—Bill and Sue!"

1064

Three litigants waited in the hallway outside the courtroom. Two were extremely somber, and one smiled broadly. A teacher and a small group of students on a tour of the courthouse passed by and asked if the three people were concerned about their cases.

"I'm not worried," said one sour-faced individual, "my lawyer knows the law!"

"I'm not worried," said the second serious person, "my lawyer knows the judicial system!"

"I'm really not worried," said the smiling one, "my lawyer knows the judge!"

Lawns

1065

"I had a summer job as a gardener," said the teacher, "but I got fired."
   "Oh, what for?"
   "The artificial lawn died!"

1066

The math teacher had a perfectly mathematical lawn—every weed was precisely the same height!

1067

Then there was the teacher who took out his entire lawn and put in a rock garden. By the morning, half of the rocks had wilted and died!

1068

Then there was the home ec teacher who so loved seafood, she planted crabgrass on her lawn!

Leaders/Leadership

1069

"If the other class runs one mile," said the class president, "we will run two miles! If the other class saws a chord of firewood, we will saw three! If the other class climbs a hill, we will climb a mountain! Are there any questions?"

   "Just one," said a student in the room, "what class do you consider stupid enough to let you lead them on these suicide missions?"

1070

The general visited the camp and spoke to the sergeant.
   "Where is your leader?"
   "There he is," replied the sergeant, "up on the hill, with the map in his hands, yelling 'Go left; go right!'"
   "Yes," said the general, "but if he is your leader, he should be down on the field, with his arm in the air, shouting, 'Follow me; follow me!'"

1071

The best leader is not the one who points out the path, but the one who daily treads that path and invites others to share the walk.

Leave

1072

Principal to first grader: "I'm sorry, but the school does not grant students a leave of absence to search for the true meaning of life when they're in the first grade!"

1073

"Hello, this is the school board calling. Please tell one of your teachers, Mr. Johnson, that his request for medical leave has been denied."

"Haven't you heard? Mr. Johnson died of a heart attack last night!"

"Oh . . . well, in that case, he can reapply, but make sure he does it in triplicate!"

1074

"I don't think you fully understand the concept of maternity leave. We cannot grant you time off from your job to go out, find a husband, and get pregnant!"

Legality (See also: Law/Lawyers)

1075

"I think," said the social studies teacher, "that you don't understand the legality of the concept of self-defense. You cannot shoot the math teacher just because algebra is killing you!"

1076

"I know you have a rough school," said the school board attorney to the principal, "but there is simply no legal way of having the school open WITHOUT allowing students to enter the building!"

1077

"That's a tremendous idea, Jones," said the teacher, "but I'm afraid it is not quite legal to raise money for our class trip by my selling A's for five dollars and A+'s for ten!"

Lemonade

1078

The child set up a roadside lemonade stand and was soon doing volume business.

"Well," said her father when he came home from work, "I see business is really good, huh?"

"Nobody was buying anything," returned his daughter. "But when I started giving away one of your golf clubs with each drink, it really picked up!"

1079

In the cafeteria, the student fell to the floor, kicked and writhed wildly, held his throat, and banged his head against the wall.

Just then the principal walked by.

"Oh," she said, "I see the cafeteria is serving a new batch of lemonade!"

1080

"This lemonade is really different," said the teacher to the student, downing her third cup. "What's your secret?"

"Well, Mom and Dad are always talking about how things like cheese and steak are better when they're aged," the child answered, "so I made this with rotten lemons!"

Lens

1081

"Are there such things as transparent beetles?" the student asked the science teacher.

"No, there are not."

"In that case, I think I just stepped on someone's contact lens!"

"Is there anything I can do to improve the photographs I take?" the student asked the teacher.

"There is one thing," the teacher answered, tossing a stack of black paper rectangles on the desk. "Next time, take off the lens cover!"

1083

"Give me one good reason to wear contact lenses."
"So you can see."
"I asked for a 'good' reason, not an excellent one!"

Lettuce

1084

"Our cafeteria says the lettuce in the salad is just like it was when picked."
"That's true; warm and covered with dirt!"

1085

"What did the salad say?"
"Lettuce alone; we're dressing!"

1086

"Does the government ever send vegetables to people?" asked the student.

"I don't believe so," said the teacher. "Why do you ask?"

"Because," answered the child, "I heard Daddy tell Mommy that when he got finished fooling with his income tax, the government was going to be sending us a whole lot of lettuce!"

Liberal (See also: Politics/Politicians)

1087

"I think we need less dictatorial discipline in our schools!" stated the young man at the Board of Education meeting.

"Sir," asked a teacher who was present, "how long have you taught?"

"I have never taught!"

"Aha!" exclaimed the teacher, "a liberal!"

1088

"Mr. Jones," said the principal, "I just received word that a student of yours scratched the surface of your car with a bent nail. Now, we have the student, but we need to handle this with understanding; we need not be punitive; we must maintain a liberal viewpoint and seek the child's rehabilitation."

Just then the door opened and a secretary entered.

"Sir, we made a mistake before. It wasn't Mr. Jones' car that got ruined, it was yours."

"What!" shouted the principal. "Bring in that little criminal I'm going to expel!"

1089

"Where are we going to get the money for all these new programs in school?"

"Why from you, the taxpayers."

"But, you don't even live in this town. All you're doing is spending our money!"

"Of course. I've always been a liberal at heart!"

Liberty

1090

"Liberty means responsibility; that's why most men dread it."

— George Bernard Shaw

1091

Few things have been more difficult to obtain, more costly to retain, and more abused when maintained than LIBERTY!

1092

Quoted the student, "In Patrick Henry's words, 'Give me liberty or give me the cafeteria!'"

"No! That's 'Give me liberty or give me death!'"

"Same thing!"

224

1093

"Liberty is a little like copper."

"What? How can you say that?"

"'Cause my folks took me to see the Statue of Liberty, and that's what it looked like it was made of to me!"

Library

1094

"For as long as I can remember," said the teacher, "my parents have always given me one book on my birthday."

"Gosh!" said one child in class. "By now, you could start a lending library!"

1095

"Who wrote that song, 'Whistle While You Work'?"

"I don't know, but I'll bet it wasn't a librarian!"

1096

I have my personal library divided into three sections; the books I have read, the books I intend to read some day, and all those whose bindings match the color scheme of the room.

1097

"I'd like the book on the red sailboat that my teacher told me about."

"Red sailboat," said the librarian. "Can you be more specific?"

"Yes, it's called 'The Ruby Yacht' by somebody named Khayam?"

Lies and Liars

1098

"I don't have my homework," said one second grader, "because this big giraffe put his head in the window and ate it!"

"He's lying!" whispered another student.

"Yes," said a third, "and rather poorly!"

1099

"I'm happy to meet you," said the teacher to the small student.

The child said nothing, just stood there.

"Why don't you say that you're happy to meet me?" asked the teacher.

"Because," answered the child, "I'm not supposed to lie!"

1100

"Billy," said the teacher to the student on Parent Visitation Day, "why don't you stand up in front of the class and tell the parents how much you enjoy this class?"

"Let me get this straight," mused Billy. "You WANT me to lie?"

1101

"I told you that you would enjoy this school year," said the teacher to the class. "The principal told you that you would enjoy it, and your guidance counselor told you the same thing. Now, what does that prove?"

Answered one student, "That liars come in all shapes and sizes!"

Life

1102

Sign in a classroom: THIS is real life; when things go bad, you can't just change the channel!

1103

The lives of people are like books—different covers; different stories; same ending!

1104

"I think I'm living my life in a shower," said one student.

"Why do you say that?"

"Because," moaned the child, "every time I turn around, I'm in hot water!"

1105

Life is like an elevator, it has its ups and downs, and sometimes you get off on the wrong floor!

1106

Life is like a bowl of corn flakes; if you don't go after it right away, it has a tendency to sit there and get soggy!

1107

Life is like a bowl of chili; the spicier it is, the more likely you are to get heartburn—but the better it tastes!"

Lightning

1108

"Why does lightning never strike twice in the same place?" asked the teacher.

Answered one child, "I've seen a house struck by lightning, and believe me, it has no need to come back to finish the job!"

1109

Outside the bedroom window the lightning flashed. Inside, the child stood with her face pressed tightly against the windowpane.

"Wow, God!" she said. "You must have one gigantic electric bill!"

1110

"The teacher gave me a nickname today," said the child. "She called me 'Lightning Bolt.'"

"Oh," said mother, "is that because you are so brilliant and dynamic?"

"No," answered the child, "she said it was because I cause so much damage wherever I touch down!"

Line/Lines

1111

When the teacher and her class got to the theater, they found a long line already formed. With a deep breath, the teacher placed her class in the queue and waited.

"Is this the first time you've brought a class here?" asked an usher.

"Why, yes," answered the teacher. "How did you know?"

"Because," the employee stated, "the show started three minutes ago, and you're all standing in line for the ladies room!"

1112

Outside the door to the cafeteria, the new student sniffed and said, "Do they actually make you eat that food?"

"Worse!" answered a school veteran, "They make you stand in line so you can anticipate the agony!"

1113

The kindergarten child began to wander from the group.

"Now, Henry," said the teacher, "Don't you know that you have to stay in line if you want to use the lavatory!"

"Lines and lavatories are fine," stated the precocious lad, "but what I know is that if I don't find a bathroom soon, we are both going to be embarrassed!"

Linguist/Linguistics (See also: Language)

1114

Asked the registrar, "Would you like to have linguistics?"

Answered the college student, "With red or white clam sauce?"

1115

"Professor?" said the voice on the telephone, "I wonder if you could come and give a talk to our club?"

"Are you sure you have the right number? After all, I am a linguist."

"That's OK," said the voice. "Just tell us about the care and feeding of Ling's!"

1116

"Professor Jones is a fantastic linguist!"

"Really? I didn't know he spoke any languages."

"Oh, yes! He can avoid paying the check in fourteen different tongues!"

Literature

1117

"What did you think of the story I gave you, professor?"
  "I think it was the worst tripe I ever read . . . "
  "Aha! That was a story YOU wrote in college!"
  " . . . but, then, all great literature has its critics!"

1118

A truly great teacher is one who teaches the classics in such a way that his or her students are enjoying them too much to realize that they're literature.

1119

"We'd like to know about a bank loan," said the very young couple.
  "Certainly," said the bank officer, "I'll give you some literature."
  "Please don't!" came the reply. "We had to take that in high school, and both of us darn near failed!"

1120

"At home I have one whole wall of literature," said the teacher, "and I also have books I really enjoy!"

Logic

1121

"Be logical for a moment," said the teacher to the student. "You didn't do your homework; and that's why you got an 'F.'"
  "You call that logical?" returned the student. "I'd like to know how you could possibly fail a paper you didn't even have to see if it were wrong!"

1122

"Two things equal to the same third thing are equal to each other," stated the teacher. "That is a fact of logic."
  "I don't know," said a student. "A filling station and a pepperoni pizza both give you gas, and they are NOTHING like each other!"

1123

"I'm gonna beat up Johnny Jones!" announced one student.

"No, you're not," stated another student who blocked the way.

"Give me one good reason why not?"

"Because, if you touch him, I'll put you in the hospital for a month!"

"You know," said the first student as he headed back the way he had come, "there are times when we simply must allow logic to prevail!"

Loquacious

1124

"Thank you," said the principal to the elder teacher who had finished a speech, "I really enjoyed your loquacious manner."

"What did he say?" the teacher asked his wife.

She replied, "He said you run off at the mouth!"

1125

"My only criticism of your speech," said the forensic coach, "was that it tended to be loquacious."

"That's only 'cause I cut about forty minutes from it," said the student. "I could put it back in!"

1126

"What did you think of Jack?" the daughter asked her mother.

"Well, he is rather loquacious for his age."

"I thought so, too, and I think we could really get on if he didn't talk so much!"

Love

1127

There is no pain hot enough, no hurt deep enough, no problem tall enough that it cannot be cooled through, filled up with, or laid to peaceful rest by the hand of love.

1128

"I fell in love with my wife at first sight."

"At first sight, eh? Isn't that a bit unusual?"

"Well, I was on my coffee break, so I didn't have much time . . . "

1129

"Is it true," someone asked the teacher, "that your class comes to love you?"

"Oh, yes," answered the educator, "you have no idea of what it feels like to leave school and find the words, 'Mrs. Johnson, We Love You!' written in red lipstick across the side of your brand-new car!"

1130

" . . . in conclusion," said the student speaker, "I would remind you of what the famous sixteenth-century scholar Francis Bacon wrote, 'It is impossible to love and be wise!'"

Shouted one student member of the audience, "You mean everybody in this class is in love?"

1131

"What I would like more than anything," said one young teacher, "is to be loved for myself!"

"Actually," commented a slightly more mature educator, "I'd like to be loved in spite of myself!"

1132

"When I was twenty-two, I thought I knew everything there was to know about love, but then I matured, I experienced the wonder and the pain of love, and now I understand love far more deeply than I ever could have at twenty-two . . . "

"How old are you?"

"Twenty-three."

1133

"Hey, Mary Jones!" yelled the second-grade boy on the playground, "You're a real dog! Woof! Woof!"

Whereupon one of the boy's classmates stepped forward and knocked him to the ground.

"Hey," sputtered the conquered lad, "why didn't you just tell me you two were in love?"

1134

"I called Mary Jones a dog," the second-grader explained to the school nurse, "and Bobby Smith comes up and socks me in the eye!"

"Did you learn anything from this?"

"Yeah," moaned the youth, "I learned that when you're in love, you lose your sense of humor!"

1135

"Johnny Jones is in love with me!" said the high school girl to her friend.

"How do you know?"

"How do I know?" she exclaimed. "He dissected my frog for me in science class!"

1136

"I love you, Mrs. Johnson," said the first-grader, "and I want to marry you."

"Why, thank you, Johnny," returned the understanding teacher, "but I'm already married, and I have three children of my own."

"No problem," the youth continued. "I'll have Mom and Dad redo the attic, and your husband and kids can stay there!"

1137

Love is a quality that allows a man and a woman to look at a child who has just scratched his name into the side of their brand-new Mercedes and say, "How wonderful! Our child can spell!"

Luck

1138

"This rabbit's foot gives me good luck!" said one student.

"I wouldn't depend on that if I were you," said a classmate. "It didn't do one bit of good for the rabbit!"

1139

"Of course I believe in luck," said the teacher. "How else can you explain Jones being made principal instead of me!"

1140

"I was made captain of the team due to my physical conditioning, my athletic talent, and my leadership abilities!"

"What about your co-captain?"

"Now, there is an example of what LUCK can do!"

1141

I'm really not a very lucky person. I packed up the family one year and we went to see the Pacific Ocean—it was closed for repairs!

1142

"You didn't have your homework in four classes," said the principal to the student. "You put bubble gum in a student's hair; you were pushing and shoving during the fire drill, and you threw a plate of spaghetti in the cafeteria! Now, can you offer me any explanation for your behavior?"

"Would you believe," answered the pupil, "that this is NOT one of my lucky days?"

Lunch (See also: Cafeteria)

1143

"So, what's your favorite subject in school?"

"Lunch!"

1144

"I will do everything in my power," announced the principal over the loudspeaker system, "to see to it that every student has a hot, delicious lunch every day!"

"Did you hear that?" said one student to a friend. "She's going to close down the cafeteria!"

1145

"Honestly, Ma'am," explained the student, "my poor grades are the result of lunch!"

"Oh, come, now!" said the teacher. "How does lunch affect your grades?"

"Well," the student offered, "before lunch I'm too hungry to concentrate and after lunch I'm too content to care!"

1146

"If it weren't for school lunch," said the teacher, "you would not have the energy to keep up with your classes in the afternoon."

"If it weren't for school lunch," whispered one of the students, "half of us wouldn't get the homework done for those subjects, either!"

Luxury

1147

Then there was the kindergarten teacher whose idea of luxury was to have someone to help put on HER boots at the end of the day!

1148

Then there was the teacher whose idea of luxury was teaching in an orphanage, so there wouldn't be any parental conferences!

1149

"What would you call," asked one teacher of another, "a class of twenty children who were all ready and anxious to learn?"

Answered the colleague, "One of those luxuries I shall never be able to attain!"

1150

"Sometimes, I just don't understand education," commented one student. "Here I am in school carrying around forty pounds of books, sitting in desks with splinters, and eating something they call lunch in the cafeteria, when I could be at home, learning to adapt to luxury—and they tell me it's for MY good!"

Machinery

1151

The device sat on the student's workbench in the machine shop. It buzzed and whirred, and lights flashed on and off.

"Incredible!" said the teacher, "but what does this machine do?"

"Not a darn thing," answered the student, "but I made it, and ain't it wonderful!"

1152

"I'm sorry," said the patent attorney to the social studies teacher, "but I don't think we can copyright a machine that goes around in circles doing nothing and going nowhere as a learning device to teach children about politics!"

1153

"Do you think they'll ever replace teachers with machines?"

"Of course not! You tell me of any machine you know that can look at a kid and tell if he really has to go to the bathroom or only wants to get out of class!"

Magic

1154

The magician placed a white rat with beady red eyes into a box, tapped on it with his magic wand, and when the box was opened, the rat had turned into a cuddly bunny!

"How about that!" said one of the students in the audience. "There is hope for my little brother after all!"

1155

"Is there any trick you'd really like to see me do?" the magician asked the class.

In one voice they answered: "Make the teacher disappear!"

1156

After the show, the magician found two boys waiting at the stage door.

"Would you like my autograph?" asked the performer.

"Not really," said one. "Actually, we were wondering how much you'd take to make all our homework for the next year appear in one place right now?"

Magnet

1157

"What does it mean to have a 'magnetic personality'?" asked one student.

"It means," answered another, "that YOU are always the one who sits on the steel tack!"

1158

"Good morning, Professor," said the student, "did you forget to return the magnet to the science demonstration kit?"

"Why, yes, I did. However did you know?"

"Oh, it had something to do with those paper clips and thumbtacks hanging from the outside of your pocket!"

Mail

1159

"Do you get your mail quickly around this school?" asked the new teacher.

"Oh, yes," answered a veteran of the establishment. "Why, just yesterday, I received an offer for a free flight on the *Hindenberg*."

1160

"John, I received a letter from your mom requesting me to give you no homework for the rest of the marking period, but I'm not going to do it."

"You're not! How come?"

"Because somehow I have no faith in a letter that's signed, 'Yours truly, My Mother'!"

1161

"I always divide the mail into two groups," stated the school secretary. "There are those that have no bills and those that do have bills. I guess you might say that I divide them into mail and fee-mail!"

Make-up

1162

"Do I have on too much rouge?" asked one student in the girl's room.

"No," answered her friend, "I'd say you were reddy!"

1163

"Do you use a lot of make-up?" asked one student.

"No," answered another, "but I am wearing a little pancake on my face."

"Don't worry about that," said yet another, "Mr. Jones has egg yolk all over his tie!"

1164

"I know I called this a 'make-up test,' young lady," said the teacher, "but that doesn't mean that you can mark the right answers with eyebrow pencil and lipstick!"

Malice (See also: Hate)

1165

"So you're the one who wrote on the wall," stated the principal to the student. "You know, I believe that you did that with malice!"

"Naw!" said the lad, "I did it by myself; I don't even know no girl named Malice!"

1166

"I want you to know that there is no malice in me," said the teacher who had not been given the post of principal. "You're the principal now, and I am here to support you."

"Why, thank you . . . "

"And I'll be right here to step in and take over the minute you have your nervous breakdown!"

Man/Mankind

1167

"Remember," said the social studies teacher, "man has made the world we have today!"

"Wow!" exclaimed one young lady in the class. "And you admit it?"

1168

MAN—a creature made at the end of the week's work when God was tired.

—Samuel Clemens (Mark Twain)

Manners

1169

"Hi, Johnson!" said the student to the teacher.

"Just a minute, young man!" snapped the teacher. "Where are your manners? You will call me Mr. Johnson!"

"Sorry!" said the lad, "I didn't know you were married!"

"I tell you," said the teacher to his friend, "my brother-in-law has the manners of a gentleman."

"Does he, really?" inquired the colleague.

"Oh, yes!" the educator replied. "He orders everyone about and refuses to do a lick of work!"

Manufacture

1171

"In order to manufacture popcorn, first you have to go to the U.S. Army!"

"Just a minute," said the teacher. "Why do you need the army to make popcorn?"

"Well, my mom says that first you have to get some kernels . . ."

1172

"Who can tell me something that is NOT manufactured?" asked the teacher.

"Babies!" answered a student. "They're WOMAN-ufactured!"

Marriage
(See also: Court; Engagement; Wedding)

1173

Marriage is a fine institution—providing you don't mind living in an institution.

1174

My spouse considers our marriage an institution—but have you ever tasted institutional food?

1175

I truly believe that marriages are made in heaven—unfortunately, they are lived on earth!

"What is one reason why people get divorced?" asked the teacher.

Answered one student, "They got married!"

1177

"Mrs. Jones," said the first-grader to his teacher, "can we get married and live happily ever after?"

"Thank you, Billy," answered the teacher, "but I have a husband, and he would be very, very angry if I married someone else."

"In that case, forget about it!" stated the lad. "I'm too young to be marred forever by a nasty divorce!"

Martial Arts (See also: Kung Fu)

1178

Then there was a student who was so peaceful, he thought martial arts were paintings by a guy named Marshall.

1179

There was a martial arts expert who turned to a life of crime. He figured he could break into anyone's house because he knew Karate and he knew kung fu.

Unfortunately, in the first house he broke into lived a guy who knew how to pull the trigger on a double-barreled shotgun!

Mascot (See also: School Spirit)

1180

"Your school mascot is a SNAIL? I don't understand."

"Ah ha! Just think of the false sense of security it gives the opposing team!"

1181

"Principal Jones," said a student one Friday afternoon, "We got a big game tonight, and we are hoping that you'll help us out."

"Of course," returned the principal, "you want me to give you a couple 'special' plays, eh?"

"Actually, our mascot, Jerry the Jackass, isn't feeling well, and we were wondering if you could fill in?"

Math

1182

"I added up that column of figures," said the teacher to the pupil, "and I get a completely different answer. How do you explain that?"

"Well," said the math student, "I guess I'm just a no account!"

1183

"You have the right answers," stated the math teacher, "but you don't show any of your work. Why not?"

"Well," returned the student, "I guess that paper was something I just didn't figure on!"

1184

"I don't approve of your taking math! Say something in algebra."

"X!"

"You see! Already he's talking dirty!"

Media

1185

The man came into the adult school and stated, "I want to learn how to paint pictures!"

"Medium?" asked the teacher.

"No, Ma'am," he replied. "I don't even believe in fortune-telling!"

1186

"In today's world of mass media," said the teacher, "what is done today is known around the world tomorrow."

"Good grief!" exclaimed one student, "you mean a kid can't skip homework even once without his mom and his relatives knowing about it? That doesn't seem fair!"

Medicine

1187

"Are you all right?" the teacher asked her colleague. "You're looking really pale."

"I'm OK," the other sighed wistfully. "I just wish somebody could invent a pill that would cure childhood!"

1188

"If you know so much about medicine, what would you do with a case of amnesia?"

"I'd forget it!"

1189

"I'm sorry," said the student to the teacher, "but I can't answer you now; I'm taking my medicine."

"Really?" commented the educator. "It looks to me as if you're eating a chocolate bar!"

Responded the student, "You cure a cold your way, and I'll cure it my way!"

1190

"I had one class that was so bad, I went to the doctor for tranquilizers."

"Did they help any?"

"No, I could never get the kids to take them!"

1191

"The school nurse told me that to get rid of my headache, I should walk around the school three times."

"Personally, I'd take that with a grain of aspirin!"

Medieval

1192

It was the time for the Knights of the Round Table to ride forth, but Sir Gawain's horse was ill. Search as they might, the only mount they could find for Sir Gawain was a large St. Bernard, which they saddled up.

"Stop!" said King Arthur when he saw the arrangement. "I wouldn't send a knight out on a dog like this!"

1193

"You have to understand," said the teacher, "that in medieval times, there were no cars to take a ride; no movie theaters to pass an evening; no telephones to stay in contact with friends."

"Oh, no!" said one student, "You mean all they could do at night was to sit home in some dark castle and watch TV?"

Melancholy

1194

"You look somewhat melancholy today."

"I do? Maybe that's why I'm so depressed."

1195

Did you know that when Lassie, the great movie dog, had puppies, they were fed watermelon. Oh, yes! In fact, the trainer would come to them singing, "Here's another melon, Collie Baby!"

Memo (See also: Notes)

1196

"When the school was being attacked in the press," the principal told her faculty, "the superintendent sent me a one-word memo—defend! Later, during the budget crisis, she sent me another one-word memo—attack!

"That's why I knew I had to call you together today. This morning I got another memo from the superintendent. It says—pray!"

1197

"I'm not so sure about my new secretary," said one principal to another.

"What do you mean?"

"This morning, I asked her to take a memo, and she said, 'Thanks!' and left the office for an hour and a half!"

Memory

1198

"Mrs. Johnson, our teacher, has a really terrible memory," one student told another.

"She does?"

"Yeah," said the student with a great sigh, "she remembers EVERY-THING!"

1199

"If you want to help people's memory to improve," wrote one student, "borrow money from them. See how fast they start to remember!"

1200

The one extraordinary thing about always telling the truth is that you never have to expend the energy to remember whom you lied to!

1201

"Listen," said one teacher to another, "I do not owe you five dollars. I would remember if I did; I have a photographic memory!"

"Really?" commented the colleague. "You may have a photographic memory, but this is one time you left on the lens cap!"

1202

"Welcome back to the school," said the principal to the student who had returned to the school a mere three weeks after he had left. "It certainly is unusual that your parents were transferred back to this area in such a short time. Can I do anything for you before I send you to class?"

"Just one thing," answered the student. "Please put me in a class with a teacher who has a bad memory about how I told them all off when I thought I was leaving for good!"

Men (See also: Men and Women; Women)

1203

"Let it be said of our friend," intoned the speaker who delivered the eulogy, "that he was a real man—he loved sports; he loved money; he loved sports and money!"

The teacher was holding a make-up class for members of the football team, and he arrived one afternoon to find the team waiting for him in complete darkness.

"My goodness," said the teacher, "why didn't somebody turn on the lights?"

Replied one player, "Men ain't afraid of the dark!"

Men and Women (See also: Men; Women)

1205

"Now, let's begin our study with the fact that there are men, and there are women."

"Just a minute! Just a minute! Give me time for the concept to sink in!"

1206

"Boys are better than girls!" bellowed the boy in the hallway of the school.

"Girls are better than boys!" the girl screamed back.

"Should we break that up?" a passing teacher asked a colleague.

"Better not," answered the second teacher. "It's been going on for the last million years, and who are we to interfere?"

Mental Health

1207

In any given situation involving school, mental health is what you possess while everyone around you is obviously teetering on the brink of insanity!

1208

"Tommy, you haven't handed in your homework on mental health."

"I don't see why I should be punished just because I understand the subject."

"What do you mean?"

"Well, I want good mental health for myself, so I'm taking a mental vacation to get back my strength and vitality!"

Military

1209

It has been said that military intelligence is to intelligence what military music is to music!

1210

The military man stood before the class in a pristine uniform and gave a flawless speech about the military. When he finished, he faced the class and asked if there were any questions.

"Yes," said one young student. "With all those metals on the left side of your coat, how come you don't walk lopsided?"

1211

"And so," said the teacher, "the six hundred men marched to certain death against an overwhelmingly powerful enemy. Now, what would you call that?"

Answered one student, "Military intelligence?"

Milk

1212

"Here in school," said the principal to the class, "we try to be like your parents . . ."

"Oh, yeah?" shouted one student, "then how come when we get milk in the cafeteria, it doesn't come with cookies?"

1213

"Drink your milk! It will help you grow!"

"No way! Who wants to become a cow?"

1214

"A cow," said the teacher, "is an animal who gives milk."

"She does not!" exclaimed one child who had been raised on a farm. "You gotta get in there and take every ounce!"

Milky Way

1215

"Today," declared the teacher, "we are going to learn about the Milky Way."

"School is getting better," a student whispered to a friend. "A whole class, just on one candy bar!"

1216

" . . . so we see that there are billions and billions of planets in the Milky Way, which is our home. Are there any questions?"

"Yeah!" offered one student. "If there are so many planets, how did we ever figure out which one to be born on?"

Mirror

1217

"Do you think Mr. Jones is vain about his looks?"

"I don't know, but he's the only teacher I know who puts mirrors on every wall of his classroom, so he can see himself teach from all angles!"

1218

"Do you think Mrs. Johnson has put on weight?"

"I don't know, but yesterday I saw her standing in front of a mirror, and she was screaming, 'You lie! You lie!'"

Misfortune

1219

"My bad grades are all a matter of misfortune," claimed the youth.

"How do you figure?"

"Unfortunately," he answered, "I got assigned to a class with a teacher who checks homework!"

1220

"Now, there's a child who really looks sad," commented one teacher to a colleague.

"He should be," answered the other, "he's had a great misfortune."

"What happened?"

"Last night when I called his home, his mother answered before he could!"

Mistakes

1221

Mistakes are what others make while you are being a victim of circumstance!

1222

"You gave me an 'F,'" said the student. "Isn't that a mistake?"

"Yes, it is," answered the teacher, "but the school doesn't have a grade any lower!"

Misunderstanding

1223

"I hope that we can overcome our misunderstanding," the teacher said to the student.

"What misunderstanding?" asked the student.

"The misunderstanding on your part that I wouldn't recognize the book report your brother handed in three years ago!"

1224

"My bad grades are all a matter of misunderstanding," said the student to the teacher.

"How do you figure that?"

"Because you simply fail to understand that not doing homework is a part of my personality!"

Model

1225

"Do you always throw the directions away before you make the model?" asked the teacher.

"How did you know that?"

"Well, it's just that most jet planes don't have a wing sticking out of the cockpit!"

1226

"Who is that beautiful woman?" said one student.

"She's giving a talk to home ec class; she's a model."

"A model!" exclaimed the student. "Gosh, her assembly instructions must be a mile long!"

Money

1227

"What do you want for your birthday?"

"Money!"

"Come, now! There must be something else . . . "

"OK, I also want a big suitcase to carry the money in!"

1228

"All you ever talk about is money!"

"I do not! I talk about a lot of things that make sense!"

"'Things that make cents!' There you go talking about money again!"

Mother

1229

MOTHER—a person with a heart large enough to withstand the strongest blasts that life can give and small enough to hear and shelter the tiniest cry . . .

1230

Student definition on a quiz: "A Mom is the person you go to after Dad says it can't be done!"

1231

Junior had been a perfect gentleman. On top of that, he had cleaned his room, washed the dishes, and even helped his baby brother.

"You know," Mother told him, "there has been a wonderful change in you . . . "

"Mom," he interrupted, "today is Mother's Day, and I couldn't afford to get you a present, but don't get used to it, OK?"

Mother and Child

1232

"Frankly," said the principal to the student, "I find it difficult to believe that your parents cannot come to school for a conference with the teacher because your mother never had any children!"

1233

The art teacher looked at the student's painting, which depicted a room with the wall dripping mud and clothes scattered everywhere. In the center stood a woman obviously ripping out her hair.

"What do you call this?" asked the teacher.

Answered the student, "Mother and Child!"

Mother and Father

1234

"Who can name two major lending institutions in the United States?"

Answered a student, "Mom and Dad!"

1235

Asked the teacher, "Can you name something that makes a couple a good mother and father?"

"I would think," answered one precocious student, "that it would help a great deal if they had children!"

Movies

1236

Movies have a definite influence on a student's learning. One social studies teacher assigned her class to watch a movie on TV about the

Revolutionary War and then had a difficult time convincing the class that Paul Revere did not take his ride because he wanted to visit his girlfriends in Lexington and Concord!

1237

"If you don't give us all A's," said one small student, "we're gonna put out a contract on you!"

"That's terrible!" exclaimed the teacher. "Where did you ever come up with such a horrible idea?"

"Easy! It was the Movie of the Week on TV last night!"

Mugwump

1238

From the time of Abraham Lincoln, a MUGWUMP is someone who straddles a fence on an issue with such dexterity that the MUG is one side and the WUMP is on the other!

1239

The classic example of a MUGWUMP is someone who, when asked if he agrees that people should take strong stands on issues, answers, "Yes and no . . . "

Muscles

1240

"Did you see that Johnson kid?" asked a teacher. "He just lifted an entire case of books all by himself. You've got to admire his muscles!"

"Yes," said another teacher, looking at the boy's test paper, "Especially those in his head!"

1241

"Now, this chart shows the things in your arm that make it work. They're called muscles."

"Oh, no! Do you mean that my father ate a plate of those with spaghetti last night?"

Music

1242

"'If music be the food of love, play on . . . ' Shakespeare, William, *Twelfth Night*," said the professor.

Stated a student, "'Beat me, Daddy, eight to the bar . . . ' Gillespie, Dizzy, Trumpet!"

1243

"Modern music goes beyond the ability to be defined!" stated a member of a student rock band.

"True," answered a teacher, "and sometimes it goes beyond the ability to be listened to!"

Music Instruction

1244

The school's music teacher got the normal supplies—piano, baton, ear plugs . . .

1245

"That was the best rendition of 'Jingle Bells' I have ever heard," said the music teacher. "Unfortunately, you were supposed to be playing 'Moonlight Sonata'!"

1246

"So, you think I have a future in music?"

"Oh, yes! We always need someone to set up the music stands!"

Music Recitals

1247

The neighbor came running over and shouted, "Good grief, I heard the noise and the moaning and the wailing! Did your furnace explode?"

"No, but my son is giving a recital on the electric guitar, and he just turned up the amplifiers so the neighborhood could appreciate it more fully!"

1248

"Your son gave a recital on the drums, and you didn't invite me," said Uncle George. "How come?"

"Because," came the answer, "you really ARE my favorite uncle, and I want to keep it that way!"

N

Name

1249

The teacher looked at the class list and saw a "Norman Playauer" listed. The boy, however, did not appear for the first few days. Therefore, she went to the principal.

"Tell me," she said, "do we have a Playauer here?"

"Of course we don't have a Play-hour," returned the principal, "we barely have time enough for a coffee break!"

1250

"You! What is your name?"

"Why do you want to know?"

"I want to report you for cutting class."

"Washington, Sir! George Washington at your service!"

Nap

1251

"Really, Ma'am," said the student, "I have read that children benefit from a nap every afternoon."

"Very true," returned the teacher, "but NOT in the middle of my English class!"

"I like to take a nap every afternoon," he said. "I like to take my blanket and curl up with my stuffed bunny rabbit and go off to dreamland!"

"I know you like that," she answered, "but you've got to stop it. You're the principal, and people need to talk to you!"

Nature

1253

In the tent, father and son huddled together for warmth. It was cold, damp, and wet. Outside, thunder rumbled, lightning flashed, and winds howled. Inside, the tent had just sprung a leak.

The little boy looked up at his weary father and said, "Gee, Dad, nature is wonderful! Ain't this great!"

1254

The girl opened her locker, saw the snake, screamed and ran.

A few feet down the hall, two boys leaned against a wall, smiling and observing.

"I tell you," remarked one, "we have just begun to scratch the surface of the uses to which nature may be put!"

Natural Resources

1255

"Name a natural resource."

"My father!"

"How can you say that?"

"Because everytime I go to him with my math homework, he just naturally does it for me."

1256

"Jones," said the teacher looking at the test paper, "I can sympathize with you, but I doubt that I can accept an answer that states that the two most used natural resources in the United States are TV games and bubble gum!"

Nature Study

1257

The teacher looked into the student's locker to find the textbook for her subject lying there covered with spider webs, obviously not disturbed for a long time.

"Aha!" she said, removing the cobweb-covered tome.

"Really, Mrs. Johnson," remarked the student, "I thought you were the kind of teacher who would appreciate a student doing independent nature study!"

1258

Two boys were caught trying to peek into the girl's locker room.

"Well?" bellowed the principal.

Ventured one student, "I guess you wouldn't believe that this was all part of a nature study for human growth and development class?"

Nausea (See also: Illness)

1259

"Has this frog dissection inspired you?" asked the science teacher following the activity.

"It has inspired me to keep studying," said one.

"It has inspired me to respect nature," said another.

"It has inspired me to nausea," said a third. "Excuse me, please!"

1260

The art student showed the teacher her modern, abstract painting.

"Does this remind you of anything?" the student asked.

"As a matter of fact," answered the teacher, "I have felt rather nauseous all morning!"

Need

1261

"Have you learned anything about the difference between a WANT and a NEED?" asked the teacher.

"Sure," answered the student. "I learned that if I really WANT something, I'd better tell my Mom that I really NEED it!"

"I know I asked you to list your classroom needs," the principal said to the kindergarten teacher, "but I really don't know how I can justify an order of shin guards, shoulder pads, and a hockey goalie's face mask!"

Needle
(See also: Home Economics)

1263

"I had a whole package of needles here," said the home ec teacher, "and now they're gone, gone, gone!"

"Yike!" exclaimed one student jumping up. "Well, now they're found (Ouch!), found (Ouch!), found!"

1264

"Come now," said the school nurse to the teacher, "are you going to allow a little needle to intimidate you?"

"Intimidate? No!" said the educator, "but scare, frighten, and horrify—YES!!!"

Neighbor/Neighborhood

1265

"I think our neighbors feel that we need tighter control over our students," stated the principal.

"Have they said anything?"

"No, but when I see them putting up barbed wire and digging moats around their houses, I can't help thinking they're trying to tell us something!"

1266

It was such a tough neighborhood that the schoolteachers all held Golden Gloves rankings!

Nerve (See also: Courage)

1267

"I know where we can get samples, now that we're studying the nervous system," said the student to the teacher.

"What do you mean? Where could we get nerves?"

"Well," stated the pupil, "last night my aunt was over, and I heard my mother tell her she had a lot of it. Maybe she can spare some?"

1268

"Are 'nerves' anything like a train or bus?"

"Why do you ask?"

"Because, you can 'get on' a train; you can 'get on' a bus; and the teacher says I've been getting on his nerves for months!"

News/Newspaper
(See also: Current Affairs; Media)

1269

"You can't believe everything you read in the newspapers," commented the teacher.

"Thanks, Man!" said one student. "I read an article about you talking about how good a teacher you are, and those bozos almost had me convinced!"

1270

"I have news for you," said the teacher. "You are going to have to make up this course in summer school!"

"That isn't news," moaned the student, "that's a documentary special with film at eleven!"

Nickel (See also: Money)

1271

"Why, when I was young, I'd clean the whole house and do the laundry for a nickel!" said the teacher.

"Wow!" exclaimed a student, "come over to our house and do that, and I'll personally give you a DIME!"

1272

"What can you buy for a nickel nowadays?" bemoaned one student.

Answered another enterprising lad, "If you have one on you, I'd be glad to sell you the answer to that question!"

Nickname (See also: Name)

1273

"Nicknames are interesting; sometimes they really capture a personality."

"I'd like to talk to you, but I have to go deal with a student."

"Do I know him?"

"I don't think so. He's that kid in the eighth grade, Hooky Johnson?"

1274

"He was called 'Richard the Lionhearted,'" the teacher went on, "because he was a very brave and courageous king. I often wonder what they would have said of me, had I lived in those days."

Whispered one student, "'Oh, look, here comes Johnson the Boring!'"

Night

1275

"Come, now!" said the teacher. "You're a big boy; surely you're not afraid of the night?"

"I don't mind the night," answered the tike, "as long as the lights are on and Mommy and Daddy are home!"

1276

"Please," said the student to the teacher, "can we hold the parent conference with the principal at 8:00 P.M.?"

"Yes, but why do you want it then?"

"Because, my father works nights, and I'm hoping that's the only time he CAN'T come!"

1277

"Someday," said the student, "I'd like to be the first person to land on the sun!"

"You couldn't possibly do that," remarked the teacher, "you'd burn up!"

"No, I wouldn't!" the pupil answered. "I'd wait and go at night!"

No (See also: Discipline)

1278

NO—a word that could work wonders if applied judiciously by parents to today's youth!

1279

The first thing I learned about school was that it wasn't like home. When the teacher said, "No!"—she really meant it!

1280

The principal turned down so many requests from students and teachers that he had a plaque on his desk that read, "I NO that!"

Nocturnal (See also: Night)

1281

"Name a nocturnal animal that is very ugly, has sharp teeth, and eats insects," asked the teacher.

"My brother!" said one student. "I'm lying about the insects, but he fits all the other characteristics!"

1282

"Let me get this straight," said the guidance counselor, "your grades are bad because all your classes are held during the day and you claim to be a nocturnal learner?"

Noise

1283

"How can you stand all that noise?" said one teacher to a colleague who stood in the cafeteria in the middle of a raucous lunch hour.

"What?"

"I said, 'How can you stand this noise?'"

"Just a minute," answered the first teacher, "I can't hear you. Let me turn up my hearing aid!"

1284

The class visited a local power plant, and in the engine room the noise was incredible. The children pressed hands against ears, and it was all the teacher could do to stay in the place.

Once outside, they were introduced to a man who had worked in that room for 32 years.

"How could you stay in a place with that kind of noise for so long?" asked the teacher.

"Noise?" returned the man. "What noise?"

Normal

1285

"Well, said the school psychologist, "we've checked him out, and he has no learning difficulties, no neurological impairment, and no psychological disturbances—we have, therefore, come to the conclusion that he is a perfectly normal little brat!"

1286

"Your temperature is normal," said mother one morning at the breakfast table. "You're going to school."

"Mom," said the lad, "why don't you go see about the baby for a minute; I'll watch to see that nobody spills your cup of hot coffee, and we'll see what the thermometer says when you get back!"

1287

"The name of the family that lives next to us isn't 'Normal,' is it?" asked junior.

"No, but why do you ask?"

"Because," continued the lad, "my guidance counselor is crazy and doesn't know what she's talking about! Today, she told my teacher that I was right alongside of Abby Normal!"

Notes

1288

"Sandra," said the teacher, "are you and Henry passing notes back there?"

"Oh, no!" came the answer, "we are exchanging personal information."

"Thank goodness," sighed the teacher, "for a moment I thought you weren't paying attention."

1289

"Mr. Jones," said the student to the music teacher, "I have a note for you from the office."

"What is it?"

"F sharp!"

1290

"But," said the student reading the slip of paper, "this says, 'Don't let Mr. Jones find the other note!' What other note?"

"That's just it," explained the other pupil, "there is none! We let Mr. Jones see this one on the floor, and then we watch him go crazy trying to find the other!"

Notes from Home

1291

"Please excuse Melissa's being. It was definitely her father's doing!"

1292

"Please allow Maria to stay after school and take the late bus home. I'm having an affair, and I don't want to be disturbed in the middle of everything!"

1293

"Please excuse Allison for being late this morning. Look . . . I have five kids, either you understand, or you don't!"

1294

"Please give Jason more math homework; his father needs the practice!"

Notes from School

1295

"Dear Mr. Jones—I'd like to invite you to an intimate little gathering. It'll be just you, the principal, your son, and me!"

1296

"Dear Mr. Jones—Since your son has told me that he couldn't do his homework because you had passed away suddenly, you have no idea how delighted I was to see you pick him up after school yesterday!"

Notice
(See also: Memo)

1297

Sign on a Faculty Room bulletin board: NOTICE: It is important that you disregard this notice!

1298

"You have ignored all previous notices," read the note from the school library. "Return the book now! This is your FINAL NOTICE!"

The student brought back the book and remarked, "Sorry I'm so late, but honestly, I never got any other notices to return the book."

"I know," said the librarian. "Doesn't it work well!"

Nourishment
(See also: Cafeteria; Cooking)

1299

The little boy had worked on the neighbor's lawn all afternoon. Finally, the neighbor called the young man to the door.

"You've done a wonderful job on the lawn," she said. "Now won't you stop and take some nourishment?"

"Thank you, Ma'am," returned the lad. "Nourishment would be nice, but if it's all the same to you, do you think I could have a Coke and a Twinkie instead?"

1300

"This homework will nourish your mind," said the teacher.

"Maybe," remarked one student, "but I don't think it will ever take the place of a hot dog and sauerkraut!"

Numbers
(See also: Arithmetic; Math)

1301

"Last night, I assigned my first-grade class the learning of their numbers from 1 to 100. Do you think they'll do it?"

"Well, I wouldn't count on it!"

1302

"Sir," said the teacher to the principal, "I think your being a former math teacher has influenced your school administration."

"Oh," mused the principal, "what makes you say that, 47?"

1303

"I think I am in trouble this year," said one teacher to a colleague. "Look at the numbers for my classes!"

"This isn't bad at all," commented the other teacher. "Why these numbers indicate a very small class size."

"That's just it! That's not class size; that's their collective IQ!"

Numismatist

1304

"As a numismatist, do you believe that George Washington actually threw a silver dollar across the Potomac?"

"Certainly, you know a dollar went a great deal further in those days!"

1305

"So, a 'numismatist,'" the visitor told the second-grade class, "is a person who collects coins."

"That word's too hard," volunteered one child. "I collect coins, and do you know what I call myself?"

"What?"

"A 'Piggybankologist!'"

Nurses

1306

"When I grow up, I want to be a nurse," said the child.

"Is that because you want to serve others," asked the teacher, "and help suffering humanity?"

"Gosh, no," answered the youngster. "It's because I like to stick people with needles!"

1307

"Are you sure you want to be a nurse?" asked the counselor. "Just think of what they have to do with bedpans and when people get ill!"

"That's OK," answered the student. "Finally, I'll be in a profession where I'll be cleaning up!"

Nurse, The School

1308

The child ran into the school nurse's office and said, "Could I have some cotton, gauze, and about ten yards of bandage and tape?"

"Goodness!" exclaimed the nurse. "Is someone injured?"

"Naw!" answered the lad. "We want it so we can tie up and gag Billy Jones and toss him in a locker!"

1309

School nurse to young student: "I don't care how much you promise that it's true, I will need a note from your doctor before I can consider a chocolate bar between each class period as a medicine to be dispersed through this office!"

Nursery

1310

The new parents looked in at the hospital nursery. The babies were making a terrible racket, when one infant pushed up slightly and let go with a tremendous wail that silenced all the other infants instantly.

"How about that," said her parent, "our daughter is going to be a teacher!"

1311

Then there was the teacher who took a part-time job in a nursery, because someone told her she really needed to change!

Nutrition

1312

We have to teach nutrition in schools, because the basic diet of most teenagers is NO-trition!

1313

"We aim at giving the student the best in nutrition," commented the cafeteria manager.

"I understand," said the principal, "but do you really think there will be much call for your Brussels sprouts sandwiches?"

1314

"Today," said the cafeteria manager to the class, "I'd like to speak to you about nutrition."

"Gosh," whispered one student, "I wish she'd talk about something with which she's familiar!"

266

O

Oasis

1315

"I have this recurring nightmare," said the teacher. "I'm at this lovely desert oasis with palm trees, cool water, and lovely serving girls feeding me dates!"

"How is that a nightmare?"

"Because," sighed the educator, "just at that point a bell rings and my second-period class comes in!"

1316

"In my dreams, I'm at this desert oasis, and I'm alone with this gorgeous princess, just the two of us . . . "

"What happens?"

"What do you mean, 'What happens?' I'm a teacher; I take out my books and tutor her in math for the next two hours!"

Obligation

1317

"Why do you misbehave so much?" asked the teacher.

"Please!" answered the boy. "My grandfather misbehaved, my father misbehaved, and you have no idea of the burden such an obligation places on me!"

1318

"I am a teacher!" exclaimed the upset educator. "I have an obligation to teach!"

"Don't get excited," returned the pupil. "I am a student; I have an obligation to resist! Nothing personal!"

1319

"Young man," said the principal, "you have an outstanding loan with this office. Are you trying to run out on your financial obligations?"

"I do not run out on my financial obligations!" stated the youth. Ask anyone you wish; I borrow from everybody equally!"

Occupation

1320

The teacher spotted a former student working in a supermarket.

"What is your occupation?" asked the teacher.

"Finding dates for Saturday night," the lad answered. "Now, would you like to know my job?"

1321

"What are you going to do when you retire?" asked the student.

"I've thought about that," answered the teacher, "and I believe I will take up an occupation where there is a great deal less stress."

"Like what?"

"I've got a job lined up driving a nitroglycerin truck over twisting mountain roads."

1322

"Yes, young man," said the employment-office clerk, "for which occupation do you wish to apply?"

"Occupation?" frowned the boy. "What occupation? All I want is a crummy little after-school job!"

Ocean

1323

The child stood at the edge of the Atlantic Ocean for the first time.

"Right over there," said an adult pointing due east, "is Europe!"

"Well, somebody must be kicking their feet like mad," returned the child. "Just look at those waves!"

1324

When the class visited the beach, a line of debris had been washed up on the shore.

"Do lots of people swim in this ocean?" a child asked.

"Yes, probably millions of people."

"I thought so," the child mused, pointing to the debris. "Just look at the ring they left around the edges!"

Odors

1325

The school bus ran over a skunk. As the bus arrived at school and the doors opened, the scent floated in.

"How about that?" said one student. "The cafeteria is trying a whole new menu!"

1326

"What if they had a perfume named after this school?" asked the teacher. "What would it be called?"

One student sniffed and said, "How about, 'Eau de Locker Room, PS3!' "

1327

"Do you know where I might find the boy who brought in the pet skunk?" asked the principal.

The teacher sniffed the air and answered, "Around the corner and down the hall . . ."

Office (See also: Secretary, The School; Principal)

1328

"This is MY office," roared the principal. "I and I alone am responsible for it; I and I alone make it function!

"Now, as soon as my secretary tells me where my phone is located, I'll get started."

1329

"When I sent you out of the room, you left school," said the angry teacher to the student. "Why did you do that?"

"It's your fault," answered the student. "You told me to go to the Maine Office, and I was on my way to New England!"

Old Age

1330

"Johnson," said the teacher to the student as she handed back a failing test paper, "I have finally figured out what you are going to achieve in this class."

"You have? What?"

Answered the teacher, "Old age!"

1331

"I don't think I'll ever retire," remarked the teacher to the class. "I don't know what I'm going to do when I reach old age."

"What?" gasped one wide-eyed innocent, "You mean you're not there already?"

Old Timer

1332

"Mr. Johnson is a real old-timer!"

"Yeah! A definite old-timer!"

"Maybe even as old as thirty!"

"Come on! NOBODY is THAT old!"

1333

"Mr. Johnson is a real old-timer!"

"How old is he?"

"You won't believe this, but he's so old he began teaching BEFORE there was a computer in the room!"

Olympics

1334

"In our study of Greece, we cannot overlook the Olympic games, but I wonder if anyone can tell me where the modern games are located?"

"I know," said one child. "Atlantic City and Las Vegas!"

1335

"In this class," said the physical education teacher, "you will select a sport and train, train, train for it as if you were training for an Olympic event!"

Whispered one student, "I don't suppose there's an Olympic event in sleeping, is there?"

Omnivorous

1336

OMNIVOROUS—a term universally applied to teenagers.

1337

"Name an omnivorous animal," asked the teacher.

"Billy Jones!" shouted a student.

"Come, now! How can you say Billy is omnivorous?"

"Because," came the reply, "he eats the 'Cafeteria Special' every day!"

Open House (See also: Parents; Visitor)

1338

OPEN HOUSE—a school function where teachers come in well-dressed, students are particularly well-behaved, and many parents find it necessary to come incognito!

1339

"I would like you to take home invitations to your parents," said the principal over the PA system, "to come to an open house where they can see what you do every day!"

"What I'd like to know," stated one student to another, "is how he expects to get us to take these invitations home?"

1340

The parents held an open house and invited the teacher, who walked about looking carefully at everything.

"Are you interested in the decor?" asked mother.

"Actually," answered the teacher, "I'm looking for the huge cracks in the wall that your son told me about. You know, the ones where the wind blows through and freezes his fingers so he can't write out his homework!"

Opening Day

1341

"So, D-Day, the invasion of Europe during World War II was planned for years and years. Can you think of anything else that requires such planning?"

Just then the principal walked by and shouted in, "The opening day of school!"

1342

"This is the opening day of school," said the principal to the student, "and you've already been sent to my office! What have you to say for yourself?"

"I'm off to a slow start, I'll admit," the student answered, "but by the time midterms roll around, we should know each other really well!"

1343

On opening day, the principal addressed the student body.

"I know you are here to work hard," he said. "I know you are here to write reports and do homework; I know you are here to spend hours in academic research . . . "

"Say," whispered one student, "do you think somebody should set him straight before the school year officially begins?"

Operation

1344

"I had an operation once, and I was awake throughout the whole thing!"
"Good grief! What kind of an operation was it?"
"An IRS audit; they removed my bank account!"

1345

"No, Tommy, I'm afraid that while they are operating to remove your teacher's appendix, they cannot also remove all memory of the homework you did not turn in!"

1346

"Charley," said the teacher, "I know that your project involves charting your weight gain as you eat only cafeteria food for lunch every day, but I really think we should call it something other than 'Operation Up-Chuck'!"

Opinion

1347

"I have a right to my opinion!" proclaimed one student debater to another.
"True," said the other, "and you also have a right to be stupid; a right which I see you are exercising quite well!"

1348

"I think," said the principal to the student, "that you would benefit from being suspended from school and not being allowed back until we have a conference with your parents. What do you think?"
Said the student, "I think I'd like a second opinion!"

Opinion Polls

1349

Question: How can we keep students from not doing their homework?
Answer (on a student opinion poll): Don't give homework!

"You know," commented the principal, "we should use student opinion polls to guide us in our approach to our students, don't you think?"

"The latest student opinion polls state that you should be fired."

"Hey! What do these stupid polls know?"

1351

"I'm conducting an opinion poll, young lady," said the reporter. "What do you believe is the major cause of drop outs?"

Answered the student without hesitation, "School!"

Opportunity

1352

Opportunity is that which many people wait years for, only to find that its been hanging around them all this time just waiting to be recognized.

1353

Opportunity is not something to be taken; it is something to be made.

1354

"I hope you will look upon detention as an opportunity to build your character," said the teacher.

"And I'm hoping," whispered the student to a friend, "that when I cut that detention, the teacher will look upon it as an opportunity to get home early!"

Orange

1355

"Yes, Honey," said the kindergarten teacher, "I know you need Vitamin C, but you will NOT get it by eating the orange crayon!"

1356

"Every day you come to school," said the teacher, "you bring an apple and an orange. You put the apple on my desk, and you eat the orange. Today, you placed the orange on my desk and you ate the APPLE. How come?"

"Well," said the child, "usually the apple has a rotten spot in it, but today it was the orange!"

Orator

1357

What a public speaker becomes when he finds a group willing to pay for his speech!

1358

Any public speaker who has sense enough to quit before the audience does!

1359

An "orator" is any public speaker with whom you happen to agree!

1360

ORATOR—a person of few words, but only if the audience is very, very lucky!

Orchard

1361

"Why so glum?" asked Mom. "This morning you were all excited about your class trip to the orchard. Didn't you go?"

"We went all right," said her daughter, "but I was so disappointed—it was nothing but trees!"

1362

A reporter once asked a farmer what would be the quickest way to rid his orchard of pests?

Answered the farmer with a wink, "Make it illegal for kids to want to climb trees!"

Ordinary (See also: Normal)

1363

"Now," said the guidance counselor to the new student, "for Language Arts, we have Gifted and Talented, Remedial Instruction, Resource Room, Enrichment Classes, and Basic Skills . . ."

"Gosh!" muttered the confused student, "Don't you have some kind of course called, 'Just Ordinary-Kid English'?"

1364

"How would you describe yourself?"

"I'm an ordinary plus ordinary person."

"I don't get it?"

"You know, that's one extra 'ordinary' person. After all, I do want to be modest!"

Ostrich

1365

The ostrich hides its head in the sand when trouble comes along. What a stupid bird, always imitating mankind!

1366

At the zoo, the small child watched as the ostrich put its head to the ground with its hindquarters uppermost.

"Look, Mommy," said the tot, "it's gonna have its temperature taken!"

Outdoors (See also: Nature; Transportation, Travel and Trips)

1367

I love the great outdoors, particularly when I'm looking at it through the picture window of my air-conditioned hotel room!

1368

"Think of it," said Dad, "the great outdoors—hiking twenty miles; building our own camp; struggling to find food; braving all kinds of weather. We are going to have fun!"

"'WE?'" returned the boy. "Were you planning on taking someone with you?"

1369

Asked the teacher, "What is meant by the great outdoors?"

Answered the student, "Exit 1 by the Main Office; Exit 2 by the gym . . . "

Outlaw

1370

"Uncle Harry is my father's outlaw," stated the child.

"You mean," corrected the teacher, "that he's your father's in-law."

"Hey," returned the boy, "you ain't never met Uncle Harry!"

1371

"Today," said the social studies teacher, "we will study the famous outlaws of the West."

"Like Betty the Kid?" asked one student.

"You mean 'Billy' the Kid, don't you?"

"What's the matter," returned the student, "you ain't never heard of 'Affirmative Action'?"

Oven
(See also: Home Economics; Kitchen)

1372

"I know they're called 'oven mitts,'" said the home ec teacher through the cloud of smoke, "but that does NOT mean that they are to be kept in the oven while the chicken is roasting!"

1373

Then there was the mother who asked her teenaged son to turn off the oven, so he went up to it and said, "You're ugly, and your breath smells!"

"These kids really know nothing coming into home ec," said the teacher. "Last week I asked a student to turn down the oven, so he fluffed up a pillow and threw it and a quilt inside!"

Overachievement

1375

An overachiever is one who, when asked the directions to Times Square, writes a "Traveler's Guide to New York," sells a million or so copies, and retires at age 40!

1376

"All I asked for was the answer to one math problem," said the teacher to the overachiever. "You did not have to include the dead batteries from your calculator!"

1377

The first time the teacher saw the Grand Canyon, he looked straight upward and intoned, "OK, God, now THIS is overachieving!"

Overcome
(See also: Victory)

1378

"Depressed?" said the lad to his friend. "You have no need to be depressed. Why, together, we can overcome anything!"

"Glad to hear you say that," commented the other boy. "I was depressed because I had no money for a date, but if you'll come across with twenty bucks, I'll gladly overcome the depression with you!"

1379

"What does it take to overcome adversity and rise to the top?"

Answered a student, "To overcome adversity, you must start with courage, determination, and about a million-five in liquid assets!"

"Ma'am," said the student to the teacher, "I want to thank you for help-ing me to overcome my shyness; overcome my doubts; overcome my fears . . . "

"Why . . . why, thank you!"

"And, now, Ma'am," the student continued, "would there be a way you could help me overcome the homework I didn't do last night?"

Overeater
(See also: Diet/Dieting; Weight)

1381

Well, I wouldn't say that he's an overeater, but he does wait until every-one has gone through the cafeteria line and then walks in with a tray in each hand yelling, "Give me everything that's left!"

1382

"There's a marvelous new diet out," said one teacher to a colleague. "It's called the overeater's diet."

"Oh, how does it work?"

"Very simple! You may eat as much as you want of everything you hate!"

Overheat

1383

Then there was the day it got so hot they had to evacuate the school. It seems that when the air temperature mixed with all the normal hot air, it threatened to melt down the building!

1384

"So," continued the shop teacher, "without the proper lubrication and cooling fluids, any engine will overheat and stop."

"In that case," called out one student, "could I go get a soda? I'd hate to seize up in the middle of class."

Oversight

1385

"Bobby," said the teacher, "I'm sorry I didn't call your name just now. It was an oversight on my part."

"That's OK," sighed the small boy. "I'm so short, people have been sighting over me for years!"

1386

"How was school today?" mother asked as Junior came through the door.

"OK," he said, "except for a small oversight."

"What was that?"

"Well," sighed the boy, "I forgot to attend five of my classes!"

Oxidation

1387

"I have spent a lifetime," said the principal, "keeping my mind like a steel trap; I guard against apathy; I guard against complacency . . . "

Commented one listener, "He should watch out for oxidation, too!"

1388

The shop teacher built a large iron sculpture and requested Central Administration for "a protective coating in order to retard oxidation."

Central Administration wrote back that the request was denied and added, "but we will send a crew to paint the thing; otherwise, it will rust like a son of a gun!"

Oysters

1389

Then there was the science teacher who got a job as a waiter in a seafood restaurant. It didn't last. It seems that every time somebody ordered oysters, he'd yell, "One plate of living bivalve mollusks on their external support structures!"

1390

Two oysters were talking.

"Don't you pity those humans?" said one.

"Sure do," commented the other. "They travel around in schools for years and years, and they don't ever get to be blue-plate specials!"

P

Package
(See also: Mail)

1391

"John," said the teacher, "you know that package I gave you last week to mail on your way home? You didn't forget, did you?"

"No, Ma'am!" answered the boy, "I remembered exactly!"

Then he added in a whisper, " . . . and I also remember exactly where I left it at home after I forgot to mail it!"

1392

"Take a lesson from experience," stated a teacher. "Good things come in small packages!"

"Take a lesson from science," quipped one student. "So do germs and bacteria!"

Page
(See also: Books)

1393

"Did you do ALL of last night's reading assignment?" asked the teacher.

"Yes, Ma'am," returned the student, "and I will gladly answer any question you'd care to ask . . . about the title page."

"If you were a book, what would your pages say?"

"They'd say, 'These pages are blank, but give me a break; I'm only nine years old!'"

Palm

1395

"I'd like to buy that plant that's real handy."

"A 'handy' plant?"

"Yeah, you know—a palm!"

1396

"No more stalling!" exclaimed the teacher. "Take your homework and place it on my palm!"

So the student pulled out a sheet of paper from a notebook and shoved it into the potted plant in one corner of the room!

Pants
(See also: Clothing)

1397

"Today," boasted the teacher, "I outlined material on the chalkboard, and the class had their eyes glued on me!"

"You know," said a colleague when the teacher had left, "I just didn't have the heart to tell him he had ripped his pants up the back!"

1398

The teacher saw the boy come in wearing a pair of ripped, frayed, faded, and torn pants. The teacher quietly approached the boy and gently explained that if there were financial problems in the family, perhaps the school could get him a new pair of pants.

"But," said the lad, "these are new. Hey, it cost a fortune to buy them this way!"

Parallel

1399

"Now," said the math teacher, "do you understand about parallel lines?"
"I think so," said the student, "but why are they side by side?"

1400

"Your brother gave me fits when I had him in class," said the teacher, "and you're doing the same thing!"
"Well," shrugged the student, "it sort of gives you a new respect for the theory of parallel development, don't it?"

Parents

1401

You know you're a parent when you find yourself doing the same things to your children that your parents did to you, which you promised you would never do to your kids!

1402

"The problems of today's youth may be reduced to a single word," said the teacher to the class. "And do you know what that word is?"
Answered the class in unison, "PARENTS!"

Parents and Children

1403

"Parents," said the speaker, "are made by love, devotion, and toil!"
Came a voice from the back of the room, " . . . and a couple of kids don't hurt none, either!"

1404

The teacher's doctoral dissertation was on the hereditary nature of mental illness—claimed parents inherited insanity from their children.

Parents and the School

1405

" . . . so all parents are invited to visit school tomorrow," said Junior.

"Fine," replied Mom and Dad, "but how will we recognize your teachers?"

"Don't worry," replied the lad, "I think they'll be waiting in line for YOU!"

1406

Wrote the kindergarten teacher to the parents: "You have given us your children, and all contributions, no matter how small, will be cherished and deeply appreciated."

Parent/Teacher Groups

1407

"Well, now that the last of your six children has graduated from this school, what do you look forward to the most?"

Answered the parent with a deep sigh, "No more PTA meetings!"

1408

Said one distraught parent, "I've been in PTA, PTO, PFO, and PFA, and if I don't get out of them PDQ, I'm going to go N-U-T-S!"

Park (See also: Nature; Nature Study)

1409

"Name three good things about going to the park," asked the teacher.

Wrote one student, "It's not school; it's not school; it's not school!"

1410

"Why do you like the park so much?" asked the teacher. "What's there that's so attractive?"

"It's not what's there; it's what isn't there!"

"Oh, and what's NOT there that gives you such pleasure?"
Answered the student, "Teachers!"

Parking (See also: Automobiles; Buses; Driver's Education)

1411

"Do you have a parking problem at this school?" asked the visitor.

"Not at all," answered the principal. "Now, if you'll wait a moment, I'll get a taxi to drive you to your car."

1412

"Now," said the inspector to the student, "I'd like you to successfully parallel park."

"So would I," remarked the student. "Can't I just promise never to put the car in reverse?"

Parliament (See also: Government)

1413

Parliament and Congress have one great thing in common—they both talk too much!

1414

In Parliament, there's the House of Commons and the House of Lords. That makes sense; in America, politicians from one House usually Lord it over those from another.

Partner

1415

"Did you have a partner on this science project?" asked the teacher.
"Why do you ask?"

"Because it's magnificent!"
"In that case," said the student, "I did it all alone!"

1416

"Pick a study partner you really can't stand," advised one student. "In that way, you'll be so anxious to get away from one another, you'll get your studying done in half the time!"

Pastimes (See also: Hobbies; Sports)

1417

"Look," said the guidance counselor, "this survey is for our records; you can't put down 'making the teacher's life miserable' as one of your pastimes!"

1418

Commented the teacher, "I asked him for his favorite pastime, and now I have to explain why 'The Days of King Arthur' is not an acceptable answer."

Patience

1419

It's difficult to develop patience; you have to wait so long for it!

1420

"Name an endeavor in which you have to have patience to succeed."
    "Being a doctor!"

Peace

1421

"I would like," said the student, "to have peace of mind."
    "Fine," replied the teacher. "From now on, I'll give you a piece of my mind every day!"

1422

"If I were King of the World," reflected the student, "I would have world peace . . . and I'd go to war with anyone who disagreed with me!"

Peanut Butter (See also: Cafeteria; Lunch)

1423

Our cafeteria is so bad, the peanut butter and jelly sandwiches are underdone!

1424

"I think peanut butter is the most nutritious food in the world," stated one student.

"Do you have a reason for saying that?"

"Sure," answered the student, "if it sticks to the roof of your mouth the way it does, just think of how it must stick to your ribs!"

Penmanship

1425

"This is atrocious penmanship," said the teacher. "It's sloppy, and I can't read a word of it!"

"Sorry," answered the student. "I gave you the wrong paper. What you have there is the note YOU gave me to take home to my mother!"

1426

Did you hear about the student who got into medical school on the basis of one written essay? No one could read his handwriting, so they figured he'd make a natural doctor!

Penny (See also: Money)

1427

Said the student to the teacher, "I'll give you a penny if you'll explain that again."

"I'll do it for nothing," smiled the teacher, "but don't you think that's rather a small price to offer?"

"Hey," replied the student, "take it or leave it; that's all it's worth to me!"

1428

"Have you ever heard the expression, 'A penny for your thoughts'?"

"And, have you ever heard the expression, 'Make it worth my while, or I'm clamming up'!?"

Pensions

1429

"Just think," said a young teacher to an elder colleague, "one more year and you'll be out of here collecting your pension!"

"Yes," returned the other teacher, "and then if I can only hold down three part-time jobs, I should be able to live!"

1430

"I'm sorry you're not feeling well," said the principal to the elderly, ailing teacher. "Just think about the pension you'll soon be receiving!"

"Come on!" said a companion. "Do you want to depress the poor guy completely?"

Perception

1431

"You know," said the teacher to the student, "it isn't a problem until we choose to perceive it as a problem, and right now, you're coming into 20/20 focus!"

1432

Reality is not half as important as the way in which we perceive that reality.

Perfection/Perfectionists

1433

"Why do you work so hard at being a disruption in class?" asked the teacher.

"Please," came the reply, "I'm a perfectionist!"

1434

"I want perfection in your homework," said the teacher, "for I am a perfectionist!"

"Well, you won't find it in mine," whispered one student, "for I am a NEGLECT-IONIST!"

Period (See also: History; Time)

1435

"Excuse me," said the student to the teacher, "but what period is this?"

"Last period of the day, but why do you ask?"

"Last period, and I haven't gotten in trouble once! Wow! I'm really going to have to work hard to make my daily quota!"

1436

"What's your favorite period of the day?" the principal asked the student in the hall.

"It's hard to choose," answered the student, "between science, math, or English—science, I think . . . "

The principal left, and the student turned to a companion.

"Actually, my favorite period is lunch, but she seemed in such need of a positive message!"

Perseverance

1437

"I warned you five times!" said the teacher. "Now, I am assigning you detention! What do you have to say for yourself?"

"Well," smiled the lad, "you have to admire my perseverance!"

"To succeed in this subject," explained the teacher, "all you need do is take your homework and persevere, persevere, persevere!"

"Personally," whispered one student to a companion, "I've found it easier to take an encyclopedia and copy, copy, copy!"

Pets (See also: Animals; Nature; Nature Study)

1439

"I don't care what you say, young man, these moths in your locker do not qualify as family pets!"

1440

"Mrs. Jones, you don't understand," said the teacher on the phone. "Bobby is quite right. Tomorrow is a special day when we encourage students to bring in their pets, but only if they're in cages."

"It's you who doesn't understand," replied the parent. "Bobby has just gotten a wire basket, and he's trying to stuff his baby sister in it!"

Philosophy

1441

"Yes," said the student, "I do have detention every afternoon for the next three weeks, but just think of the wealth of learning and experience I will attain."

"Well, you certainly have a good attitude."

"Look," sighed the student, "around this asylum, you are either philosophical or you're insane!"

1442

"Philosophy is most important to mankind," said the teacher, "for it helps us discover who we are."

"Big deal," remarked one student, "I can get the same information from a phone book in half the time!"

Philosophy of Education

1443

"Young man!" said the teacher to the disruptive student. "Would you like to teach this class?"

"Not really," answered the student, "but I wouldn't mind sharing my philosophy of education with you!"

1444

"Bobby," said the teacher, "I give homework because that is part of the philosophy of education."

"Yes," said the lad, "but I don't do it, because that is part of the philosophy of Bob!"

Photography/Photographer

1445

"Come on," said the school photographer, "won't you please smile?"

"I've seen your photos," replied the student. "Believe me, I have nothing to smile about!"

1446

"Wow!" exclaimed the photography student after the first day of class, "it's photography for me! It was so great taking all those photos! I can hardly wait until next week, when we get to put film in the camera!"

Physical Education

1447

"What would this class rather do?" asked the physical education teacher. "Would you rather run five laps around the track or do fifty push-ups?"

"Actually," answered one member of the class, "I'd like to form a committee to come up with alternate suggestions."

1448

"Remember our goal," said the physical education teacher, "a sound mind; a sound body; a well-rounded person!"

"Wow!" remarked one student, "a person could go crazy from all these choices!"

Pigeon

1449

"I've decided on my science experiment," said the student. "I'm going to get a pigeon from the city, bring it to the country, and see if it mugs the other birds!"

1450

"So, you went to the city and saw statues of famous people. Did it teach you anything?"
"I'll say! I never realized that all those Civil War generals went into battle with pigeons on their hats!"

Pills (See also: Medicine)

1451

The doctor gave me red pills and green pills. They don't do anything for me physically, but I look at them and get in the Christmas spirit!

1452

"The doctor gave me some pills to lose weight."
"Do they suppress your appetite?"
"No, I throw them on the floor and pick them up one at a time, three times a day!"

Pinch

1453

The home ec teacher said, "This needs salt; give me a pinch."
He did.
Five days detention!

1454

Said the student to the home ec teacher, "I kept putting in a pinch of this and a pinch of that, and I guess it was all those pinches that made the soup turn black and blue!"

Plaid

1455

My science experiment was to take a chameleon, place him on a square of plaid, and observe how long it took the little lizard to go insane!

1456

"This kid was so far out," said the teacher, "that she wore plaid!"
    "But, lots of people wear plaid jackets!"
    "What jacket? I'm talking about her hair!"

Plays

1457

Said one teacher in the faculty lounge, "The stage is no place for bad actors!"
    "Of course not," answered a colleague. "They're all in my fifth-period class!"

1458

Then there was the English teacher who became the football coach; he made the team memorize all the plays—starting with HAMLET straight through to MACBETH!"

Plays, School

1459

"Now," said the first grader to the audience at the school play, "I will tell you the long story of John Smith and Pocahontas . . . "

Then, he paused and added, " . . . but I'd better go to the bathroom first!"

1460

The visitor was being given a tour of the hospital when they came to one ward where there was bed after bed filled with individuals who were obviously in a deep sleep portraying every symptom of complete and total exhaustion.

"Teachers," explained the head doctor, "who volunteered to direct the school play!"

Pledge

1461

"We're going to say the Pledge of Allegiance!" yelled one small child. "Oh, boy! The Pledge of Allegiance! Mrs. Jones?"

"Yes, honey."

"What's 'pledge' and what's 'allegiance'?"

1462

"Will you pledge to me you didn't do it!" said the teacher.

"Pledge, heck!" returned the student. "I'll swear to it!"

Point of View (See also: Opinion)

1463

"We have a problem of point of view," said the teacher to the student. "You see yourself as a comedian who has just brought down the house, and I see you as a candidate for detention from now through your senior year in high school!"

1464

"I don't think I'll pick on kids anymore," said the former bully.

"Wonderful! What changed your mind?"

"I picked on the new kid, and he knocked me to the ground. It's amazing what that new point of view did for me!"

Poise

1465

POISE is the ability a teacher has of standing in front of a student who is covered with dripping glue to which are stuck various pieces of lab equipment and remark, "Need a little help with our science experiment, do we?"

1466

POISE is epitomized by the home ec teacher who tastes every one of the concoctions made by students, compliments each one, and never becomes physically ill!

Political Science

1467

"No, political science is not the art of buttering up your congressman so you can get a government grant to do scientific research!"

1468

"What are you studying?"
　　"Political science."
　　"You mean those politicians have got it down to a science! Oh, no! We're all doomed!"

Politics/Politicians

1469

There are stranger and more devious professions than politics . . . but no one's come up with one yet!

1470

"I see we're cutting down on expenses; Mayor Smith will be coming to speak to the school."
　　"How is that cutting down on expenses?"

"After he's done there will be enough hot air left over to keep the school warm for a month!"

Pregnancy

1471

"Are you all right, Mrs. Johnson," asked the first-grader. "You're putting on weight."

"Honey," answered the teacher, "I'm pregnant."

"What a relief," sighed the student. "For a moment there, I thought you were going to have a baby!"

1472

Then there was the English teacher who said that she didn't mind a pregnant pause, as long as what was delivered at the end of it was healthy, fresh, and new!

Prejudice

1473

Prejudice is a practice unique in the fact that while it may hurt its target, it slowly corrupts and kills the soul of the user!

1474

"No," said the teacher to the student, "you cannot claim that you are not prejudiced, just because you hate everybody equally!"

Pretzel

1475

PRETZEL—a breadstick in need of an attitude adjustment!"

1476

"After a hard day in school," said the teacher, "I feel like a pretzel from our cafeteria."

"You mean all twisted up?"
"No, ASSAULTED!"

Principal, The School

1477

The principal is the chief executive and leader of the school . . . whenever his secretary allows him to be!

1478

A vicious dog had begun to snap at a person in the street when a man stepped forward. He stood before the raging dog and said, "Go!" The dog snarled, turned, and ran away.

"Are you an animal trainer?" asked the would-be victim.

"No, I'm the principal of a school, so I've had a lot of experience and lots of practice!"

Problems and Solutions

1479

Remarked one teen, "I've got all the solutions, it's just that I haven't discovered any problems they fit!"

1480

Then there was the student who had an innovative solution to the problem of students cheating on tests—don't give tests!

Professors (See also: College)

1481

PROFESSOR—a high school teacher with an attitude.

1482

PROFESSOR—An expert, but not necessarily in teaching!

Psychologist, The School

1483

Two school psychologists were walking in opposite directions down the hall of a school.

Said one, "Good morning!"

Said the other, "Now, what did she mean by that?"

1484

"We have the results of the testing," the school psychologist told the principal, "and the child is neurotic and borders on being a paranoid schizophrenic!"

"Well," said the principal, "sounds like he'll fit right in!"

Pulse (See also: Nurses; Nurse, The School)

1485

School nurse to student: "It will not hasten this examination if every time I try to take your pulse, you start singing, 'And the Beat Goes On!'"

1486

"The first thing I must do," said the new principal to the student council, "is to take the pulse of the school. What do you think I'll find?"

Commented one student, "That we're off-beat?"

Pumpkin

1487

PUMPKIN—an acorn squash with a thyroid problem.

1488

The kindergarten student came in with a huge jack o'lantern complete with fierce eyes and fangs.

"I got this for you, Mrs. Johnson," said the child, "because it looks just like you!"

Punch (See also: Fighting)

1489

"You know," said the teacher at the class party, "this punch tastes a little stale."

"That's funny," answered one of the students, "it was fine when we stored it in the closet after last year's party!"

1490

"So, you started the fight, eh? You threw the first punch?"

"I did not!"

"You didn't throw the first punch?"

"That's right, I didn't throw it. I sent it special delivery!!!"

Q

Qualified

1491

The teacher had locked his keys inside the car and was trying unsuccessfully to open the door when along came a former student of his. The ex-student looked both ways, bent over the door, and had it opened in less than five seconds.

"Thank you," said the teacher.

"Hey, Mr. Johnson," said the ex-student, "I been in jail three times since I graduated. If you want something done, get somebody who's qualified!"

1492

Anyone who has ever taught will tell you, it is not the degrees after your name that qualifies you to teach, it is whether you can survive that first week of teaching with your sanity and your skin intact, still loving children!

Quality

1493

"This is really a quality book report!"

"After all the time my father spent on it—it better be!"

1494

Whether it comes through money, effort, time, or the tears expended, one of the facts of life is that you cannot get a high-quality education at a bargain-basement price!

Quarrel (See also: Argument; Fighting)

1495

The teacher broke up the brawl and asked, "Are you two having a fight?"

"No, Sir," said one, "we are having a quarrel using nonverbal communication!"

1496

Said the student, "I want to talk to you about my grade in English."

"Please," answered the teacher, "let's not quarrel over something so small!"

Quart

1497

The home ec teacher said, "Please bring me a quart of flour."

Replied one student, "Is that more than a 'pinch' and less than a 'smidgeon,' or right in the middle around a 'touch'?"

1498

"Last night I drank a quart of that lemonade my sister made!"

"Did it make you sick?"

"No, but for a while there, I sure could whistle good!"

Quarter (See also: Money)

1499

"At the end of the period," stated the teacher, "I'll give you your grades for the quarter."

"Wishful thinking," whispered one student. "With my grades, I wouldn't pay a nickel to know them, much less twenty-five cents!"

1500

"We need butter," said the home ec teacher, "please bring me a quarter."

"OK," said one student fishing in his pocket, "but at today's prices, that's not going to get you very much!"

Quartet

1501

"Did you enjoy the opera?" asked the teacher.

"Sort of," came the reply.

"But, surely, you must have enjoyed the quartet?"

"Not really. The only part I liked was when the four fat guys sang!"

1502

Then there was the music teacher who was so wrapped up in his work, he stopped by a convenience store and asked for a quartet of milk!

Quatrain

1503

"Today," said the English teacher, "we are going to study the quatrain."

"Finally," stated one of the students, "something I can relate to! My Mom takes it into the city every day!"

1504

A quatrain is a four-line poem
That's rhythmic, lively, short, and terse,
But those which students write at home
Quite often go from bad to verse!

Queen *(See also: Royalty)*

1505

"And this," pointed out the science teacher, "is the queen bee."
"Where's the king bee?"
"There is no king bee."
"Wow!" said the student, "another single-parent family!"

1506

Billy had just learned about the functions of the queen in a bee's nest when he came home to find his sister jubilant, because she had just been chosen Homecoming Queen.
"Wow!" said the boy, "My sister is a queen! I can hardly wait to watch her lay all those eggs!"

Quench

1507

"When we have a barbecue," said the child, "my Dad always sets out a big pitcher of ice water."
"Of course," commented the teacher, "to quench your burning thirst."
"No," continued the child, "to quench the burning steaks!"

1508

"I promise," said the teacher, "that during this school year, I will never quench the fire for learning and work deep inside of each of you!"
"And we promise," whispered one lad, "to quickly relieve you of that delusion!"

Quest

1509

"So, many knights set off on impossible quests," said the teacher. "You know what an impossible quest is, don't you?"
"Sure," whispered one, "trying to find something interesting in all this!"

"How lovely to see a class on the quest for the knowledge that means the start of education!" said the teacher.

"I guess we shouldn't tell her," commented one student, "that our real quest is for the bell that means the end of the school day!"

Questions

1511

"How high is the moon?"
    "I don't know."
    "How deep is the ocean?"
    "I don't know."
    "Forget it!"
    "Don't stop now! How are you going to learn if you don't ask questions?"

1512

"In this class," said the teacher, "you can ask any question you wish . . . "
    "How old are you?"
    " . . . as long as they're not personal!"

Questions and Answers

1513

"So, I have this question," the teacher said to her first-grade class, "Where do babies come from?"

"Ma'am," said one seven year old, "you don't have to be embarrassed just because you don't know the answer. I'll be glad to explain!"

1514

"Our principal gives such wonderful answers to questions," said one teacher.

"Come on," commented a colleague, "the other day I asked him when the book order would be in, and he answered, that the needs of Nature hang in a delicate balance with the dreams of Mankind!"

"You see," affirmed the first educator, "he always gives wonderful answers; it's just that they're not necessarily to the question you asked!"

Quicksand

1515

"So," said the teacher, "once you are in quicksand, you struggle and struggle only to find yourself being drawn in deeper and deeper!"

"Gosh," commented one student, "sounds a lot like homework, don't it?"

1516

"Where's your brother?" asked Dad on the camping trip.

"He's over playing by the fast dirt."

"Fast dirt?"

"You know, the sign that said QUICKSAND!"

Quick Thinking

1517

"Are you writing on that desk?" asked the teacher.

"I was just correcting your name," said the student. "If someone is going to write these horrible things about you, the least they could do is to spell your name correctly!"

1518

The child knocked the principal out of the way just as the truck bore down on him.

"Young lady," said the principal, "your quick thinking has saved my life!"

"Not so loud!" returned the student, "I have to live in this place you know!"

Quill Pen

1519

"Yes," said the teacher, "in those days a quill pen often came from a goose."

"Ma'am," asked one student, "what did you push on a goose to make the pen point pop out?"

1520

"In Colonial times, everyone wrote by dipping the quills of birds into ink. What does that tell you?"

Answered one student, "There must have been some pretty dirty birds in those days!"

Quilt

1521

"This is a beautiful quilt," said the art teacher to the child who had brought it in for the craft show, "but are you sure this is your work. Is this quilt yours?"

"Yes, Ma'am," said the child, "It's mine! And, if you don't believe me, I'll show you the receipt from the store where I bought it!"

1522

"Tell me," said the teacher to the first-grade class, "what can I do to let you know that school is a good place to be?"

"Well," ventured one youngster, "if it's not too much trouble, could you wrap me up in a quilt and make me a cup of cocoa?"

Quips

1523

"I'll find a joke tonight," said the teacher, "and tomorrow I shall greet you with a quip!"

"How did it go today?" asked mother later.

"Not too good," answered junior. "Mr. Johnson said that tomorrow he was going to beat us with a whip!"

1524

A quip is something you wish you had said first, and will, the next time you can maneuver the conversation in that direction!

Quitting and Quitters

1525

Get in the habit of quitting, and in no time at all, you'll be a habitual quitter!

1526

"Run one more lap," said the coach. "I didn't know you were a quitter!"

"That's nothing," panted the athlete, "you didn't know I wasn't a masochist, either!"

Quotation

1527

"My favorite quotation is Shakespeare, playwright, 'Neither a borrower nor a lender be'!"

"Mine is from Mr. Johnson, eighth grade teacher, 'Well, Son, it looks as if you finally passed English!'"

1528

Did you hear about the really rich student who, when asked for his favorite quotation, said, "General Motors, up 5 and ⅜"?

Quiver

1529

"Why do they call the arrow-holder a quiver?"

"Listen, if you were shooting at guys in armor, you'd be a little shaky, too!"

1530

"Sweetheart," said the teenaged girl to her teen date, "is it my presence that makes you quiver so?"

"No," said the boy, "it has something to do with taking you to dinner at a place where a hamburger costs six hours of my after-school job!"

Quiz

1531

I had a teacher once who used to say that it was now time for a "little" quiz. Believe me, if I hadn't studied, there was no such thing as a "little" quiz!

1532

"This is a special quiz," said the teacher. "First, write your name at the top of the paper."

"Well," sniffed one student, "if you're going to ask trick questions like that . . . !"

R

Radio

1533

"Your homework assignment was to watch a special movie on TV. Did you do it?"

"Yes, Ma'am!"

"I happen to know there was a power outage here last night! How could you have watched it?"

"Er . . . I saw it on our portable radio!"

1534

"Bobby," asked the teacher, "are you listening to your radio in class?"

"Yes, Sir," said the student, "but it's OK; I took out the batteries!"

Rash

1535

"School gave me a rash!"

"How do you figure?"

"Simple, I cut school and hid in the woods so much, I got poison ivy!"

1536

"An F in English!" exclaimed the student. "Oh, no!"

"I warned you," said the teacher, "yet you did no homework for twenty straight days."

"But, an F!" intoned the student. "Why do all you teachers have to act so rashly?"

Rationalize

1537

"Give me one reason why I should do your crummy homework!" stated the student.

"I'll call your parents, and you'll be grounded for a month."

"Of course," said the student, "your wonderful homework WOULD help develop my mind . . ."

1538

"Actually," stated the teacher, "what I'm looking for is one good reason NOT to fail you."

There was silence from the student.

"Well?" said the teacher.

"Take it easy," came the small voice. "I'm thinking! I'm thinking!"

Reading

1539

Reading is a soft key that opens doors you never knew your mind contained until you and a book became one.

1540

I used to think that my first-grade teacher was the meanest person on earth. Not only did she FORCE me to memorize letters and phonics, but she MADE ME read out loud and silently, AGAINST MY WILL! I thought her the most hardened of sadists, and I only wish she were alive now, so I could apologize and tell her what a debt I owe!

Real Estate

1541

"My uncle went to jail because he sold real estate!"
"You can't go to jail for selling real estate."
"You can if it's fake estate!"

1542

"What, oh, what can we do about our school?" intoned the principal to the faculty.

From the back of the room came a faint voice, "I know a good real estate agent . . . "

Reason

1543

Sign on a classroom wall: I wish to be an understanding and reasonable teacher. Therefore, we will do all things my way, exclusively!

1544

"Billy Jones keeps bothering me," explained the student, "but I know he'll understand and listen to reason as I explain calmly . . . just at the moment I've knocked him down and am sitting on his chest!"

Records and Record-Keeping

1545

Through almost four decades of teaching, I have kept a record of all those students who did ALL the assignments, passed EVERY quiz and test, and NEVER gave me any trouble in class—I keep it on a postage stamp in my desk!

1546

"Do you do extensive record-keeping?" the principal asked the music teacher.

"I used to," was the reply, "but I've switched to CDs."

Reducing (See also: Diet/Dieting)

1547

The superintendent sent a flyer to all teachers asking for a suggestion from each on reducing the budget. The response was overwhelming—eliminate the position of superintendent!

1548

"I understand you found a new method of reducing," said a teacher to a colleague.

"Oh, yes!" returned the other. "I eat lunch in the cafeteria WITH the students. I find I lose my appetite in no time!"

Referee (See also: Boxing; Fighting)

1549

The teacher stopped the fight and asked, "Could you guys use a teacher just now?"

"Nope," said one bruised combatant, "we know how to fight just fine; what we need is a referee!"

1550

"Who will we get as a referee for your game, coach?"

"How about Bill Johnson?"

"But Bill Johnson has a vision problem and can't see three feet in front of his face!"

"Hey," said the coach, "whose side are you on, anyway?"

Relatives

1551

Asked the teacher, "What do we call those pesky insects that invade our houses and eat away the very foundations of our homes?"

"I know," volunteered one student. "Relatives!"

"Name a major cause of bankruptcy in the United States," asked the social studies teacher.

"According to my Mom and Dad," answered one student, "it's Uncle Bill and Aunt Betty moving in with us!"

Remedial

1553

"Did he have learning difficulties? Let me put it this way—in thirty years of teaching, he's the only student I know who had to take remedial lunch!"

1554

"It's one day before report cards, son, and I'll tell you frankly, this is a poor time to come to me and ask if I'll give you a remedial course in doing your homework!"

Repairs (See also: Automobile)

1555

"I have no idea," said the principal to the school board member, "why anyone would think that we needed repairs around this building. Oh, please stand over here; you don't want to get rained on through that hole in the roof!"

1556

"I understand the Jones boy was the only one who handed back books that didn't need to be repaired," stated the guidance counselor.

"True," said the teacher. "It's amazing how clean these books stay when you haven't touched them for a year!"

Report Card

1557

"What is the warmest material in the world?" asked the teacher.

"Paper!" stated the student. "I know it is, because you should see how hot my father gets when he just LOOKS at my report card!"

1558

"What are those, Mr. Johnson?" asked the student.

"These are your report cards," answered the teacher.

"I guess," ventured the student, "it's a little late to ask if I can make up those missing assignments?"

Repression

1559

"How come you didn't choose my painting for the art show?" demanded the irate student. "I see that as repressing my artistic talent!"

"That's funny," said the judge, "I see it as saving the world from nausea!"

1560

"There are times," exalted the teacher, "when I am so happy with this class, I just want to Sing! Sing! Sing!"

Shouted the class, "Repress! Repress! Repress!"

Respect

1561

"I've always had great respect for teachers," said the parent.

"Thank you," returned the teacher. "In that case, may I ask something?"

"Of course!"

"Could you please get off my foot; you've been standing on it for the last five minutes!"

1562

"I saw you!" said the teacher. "You threw a mud ball at my car and then stood there with your hat off!"

"Of course," returned the student, "my mother taught me to show respect!"

Rest (See also: Nap)

1563

"Look," said a teacher who had dropped in to borrow something, "that student in the back is asleep!"

"Don't wake him!" cautioned the class teacher. "I need the rest!"

1564

"Are you all right?" the kindergarten student asked.

"Yes," answered the teacher, "I'm just tired and need some rest."

"What are you tired about?" the tot asked. "All you do is play with us all day!"

Restaurant

1565

"Wow!" said the youngster at the fancy restaurant, "look at these prices!"

"It's OK, son. This is a special occasion."

"Yeah, but I was just thinking about the prices at our school cafeteria. Compared to these, they almost make it worth the heartburn!"

1566

The principal took the teacher to a very exclusive and expensive restaurant.

"What'll you have?" asked the principal.

"Just coffee," answered the teacher.

"I'm paying . . . "

"Waiter!!!"

Retirement

1567

"Why so happy?" asked a teacher.

"I just checked," said the other educator, "and there are only 11,743 days until I retire!"

1568

"When I come to the end of a weary day," said the teacher, "and I am tired and discouraged, there is one thing that will renew my hope!"

"Ah," said a friend, "your family!"

"Actually," said the first, "I was thinking of my retirement fund!"

Reunion, The Class

1569

I went to my class reunion, but I had to leave—I couldn't stand how fat and bald all those OTHER people had gotten!

1570

"I know it was YOUR class reunion, but I have to tell you, I was embarrassed when you bribed the band to play 'Hail to the Chief'!"

Revision

1571

"So, you think my story needs a little revision?"

"Only the part between the title and the words, 'The End.'"

1572

If the tried and true is so archaic, how come everytime somebody calls for a revision in the teaching of reading, they end up with phonics?

Rhythm

1573

"How do you account for the fact that you are playing in a different rhythm from the rest of the orchestra?"

Answered the student, "I'm off-beat?"

1574

"My son claims you punished him for practicing his musical instrument!"

"Madam, I somehow doubt that making his desk into a rhythm section in the middle of class and practicing drum patterns on the head of the student in front of him would qualify!"

Right

1575

"Personally," said one teacher, "I don't agree with him; I feel he leans too much to the right."

"Sir," came a voice from the back of the room, "perhaps corrective footwear would help?"

1576

"But, how can you tell right from wrong?" the student asked the teacher.

"Very simple," came the answer. "Whenever I'm right; you're wrong!"

Rivalry (See also: Brothers and Sisters)

1577

"Central! Central! Central!" shouted the school board member at the pep rally.

Immediately, the principal nudged him and whispered, "Central is our rival; you're at Southside!"

"And that," roared the board member without losing a beat, "is exactly whom we are going to beat—Central! Central! Central!"

1578

"Southside is a bunch of dogs!" yelled the high school student in the candy store.

Just then a six-foot four-inch, 300-pound teenager wearing the jacket of the rival school stood up.

"Of course," continued the first student, "it (Woof!) takes one (Woof!) to know one (Whine! Whine! Woof!)!"

Roller Blades (See also: Pastimes; Sports)

1579

I'm not saying that roller blades are expensive, but they're now offering good percentage rates to those who want to take out a loan to purchase a pair!

1580

Nowadays, kids want roller blades so they can be slicker, faster, and further away when it's time to come home for dinner!

Rome

1581

"We went to Rome last summer."
"How was it?"
"Kinda dirty. They got some buildings over there that are all broken apart, and nobody ever bothers to plaster them up!"

1582

"I hate Rome," said the student.
"Why?" asked the teacher.
"Hey!" answered the child, "I failed Latin last year; I got my reasons!"

Royalty

1583

Definition on a vocabulary test: ROYAL-TY is a beverage drunk by a king and queen in England!

1584

"Guess what?" said Mom when her son came home from school, "your sister has been selected Prom Queen! What do you think about that?"
"I think," he answered, "that I begin to understand about the decline of royalty!"

Rugged

1585

"We had it tough in school," said Grandpa, "but it made us rugged!"

"Well," said his granddaughter, "we have carpeting on the floor in the classrooms!"

"So?"

"Come on, Granddad, you can't get more rug-ed than that!"

1586

"You know," observed someone, "many teachers make good outdoors people."

"Of course," ventured one teacher. "After years of fighting your way through the halls at passing time, you either get rugged or you die!"

Rules and Regulations

1587

It was a very progressive school. In fact, the rules were only one word long—DON'T!

1588

"I understand that the new student wanted a list of our rules and regulations. That sounds promising!"

"I don't know. I overheard him speaking to another student, and he said that he wanted the list to see if there were any that he hadn't broken at his old school!"

1589

"How can you say that I have no respect for the rules and regulations of this school?" said the irate student to the principal. "Why, I look up to them so much, these are the ones I have chosen to break!"

Running

1590

"I truly enjoy all forms of running," said the slightly overweight educator.

"You do?"

"Oh, yes!" came the answer. "In fact, I curl up with a box of candy and watch them on TV every chance I get!"

1591

I took up running as a hobby, but I had to give it up because it became too expensive. You have no idea how much I spent on phone calls to friends, begging them to come and pick me up!

Rural

1592

"So, you started teaching in a rural school, eh? Is it much different from the city school?"

"Not really, once I got used to the fact that the passing bell was a rooster!"

1593

Our school is really rural. When we take the kids out for a field day, we harvest twelve acres of corn!

Sabbatical

1594

"Yes, I am your new teacher, because Mrs. Jones is spending a year on sabbatical."

"Wow!" commented one student. "Does a sabbatical have one sail or two?"

1595

"I want a sabbatical in order to study psychology," said the teacher.

"That sounds reasonable," replied the administrator.

"Yes, I want to see if a year away from this school will allow me to regain my sanity!"

Safety

1596

A child was running down the hall of the school when another child tripped him and sent him sprawling.

"Safety patrol!" shouted the tripper. "Stop running or you're going to get hurt!"

The teacher came into the home ec room wearing a chest protector, shoulder pads, a plastic face plate, and thick leather gloves.

"Look," said the teacher in charge, "I know you're a bug for safety, but is all this necessary just to carve a turkey?"

Salt

1598

The principal was invited to taste the new soup of the day in the cafeteria. He took a sip and his lips puckered, his eyes crossed, and he gripped his throat with both hands.

Said the cafeteria manager, "Little heavy on the salt, eh?"

1599

We really love our home ec teacher. You've heard of people being called the "Salt of the earth?" Well, we call her the "Salter of the school!"

Sandbox (See also: Scent)

1600

Then there was the child who was taken to the beach for the first time and exclaimed, "One big sandbox, and it's mine, all mine!"

1601

"Let me get this straight," said Mother to her unhappy child, "you were pretending you were a kitty cat scratching in the school's sandbox when you got this idea to show people what else kitty cats do in sandboxes, and that's when they got angry . . . "

Sarcasm

1602

"In sarcasm, you say one thing that really means something else. Can anyone give me an example?"

Answered one lad, "Politicians!"

1603

"I would never use sarcasm on you . . ."

"Thank you."

". . . since your degree of understanding would render it useless!"

Sausage

1604

SAUSAGE is a hot dog with an identity crisis.

1605

"Yes," said the home ec teacher, "sausage is to be thoroughly cooked, but that didn't mean you had to run a blow torch over it once it was on the principal's plate!"

Saw

1606

There was both a similarity and a difference between the wood shop teacher and his saw. Both were hard-working, but the saw had all its teeth!

1607

"Excuse me for asking," said the visitor to the home, "but why are all your chairs and tables less than six inches off the ground?"

"My husband is a teacher," explained the hostess, "and yesterday, he taught our daughter what a saw was, and he taught her using the discovery method!

Scandal

1608

"This school system," stated the superintendent, "has never been touched by scandal. Embraced, kissed, and smothered by it perhaps, but never touched!"

1609

"Did you hear the scandal? The cafeteria has been putting bean-filler in the meatloaf! Did you notice any difference?"

"Outside of the gas and the fact that it tasted better, not a thing!"

Scent

1610

"What is that scent you're wearing? asked one teacher of another who had just come in from playground duty.

Replied the other without missing a beat, "Essence of sandbox!"

1611

Then there was the student who started a "Rent-a-Skunk" business. You could rent papa skunk for a dollar a day, and you could get the whole skunk family for a few scents more!

Schedule

1612

The teacher noticed the boy out in the hall for the third time in an hour.

"Young man! Do you have a schedule?"

"Nope!" replied the offender, "I just roam the halls whenever the spirit moves me!"

1613

"Do you have a very heavy schedule?" the teacher asked the student.

"Weighs less than an ounce," said the pupil. "I can carry it fine; it's all these classes I object to!"

School Building, The

1614

There is no school building more important that those who teach and are taught in it!

1615

How old is our school building? Let me put it this way: there is a wall in this building on which is carved, "Dear Martha, Meet me at the cherry tree. Love, George!"

School, Parochial

1616

One good thing about going to parochial school—if someone asks you who your teachers were, you can honestly say, "We had nun!"

1617

I asked a priest once, "Where can you possibly find the funds and support necessary to keep your parochial school going?"
He answered, "God knows!"

School, Private

1618

The motto of every private school: "The bucks stop here!"

1619

I heard of this one private school that was so expensive, they offered a course to parents call "Innovative Techniques of Creative Tuition-Raising!"

School, Public

1620

"Grandma," said the Mother, "we have decided to send Nancy to public school rather than to private school."
"Well," said Grandmother, "just make certain she washes her hands when she comes home. You know how those public facilities are!"

1621

A large banquet was held, and much food remained. One of those in charge thought the children in the local school might enjoy a change for lunch, so he called the principal and said, "Tell me, do you take leftovers there?"

"This is a public school," answered the administrator, "we take anybody!"

School Spirit

1622

"I ain't going back!" said the kindergarten child.

"Why not? Did something bad happen?"

"No, but the teacher said we was filled with school spirit, and I ain't going to any school that's haunted!"

1623

"Hey, Mister!" shouted the boy, "give us a hand. We're going to paint the wall of THIS school with OUR school colors!"

"I don't think I can help you."

"Why not? No school spirit?"

"Worse than that, I'm the principal of THIS school!"

Science

1624

Science is a study in which we learn all the rules that govern those things about which we know nothing at all!

1625

Some basic rules of science:

If it's green and wiggles, it's BIOLOGY.

If it smells and explodes, it's CHEMISTRY.

If it doesn't work, it's PHYSICS.

If it's alive, STUDY IT.

If it's dead, DISSECT IT!

Science Fair

1626

"I know it's supposed to be a science fair." said the principal to the enter-prising student, "but I cannot condone a 'Toss-a-Ring-Around-a-Microbe' game!"

1627

A school science fair is one of those places where, when one looks at all the batteries and motors and kits that have been purchased, one realizes exactly how costly a free education can be!

Science Project

1628

Principal to student: "No, I do not want to stifle your scientific learning, but your science project can be smelled from the library to the boys' lock-er room!"

1629

"After many complaints," said the principal, "we had your locker cleaned out, and we found a sandwich that had turned green! What do you have to say for yourself?"

"I guess," returned the student, "I'm going to have to start a new sci-ence project!"

Scratch

1630

"Ready to go on the school camping trip?" the teacher asked the parent volunteer.

"Oh, yes! I'm just itching to go!"

"Funny," the teacher commented, "as far as camping is concerned, most of us are itching and scratching AFTER we come back!"

1631

"So," said the science teacher, "if your experiment on the control of poison ivy doesn't work, you'll just have to start over from scratch!"

Scream

1632

"What happened? Is everyone all right? asked the teacher as she hurried into the girl's lavatory.

"We're OK," answered one girl. "In class, Mrs. Johnson said we should find what we do best in life and work to perfect it. Personally, I scream. Want to hear it again?"

1633

In the middle of the class, the third grader stood up and screamed at the top of her lungs.

"Isn't she wonderful?" said one student to the startled teacher. "Would you like to hear her do it in the key of F?"

Sea

1634

"So," said the new teacher in the New England fishing village, "the sea gives us many things . . . "

"You got that right, Teacher," said one of the children, "only she don't 'give' a one of them. You got to TAKE it!"

1635

"I'd like you to read this book, Bobby," said the teacher. "It's called *The Old Man and the Sea.*"

"Hey," remarked the startled child, "how did you know my father is nuts for fishing?"

Secret

1636

"Want to know a secret?" said the small child.

"Sure."

"Er . . . er . . . How about that? It was so secret, I forgot to remember it!"

1637

"Guess what?" said the child to the teacher, "my Mom is pregnant; the baby's going to be born around Christmas; we can't afford it, but we'll find a way; and . . . and . . . oh, yes . . . it's a secret and I can't tell anybody!"

Secretaries

1638

"Tell me," said the new superintendent to the outgoing one, "you always gave such inspirational speeches; what was your secret?"

"Simple!" replied the educator. "I put my idea on a 3" × 5" note card . . . and gave it to my secretary to write!"

1639

"Other than emergencies," came the announcement, "no one will be sent to the Main Office today for any reason!"

"Gosh," said one teacher, "is the principal out for the day?"

"Worse than that," answered another. "His secretary called in ill!"

Secretary, The School

1640

"Remember," the superintendent said to the new teachers, "if you wish to do well, find out where the power lies in your school and court it!"

The next day, they all brought flowers and candy to the school secretary!

1641

Proclaimed the principal: "I will set the tone of this school; I will walk the halls; I will visit classrooms! That is, of course, if my secretary says it's all right!"

Seed

1642

"In a way," the teacher explained, "you might say that every living thing comes from a seed . . . "

"I thought so!" commented one girl, "I've always thought of my brother as a Venus Fly Trap!"

1643

"Now," stated the teacher as the class gathered around, "we will plant this seed and watch it grow."

"You guys stay and watch if you want," commented one class member, "but personally, I'll be back in a month!"

Self-control

1644

"I saw that bully come over and taunt you," said the teacher. "You sat there and did not rise to his challenge. I admire your self-control!"

"Save it!" stated the child. "The minute I can get loose from this chair he glued me into, I'm going to bust his head!"

1645

Said one boy to another on the playground, "Self-control is everything!"

The other threw a punch that knocked the first to the ground.

"A good left hook ain't chicken-feed, either!"

Self-improvement

1646

Mother watched her daughter climb on a chair, take down a volume from the bookshelf, and they proceed to copy out of it.

"You get nothing from your homework if you copy from a book!"

"If I have something to hand in," returned the child, "I don't get detention. What's the matter? You against self-improvement?"

1647

Mother came home from work to find her little boy seated in the middle of the kitchen floor covered from head to toe with flour.

"What do you call this?" Mother asked her older daughter who was supposed to watch the little one.

The daughter thought a moment and replied, "Self-improvement?"

Sensitivity

1648

"I not only enforce the rules of this school," said the hall monitor to the principal," but I am constantly aware of others and their feelings. I am sensitive to all people and situations!"

And, as the pleased administrator walked away, the boy turned and yelled down the hall, "Hey, you weirdo idiot! Stop running!"

1649

"Excuse me," said one student to another, "but didn't Ms. Jones just tell us that we were supposed to be sensitive to the needs of others?"

"So what?"

"So get your book off my desk or I'll smash your ugly face, you stupid clod!"

Service

1650

"Remember," said the teacher, "I am here to serve you!"

"I don't know," mumbled one student, "she sure don't look like the waitress down at the diner!"

1651

"So," said the principal to the assembled first-graders, "remember that we are here to service each and every one of you."

"What does that mean?" asked one student.

Answered another, "They're going to change our oil and rotate our tires!"

Shakespeare

1652

"Repeat something Shakespeare said," directed the English teacher.

"OK," replied a student. "'Hello, my name is Bill'!"

1653

"Don't you love it," asked a student, "how Shakespeare used all those quotes in his plays?"

Shouting

1654

"Who shouted just now?" demanded the teacher.

"Sir," responded one student, "a moment ago, I expressed the eternal optimism and enthusiasm of youth in a positive manner engendering empathic response!"

"Well," said the teacher, "that's OK. For a moment there, I thought you shouted!"

1655

"Fire! Fire!"

"What? Where?"

"There's no fire, Mister. I need you to help me cross the street."

"Well, sure, kid, but why did you yell, 'Fire!'?"

"Would you have come if I had shouted, 'Street!?'"

Shy/Shyness

1656

"Your new student is rather shy," said the guidance counselor to the teacher.

"Come, now," remarked the teacher, "how shy can he be?"

"Billy," cooed the guidance counselor, "come out from under my desk and meet your teacher . . . "

1657

"Anne," said the teacher to the quiet child, "you're so shy. Come on, Anne, say something. Please, Anne, speak up."

Just then another child poked her head in the door and said, "Mrs. Johnson, when you're finished with Mary here, she's supposed to come to class!"

Silence

1658

The class was absolutely silent as they worked. Suddenly, the teacher raised her head.

"All right," she said, "I can hear the silence! What are you planning?"

1659

"I," said the teacher, "would like complete and total silence while you are working on your class work."

"And I," whined a student, "would like world peace and a personal exemption from paying taxes!"

Singing

1660

The child finished her solo number.

"Don't you just love good singing?" the child's mother asked another member of the audience.

"Oh, yes," said the other woman, "and just as soon as my daughter begins, we'll hear some!"

1661

"I sing," said the student, "for the joy of singing!"

"That's good," said another pupil, "'cause ain't nobody going to PAY you for it!"

Smoking

1662

"Have you ever smoked in school?"
"No, but I've gotten pretty steamed!"

1663

"You've been smoking," said the teacher, "I can smell it on you!"
"Oh, no!" exclaimed the student, "and that's the last time I'll help the cafeteria serve smoked ham!"

Solo

1664

"I demand to sing solo!" the child informed the music teacher.
"Certainly," the educator replied, "try singing so low you can't be heard beyond the first row!"

1665

"After my son performed his solo number," said Mother, "his music teacher wept!"
"If my student did to Beethoven what your son did," stated another member of the audience, "believe me, I'd cry, too!"

Speakers/Speaking

1666

"My speaking ability goes beyond words!" stated the educator.
"Unfortunately," quipped a colleague, "your speeches don't!"

1667

"Did the speaker the PTA had last night speak for very long?" said one teacher as they checked in.
"I don't know," said the other, "let's go see; I understand he should be winding down right about now!"

Special

1668

"I don't believe it!" exclaimed the teacher. "All the homework is in; none missing!"

"Don't get carried away," commented one student, "because it's not permanent. We knew it was your birthday, and we wanted to give you something special!"

1669

"I don't think you understood," said the teacher. "When I said you were a very special student, it didn't mean that I would serve you lunch and drive you home every day!"

Speeches

1670

Speeches are the price we pay for showing up!

1671

A good speech is rather like a robe worn on a beach—long enough to cover the subject and short enough to keep it interesting!

Spelling

1672

"All right," stated the teacher, "get ready for a surprise spelling quiz! Are there any questions?"

"Yes," said one student. "Does spelling count?"

1673

Mark Twain wrote that he had no respect for a man who could spell a word only one way. In that case, he would have idolized my second-period class!

Sports

1674

"Name a good sport," asked the coach.
    Replied the student, "My Uncle Harry!"

1675

"I think TV is running out of sports to cover," said the student.
    "Why do you think that?"
    "Last night, they had a sports special on—the Wide World of Penny-Pitching!"

Sports Medicine

1676

"Doc," asked the coach, "were you an athlete in school?"
    "Yes," said the doctor, "I specialized in the shot put."
    "That figures," the coach replied rubbing his backside, "because you sure know where to put the shot!"

1677

As one parent commented, "The fact that sports medicine has become a recognized specialty does not engender one bit of comfort when your child comes home and says, "I just signed up for the team'!"

Stairs

1678

Did you hear about the trouble they had in the local school? It seems they hired a new custodian, and he was so enthusiastic, he waxed the stairs!"

1679

"Why so glum? asked the teacher. "I thought you were on your way up the stairway of learning."

"I was," sighed the student, "but nobody told me I had to step over the homework on every landing!"

Statistics

1680

It would do well to remember the wisdom of Queen Victoria's Prime Minister, Benjamin Disraeli, who wrote, "There are three types of falsehoods: lies, damned lies, and statistics!"

1681

When thinking of statistics, just remember the three teachers who set out to tutor at the county jail. Two of them got there, but one made a wrong turn and never did arrive. Statistically, it may be reported that two out of three educators who set out to teach end up in jail!

Stimulus

1682

"Now!" roared the angry teacher, "finish your work or you'll stay after school for a month!"

"OK! OK!" exclaimed one student. "All I needed was a proper stimulus!"

1683

"I have called this faculty meeting to inform you that you will be getting thousand-dollar bonuses next week."

Then the principal continued, "Actually, you are getting no such thing, but since your attention has been stimulated, let's carry on with the actual agenda of this meeting!"

Strike

1684

"I think," said the teacher, "that since we have gotten this far, we might as well do some more enrichment work tomorrow. Let us strike while the iron is hot!"

The next day the class brought in picket signs!

1685

"How did your class react when you taught them about the labor movement?"

"I might have done too good a job; the next day they went on strike for less homework!"

Students

1686

Principal to faculty: "When I asked in my survey what would make your teaching easier, getting rid of the students was NOT an option!"

1687

"Just think," said one teacher, "if there were no students, I would be teaching to brick walls!"

"That's funny," commented a colleague, "I have lots of students, but I often feel the same way!"

Study/Studying

1688

"How can you say that you study eight hours a night when your grades are so low?"

"I don't understand it, either. I put the book under my pillow every night when I go to sleep!"

1689

"I don't know how to break this to you," said the teacher, "but flipping the pages of your textbook before you toss it into your locker does NOT constitute STUDYING!"

Substitutes/Substitute Teaching

1690

One small student sat at his desk eating a candy bar as the rest of the class ran about the room swinging from the light fixtures, while the teacher sat gagged and bound to a corner of the desk.

Said the tike, "You know what I like about substitutes? You can talk them into anything!"

1691

"Honest, Ma'am," said the student to the substitute teacher, "Mrs. Johnson never gives us homework, because she says it rots our brains!"

Success

1692

There is no success like knowing the success of a student who, until you taught him, did not know how to succeed!

1693

Remember, school never guaranteed success to anyone! What it did guarantee was a map that set you on the right road!

Summer

1694

Ask any class what was the best part of the school year, and 95 percent will tell you it was summer, when school was not in session!

1695

Summer whets the appetite for school just as surely as school whets the appetite for summer!

Summer Hiatus

1696

To most teachers, the summer hiatus offers no pressure, no parents, no papers, and . . . no paychecks!

1697

'Though reading and writing and math are exciting,
One fact, above all, is the greatest—
In the middle of learning exists a great yearning
To start on the summer hiatus!

Summer Job

1698

"I got a great summer job," remarked the teacher, "working a jackhammer on a road-construction crew. After a year of teaching school, the peace and quiet will do me good!"

1699

"My summer job was as traffic controller at the mall. I directed millions of people to the right places and settled arguments and gave directions. I tell you, the school year had prepared me perfectly!"

Summer School

1700

The teacher tossed the failing test paper on the student's desk and asked, "How would you like to go to summer school?"

"Thanks so much," returned the lad, "but I believe I have had enough already!"

1701

To those of us who can remember the endless summer days of our youth, we are well aware that all of summer is and always will be a school for growing youth.

Sunday School

1702

Said the Sunday school teacher, "The Bible states, 'Dust thou art and unto dust thou shalt return'!"

"Then you'd better come look in my locker in school," remarked one student, "'cause somebody's in there either coming or going!"

1703

"Now," said the Sunday school teacher, "suppose you found a five-dollar bill in the parking lot of this church?"

"Just a minute," asked one student, "is that WITH or WITHOUT the pastor seeing me?"

Sunshine

1704

"Is there anything sweeter than sunshine?" asked the teacher of the class.

"I don't know," answered one child, "my uncle says that he really likes moonshine!"

1705

"I'll always think of you as my personal sunshine!" said the teacher to the class on the last day.

"Thank you," said a class spokesperson, "and we'll always consider you our very own rain cloud!"

Sunshine Laws

1706

Asked the teacher, "Who can tell me what the 'Sunshine Laws' are?"

Answered a student, "According to my father, 'If the sun shines on it—tax it'!"

1707

"Sunshine Laws allow us to know what's going on," said the teacher.

"So does Mrs. Johnson," commented a student. "She's our neighborhood gossip!"

Superintendent of Schools

1708

A SUPERINTENDENT is the chief educational leader, which means that he or she gets it all when there's nobody else left to blame!

1709

"When I grow up," said the child, "I want to become a teacher and be an INTENDENT."

"Just a moment, don't you have that word a little wrong?"

"No, I figure I'm just a regular INTENDENT; I don't know enough to be a SUPER-INTENDENT!"

Suspension

1710

"What happened to Billy Jones?" asked a student.

"He got suspended today."

"Wow! Wait until I tell my Mom! Billy Jones was hung in school today!"

1711

"The only reason I throw food in the cafeteria," explained the student, "is because I am under the stress of attending school!"

"Then you can relax," stated the principal, "because you are now under the suspension from attending school!"

Tact

1712

"Bobby," said the teacher, "Billy is in the back of the room, and he's day-dreaming. I can't leave my desk, so would you please bring his attention back, and please be very tactful?"

"OK!" said Billy, who then yelled at the top of his lungs, "Hey, loser! Wake up!"

1713

"Look," said the teacher, "get Billy to move over, but please ask him nice-ly, with tact and understanding."

The student went over to Billy and kicked him sharply in the shins.

"Wait!" shouted the teacher. "What happened to tact and under-standing?"

"Well," stated the student, "first, you got to make sure he's paying attention, don't you?"

Tag

1714

"You're it!" cried the first-grader.

"I'm what?" asked the fourth-grader.

"Don't confuse me," said the smaller student, "this is my first time at the game!"

1715

The kindergarten teacher wrote a note to each parent on a large tag and placed one on each child's coat.

"What's she doing? one child asked another.

"I think," answered the other tike, "she's marking us down for quick sale!"

Talking

1716

"Billy!" said the teacher, "I don't want to hear any more from you. I am assigning you detention because your talking has disturbed the entire class!"

"I can't understand it," mused Billy as he scratched his head. "I finally talked myself into something I couldn't talk myself out of!"

1717

"There will be no talking in this class!" stated the teacher.

"Now," whispered a student, "if she'd only keep that rule herself!!!"

Tangle

1718

"Sweetie," said the teacher gently and in private, "I've noticed that your hair is in a real tangle today, and I thought someone should tell you about putting a comb through your hair."

"Great!" returned the child, "and maybe somebody should tell Billy, who sits behind me, about parking his bubble gum IN my hair!"

1719

"It was Tennyson," lectured the English teacher, "who wrote, 'Oh, what a tangled web we weave when first we practice to deceive'!"

"Well, he sure didn't know my brother," remarked one student. "He's had so much practice, he can lie straight as an arrow!"

Tardiness

1720

"I'm tired of your continuing tardiness!"

"So am I! Why don't I just cut class altogether?"

1721

"You say your tardiness is to make me happy?" stated the teacher. "How do you figure?"

"Well," said the student, "for a little while each day, you can live under the joyous delusion that I might not show up at all!"

Task

1722

Asked the teacher, "Name a task that nobody wants to do."

Replied a weary student, "Naming tasks that nobody wants to do!"

1723

"I am a task-oriented person," wrote the student. "I will do the task as long as there is somebody there to punish me if I don't!"

Tattling

1724

"Billy Jones hit a girl!" said the child.

"He hit a girl . . . " replied the teacher.

"And he knocked down a boy!"

"He knocked down a boy . . . "

"Look," the child stated, "if you'd do something about his aggressive behavior instead of repeating everything I say, I wouldn't have to tattle!"

1725

"Mrs. Jones," whispered a student, "let my tell you about the math teacher . . . "

"Please," stated the teacher, "I will not listen to tattling!"

"Neither will I," said the student, "but this ain't tattling, it's the best gossip you ever heard!"

Taxes and the IRS

1726

" . . . so my father pays taxes to the INFERNAL Revenue System."

"You mean the INTERNAL Revenue System."

"Not the way my father looks at it!"

1727

"Did your father do this homework?" asked the teacher.

"Yes, but how did you know?"

"Because, the question was to name an animal that attaches itself to its victim and drains it dry of blood, and the answer given was, 'the IRS'!"

Taxes, Property

1728

"Your property taxes support our schools," stated the school board member.

"Support, nothing!" shouted one taxpayer, "they pick it up by the armpits and force chicken soup down its throat!"

1729

Intoned the principal, "Where would we be without property taxes?"

Came a voice from the audience, "Living in the mansions we could then afford!"

Teachers/Teaching

1730

A true teacher is a person who, at the end of the school day, still likes children!

1731

Teaching is the art of inspiration: A teacher tries to inspire in others the desire to inspire others . . .

Teachers and Children

1732

"Why yes," the teacher told the second-grader, "I have three children of my own."

"Wow!" said the lad, "When you give THEM homework, they got no place to go not to do it, because they're already there!"

1733

After a full day of dealing with other people's children, many teachers come home to children of their own. That's where the expression, "Glutton for punishment" got started!

Teachers and Home

1734

The girl was looking out the living room window when a car pulled up and her teacher stepped out.

"Mom!" yelled the girl, "I got something to tell you, and please don't answer the doorbell until you've heard MY side!"

1735

"Betty," the teacher said, "do you handle stress well?"

"I think so, Ms. Jones. Why do you ask?"

"Because, we are going to find out real soon. Your mother just invited me to dinner, and I accepted!"

Teachers and Students

1736

"How many students are in your class? asked the principal.

"Three," answered the teacher.

"That's impossible! You have to have more!"

"Well," continued the teacher, "I do have 32 children in that class, but you asked how many students!"

1737

"Do you interact with your students every day?" asked the school board member.

"Of course," the teacher answered, "why do you think I look like this?"

Team

1738

"Well, Dad," the boy stated, "you always wanted me to get into school athletics, and now I have."

"Great, Son! What's your position?"

"I'm water boy for the chess team!"

1739

"We is on the team," said the student.

"That's wonderful news but terrible English," the teacher remarked. "Say, 'are'!"

"OK," the student replied, "I are on the football team!"

Technical

1740

"I rounded off the test scores . . . "

"That's not fair! I want exactly what I got!"

"In that case, you fail by .5 of a point."

"On the other hand, there is no need to be so technical!"

1741

Knowing the procedures for teaching is fine, but there is no technical manual for touching the mind and heart of a child!

Teenagers

1742

The teenage years are years of great growth—parents grow older quicker than at any other time in their child's life!

1743

Teens are not really arrogant; they know they can be wrong . . . they just never expect to be!

Teeth

1744

"Tommy has to leave now," said Mother to the teacher at the door of the room. "He has to go to the dentist; they're taking an impression of his teeth."

"Why don't I just go with you?" the teacher stated. "Then the dentist can just take it from my arm?"

1745

"Today," said the health teacher, "we will talk about teeth!"

"Great," said one student, "I know where we can find three of them on the playground where the fight was this morning!"

Telephone

1746

"Mr. Johnson," asked a student, "may I call my mom?"

"Certainly," said the teacher.

So, the student stuck his head out the window and screamed, "MOM!!!"

1747

"Suppose there was an invader that threatened the peace and security of your home, wouldn't you fight it?"

"Be serious, will you? How are you going to fight a telephone!"

Temper

1748

"Yes," said the teacher over the phone, "I can get your son another math book, but unless your husband learns to control his temper, I can't replace every book he rips up when he's helping with homework!"

1749

"Last night we went to a Japanese restaurant and had shrimp temper," said the student.

"You mean shrimp 'tempura,' don't you?"

"Believe me, when Mom and Dad saw the bill, it was 'temper' all the way!"

Tents

1750

"So the nomads, it is said, silently folded their tents and slipped away. Now, what does that tell you?"

Answered one student, "They were made of highly compressible polyvinyl?"

1751

On the camping trip, the teacher saw one boy carrying two packs.

"Your two tents?" he asked.

"Say," stated the lad, "if you had to carry both of these, you'd be pretty tense, too!"

Terror

1752

The principal rushed into the main office, breathing heavily, his hands shaking and tears in his eyes. He gripped the wall, his eyes darting wildly back and forth. Finally, he dove under his desk and hid there, shivering.

"So," said the school secretary, "I see you made good on your promise to ride in on the school bus!"

1753

"I can't stand it! The terror of it all is getting to me; the violence; the aggression!"

"You mean the world?"

"Of course not! I'm talking about my kindergarten class!"

Texas

1754

The child pulled a wagon to the teacher's desk and unloaded a stack of newspapers four feet high.

"What's this?" the teacher asked.

"Ma'am," returned the lad, "I'm from Texas. You want current events, you got CURRENT EVENTS!"

1755

Requested the teacher, "Name somebody great who was born in Texas."

Replied a transfer student from that state, "All of us, Ma'am; all of us!"

Theater

1756

"You don't understand," the teacher whispered to the student during the field trip to the theater. "This is a live play; we can't fast forward through the dull parts!"

1757

"In the theater," intoned the guide, "one applauds the performance."

"Not so," said one student. "I was there, and they ALL clapped!"

Thin

1758

Although there is no proof of it, one boy I knew claimed he was so thin that one day before class, he fell asleep on the blackboard ledge, and the teacher used him as a pointer all afternoon!

"I would like a THIN slice of the chocolate cake," said the principal to the parent at the class party.

"Sorry," remarked the parent's child, "but when my mom makes a chocolate cake, there just ain't no thin in it!"

Things

1760

"Come on, Sally," prompted mother at the dinner table, "tell us some of the things you like most in school."

Without hesitation, Sally answered, "Billy, Josh, Marvin, Lee, Harry . . . "

1761

"Name two things about this class you like, and one thing you don't like."

"The starting bell, the closing bell; and everything in between!"

Thoroughbred

1762

"Your performance on this test," said the proud teacher, "has shown me that this is a class of thoroughbreds!"

"What did she say?"

"She said she'd bet on us every time!"

1763

"My uncle had a lot to do with thoroughbreds."

"Oh, how many did he own?"

"None, but Aunt Mary says that with all the money he's thrown away on them at the track, he COULD have owned a farm of them!"

Thread

1764

Sign of the times: The teacher read, "' . . . and so, his life hung by a thread . . . '"

Asked one student, "Cotton or polyester?"

"You said it would be invisible," moaned the student to the home ec teacher, "but I can see where my pants were mended."

"Well," the teacher replied, "it would have helped had you NOT used yellow thread to mend your black trousers!"

Tickets

1766

"I will give you a pass that will admit you to Central Detention," said the teacher.

The recipient whispered to a friend, "Things sure change fast around here. I remember when anyone would go to detention, and now you need a ticket!"

1767

"As an incentive," said the teacher, "the person who gets the highest grade on this test will get two tickets to this school's Chamber Music Society concert!"

"Quick," exclaimed one student, "show me how I can unremember what I learned!"

Time

1768

Sign covering the face of the clock in a classroom: "Time will pass—will you?"

1769

"There's never enough time!" said one conscientious student.

"Sure there is," remarked a chronic offender. "You just don't know how to waste it properly!"

Tissue

1770

The girl sniffled as she sat in the classroom. A boy next to her drew a pack of Kleenex from his pocket.

"Tissue?" he asked.

"Sure!" she said, "but not here in class!"

1771

"Oh, no!" said the science teacher, "I lost the tissue samples I was going to use today."

"Ask the teachers for a couple samples," suggested one student. "Some of them got a LOT of tissue to spare!"

Titles

1772

"I have no trouble at all writing stories," stated the student. "It's just that after the title, I get stuck for ideas."

1773

After giving the writing assignment, the English teacher asked one boy, "What's your title?"

Answered the lad, "Mister, I guess, but you can call me Bob!"

Tools

1774

"We will now pass out books," said the teacher. "After all, if I am to get into your heads, I need the right tools."

"In that case," commented one student, "might I suggest jackhammers?"

1775

"Pencil, paper, book," intoned the teacher, "tools for learning!"

"Candy, comic book, sandwich," imitated a student, "tools for cutting class!"

Torture

1776

"It is a horrible fact," commented the teacher, "that every day around this world, people are being tortured."

"And here in school," whispered one class member, "it's called homework!"

1777

"Remember," said the teacher, "torture can NEVER be justified."

"Ma'am," stated one small student, "could you come home with me and explain that to my big brother?"

Tradition

1778

"I have given detention to students every year for twenty years," stated the teacher, "but this year I had almost made it without assigning detention once. Then YOU had to act up in class!"

"Look at it this way," the student said, "who am I to break with tradition?"

1779

"How can we let you graduate," explained the principal, "when you have failed every course you've ever taken?"

"Be bold!" pleaded the student. "Start a tradition!"

Traits

1780

"You are failing," the teacher told the student, "because you are lazy, a procrastinator, and thoroughly apathetic . . . "

"Sure," said the student, "but is it fair to fail me on the basis of a few minor character violations?"

1781

Said the teacher, "You have the same traits as your brother."

"What can I do?" commented the child. "He's a year older than I am, and I get all his hand-me-downs!"

Transportation, Travel, and Trips

1782

"Yes," the student told the class, "last year my family and I took a trip around the world; this year we're going someplace else!"

1783

Guidance counselor to first-grade student: "I know you do not like riding the school bus in the mornings, but put away that ten-dollar bill because we do not provide limousine service for anyone!"

Trap

1784

"What's wrong, Dad?" asked the child as his father came in from the links looking rather dejected.

"Nothing serious," said the father, "I just had a hard time today with a sand trap."

"Come on, Dad," the child remonstrated, "who'd want to trap sand?"

1785

"I want to be a great hunter," stated one child, "and go out in the woods and hunt bear!"

"You can hunt bare if you want to," commented another, "but when winter comes, you'd best put on SOME clothes!"

Trick

1786

"First," asked the teacher, "what is your name?"

"Hey!" the student answered, "is this one of those trick questions?"

"You mean all the time we were listening to that story, we were finding out about new things we should know?" said the student. "That's not fair! You tricked us into learning!"

Trips, Class

1788

"Yes, Herbert, that is a very interesting suggestion, but somehow, I can't quite see the educational value of a class trip to your house to watch your baby sister throw up!"

1789

"Come on," said one child to another on the class trip, "hide over here with me!"

"No!" said the child, "I don't want to get left behind!"

"We won't get left behind," insisted the first. "We're just going to hide long enough to watch the teacher get all red and worried about us!"

Trouble

1790

Said the teacher, "Spell 'TROUBLE.'"

Answered the student, "H-O-M-E-W-O-R-K!"

1791

"Did you have any trouble with the assignment?" asked the teacher.

"Not one bit of trouble," remarked the student. "I ignored it completely, and it didn't bother me at all!"

Trust

1792

"I must punish you for not having the assignment," stated the teacher. "It's for your own good. Don't you trust me on that?"

"Oh, sure!" said the sorrowful student, "About as much as you trust me that I didn't have it because the dog ate it!"

1793

"I trust that you are all ready to work today!" the teacher stated cheerfully.
    "You know," whispered a student, "I just love to disillusion the 'trusting soul' type!"

Truth

1794

"Honest, Mrs. Jones, I studied for six hours for that test!"
    "Did you? Really?"
    "Well, no . . . but if I told you the truth about how long I studied, I'd never get out of detention!"

1795

"Billy," smiled the teacher, "did a kangaroo REALLY jump in your window last night and keep you from doing your homework? Tell the truth now!"
    "No, Ma'am," sighed the small student.
    "That's better . . . "
    Continued the tot, " . . . it was an elephant!!!"

TV

1796

Unfortunately, television has become our premier teacher. It teaches our children about life and how to behave and what feeling to have and not have, yet we tolerate it with far less scrutiny and criticism that we give the person who teaches junior to add up a column of figures!

1797

I won't say that TV has had an influence on our children, but yesterday a teacher started to assign homework and three quarters of the class tried to turn her off with the remote controls they brought from home!

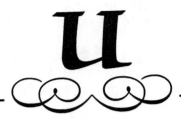

Ugly Duckling

1798

"So, the ugly duckling swam out on the lake to be with the beautiful swans."

"Story of my life!" said one tot. "We spend a year getting used to this wacko first grade, and, zap!, they put us in the second!"

1799

"So you see," concluded the teacher at the end of the story, "many of us are ugly ducklings."

"Is that why," ventured one student, "after my mother met you she said the you were one odd duck?"

Ulcer

1800

"You're quitting coaching?" said a friend. "I thought you loved coaching."

"I do," the coach replied. "It's my ulcer that's antisports!"

1801

"So," summed up the interviewer, "you'd say that teaching really hits the spot!"

"I'll say," confirmed the teacher, "I'm working on my third ulcer!"

Ultimate

1802

"When I was in school," said the teacher, "my teachers considered me the ultimate student!"

"Really?"

"Oh, yes," the educator continued. "Every time they wanted an example of how NOT to behave, they could turn to me in complete confidence!"

1803

"I have just received the ultimate report card!" said one student to another.

"What do you mean?"

"I mean," the child explained, "that I have the satisfaction of knowing that in the entire school, no one could possibly have done worse!"

Umbrella

1804

"Professor!" said a student one rainy day on campus, "I see you're carrying an umbrella!"

"Why, of course, returned the teacher. "It isn't unusual to carry an umbrella when it is raining as it is now, you know."

"No," the student commented, "but it is a bit odd to see someone standing in the middle of the quad getting soaked to the skin while carrying an UNOPENED umbrella!"

1805

"Mom!" shouted the child, "I need your umbrella to go outside and collect rain samples!"

"So . . . you want the umbrella to keep dry, eh?"

"No," answered the child, "I want the umbrella to turn upside down. How do you think I'm going to collect rain samples?"

Umpire

1806

"Yes, I would be happy to umpire your game," said the principal, "but what made you think of me?"

"Well," answered the student, "we figured that being a principal, if anyone was used to taking nothing but abuse, it would be YOU!"

1807

"Just think," stated one student player, "of what we'd have if we did away with the umpire!"

"Yeah," said an older youth, "a brawl with four bases!"

Uncertainty

1808

"Did I notice a bit of uncertainty in your answer?" asked the teacher.

"Not at all," answered the student. "What you noticed was a slight pause while my eyes adjusted to the answer written on my desk!"

1809

"So, in your classroom, then, you strive for consistency?"

"That's correct, I want them to be uncertain of what I'm going to do next."

"How is that achieving consistency?"

"I want them to be uncertain every single time!"

Underachievers

1810

One student to another on the bench in the main office: "I'm an under-achiever. What's your racket?"

1811

The child came out of the guidance office and flopped down in a chair.

"I tell you," the child sighed to another lad seated there, "you got to work harder and harder to be an underachiever these days!"

Undercover

1812

"I want to work undercover when I grow up!"
  "So, you want to be a policeman, eh?"
  "No! I want to test mattresses!"

1813

Asked the guidance counselor, "Do you plan to become an FBI agent?"
  "No."
  "Well, I was just wondering. I'm looking at your attendance record, and it seems you do so much undercover work in bed at home, that you're failing three courses!"

Underprivileged

1814

"There are teachers," the speaker continued, "who have never had problems with discipline; who have all assignments turned in; who have only 'A' students . . . "
  From the back of the room came a voice, "I'll donate my second-period class to help this underprivileged minority experience real life!"

1815

The most underprivileged people in the world are those who have had neither the opportunity nor the inclination to give of themselves to others!

Understanding

1816

"I got kept after school," the girl stated flatly.
  "What happened?" asked her mother. "Did the teacher fail to understand?"
  "The teacher understood perfectly," the child answered. "Why do you think I got the detention?"

1817

"I plead for your understanding," said the student to the principal.

"That you have," commented the administrator. "In fact, the minute I understood just what you were trying to get away with, I had you marked for suspension!"

Underwear

1818

"Now," said the health teacher to the fourth-grade class, "how can we remember always to have clean underwear?"

"Do what I do!" stated one boy. "When you get to school, take it off and keep it in your pocket!"

1819

"I'm not feeling well," said the teacher to his wife over the phone, "I feel crampy and achey and I have definite lower-back problems."

"Relax," said his wife. "It must have been dark when you got dressed this morning; you're wearing your son's underwear!"

Undressed

1820

"They forgot the soap!" said the child to the teacher at the art museum.

"What soap?"

"In that room over there," answered the student, "they got a big statue of a lady who looks like she's going to take a shower—only she ain't carrying any soap!"

1821

On the working farm, the city child watched as "Sunday Dinner" was prepared from scratch, including dressing and plucking a fowl. Later, the child was asked what he liked best.

Without hesitation, he replied, "The part where the lady undressed the chicken!"

Unemployed

1822

"And what," intoned the speaker, "what is a teacher without students?"
Came a voice from the back of the hall, "Unemployed?"

1823

"'UNEMPLOYED,'" the teacher explained, "means 'not working.'"
"That's my Dad," said one child.
"Oh, I'm so sorry," replied the teacher.
"Yeah," the child sighed, "every night when he comes home from his second job, he just lays on the couch; doing nothing; unemployed!"

Uniforms

1824

The English teacher had never been to a football game, and he finally agreed to go with his teenaged son.
"See those numbers on their uniforms, Dad?" the young man asked. "See 11 and 31 and 53? Do you know what they mean?"
"Of course, son," answered his father. "I know those boys very well, and those are their grades on the last English test!"

1825

"OK, son, why do you want to be on the team?"
"Sir, I want to serve my school to the best of my ability . . . "
"Come on, the real reason!"
"My girlfriend REALLY likes the uniforms!"

Uninhibited

1826

"One of the best things about this class," said the observer, "is that they are so uninhibited!"
"True," replied the teacher, "and that's also one of the worst things about this class!"

"On a beautiful spring day such as this," mused the principal, "I feel so uninhibited!"

"Take a look at your appointment book," suggested the school secretary. "That'll bring back all the inhibitions!"

Unions

1828

The new teacher was being shown around.

"Over there," explained the guide, "is the Student Union."

"You mean they've organized?" exclaimed the teacher. "Lord help us all!"

1829

Then there was the union representative who almost burned to death when the school caught fire. It seems he refused to leave the building until he could find "evacuation" in the job description!

Unique

1830

Children are individuals, and as such, each one is a separate and special person. Indeed, to a teacher, each student in his or her class is a headache unique unto itself!

1831

"Hey, Mom!" yelled the child, "today the principal said I was the most unique student she ever met."

"Really?"

"Yep! She said she never knew a kid who could fail every subject in school AND get kicked out of the cafeteria!"

Unity

1832

"We finally adopted the resolution by a vote of 49 to 48 with three abstentions."

"Really? What was the resolution for?"

"Unity!"

1833

"I am truly delighted that while I was out yesterday, this class held a meeting and achieved 100 percent unity. However, I cannot do away with homework and tests, no matter how you voted!"

Universe, The

1834

Asked one teacher, "Is there intelligent life in the universe?"

"I don't know," answered a colleague. "Maybe we should start searching for it here on Earth?"

1835

"When I grow up," stated the imaginative student, "I want to take a trip around the universe!"

"Even if we had the technology," commented the teacher, "such a journey would take you millions and millions of years."

"Yeah," sighed the disappointed student, "and when I got back, you'd probably be waiting to mark me tardy!"

Unkempt

1836

"How do you manage to get so unkempt?" the teacher asked the second-grader.

"Believe me, Ma'am," replied the student, "after my mother sees that I'm washed and combed and brushed each morning, it takes a lot of effort to get this dirty!"

1837

The teacher approached the extremely unkempt student and stated, "Show me a dirtier hand than that in this school, and I'll give you a dollar!"

The student withdrew his other hand from a pocket, thrust it forward and exclaimed, "Here it is! Now, where's my buck?"

Unselfish

1838

"Little children are so unselfish," remarked one teacher.

"True," confirmed another. "When they have a cold or the flu, they share it with everybody!"

1839

"Couldn't you try," asked the teacher of the student, "to do one unselfish act each day?"

"Sure," replied the child, "for a dollar I will!"

Unsung

1840

"Why did many heroes of the past go largely unsung?" asked the social studies teacher.

Ventured one child, "Their agents couldn't get them decent recording contracts?"

1841

"How would you like to hear my song, Professor?"

"If you please—unsung!"

Use, School

1842

"What do you feel is the most common use of the present-day school?" asked a school board member.

"That's simple," replied the principal, "AB-USE!"

1843

"OK," asked the teacher, "who could name a use for this building other than as a school?"

Answered one hopeful student, "Kindling?"

Utility

1844

"When you bought the house, didn't you ask if it had utilities?"

"Certainly . . . I just never asked if they worked!"

1845

"What's a 'utility closet'?" asked the student.

"That's a place where those things are that are so useful, we couldn't get through the day without them."

"Wow!" exclaimed the student, "You mean that's where our mothers go when we come to school?"

Utopia

1846

UTOPIA is a state of mind where students envision no teachers, teachers see no troublesome students, and taxpayers can imagine neither needing to be financially supported!

1847

I am more than willing to work toward the establishment of a Utopia—which means any place run exclusively by MY rules!

Vacations

1848

"It's an ideal place for a vacation," the teacher told her family. "It has sun, beaches, exciting shopping malls, and two year-round schools I can visit and observe!"

1849

"Just look at these brochures," lamented the teacher. "They all advertise places that are lively and exciting!"

"What's wrong with that?"

"After a year of teaching," replied the tired educator, "I want some place that's dull and restful!"

Vaccination

1850

"Has she had all her vaccinations and shots?" asked the secretary as Mother registered her child for kindergarten.

"Mommy," said the tot as she pulled on her mother's sleeve, "ain't that the same thing the vet asks when we take the dog in?"

Parent to child: "Look, when we said the doctor was going to give you a shot, we didn't mean with a gun! Won't you please come out from under that bed?"

Vagrant

1852

"A 'vagrant,'" explained the teacher, "is someone who has no means of support; no money."

"How about that!" asserted one student, "I've finally found my identity!"

1853

"You did poorly on the test because of your 'vagrant' answers."

"What do you mean, 'vagrant' answers?"

"I mean that not one of your answers had any visible means of support!"

Valor

1854

As we recognize valor and courage in others, part of us comes to the unhappy realization that there would be no need for those qualities if only we did what was right and just in the first place.

1855

"There's Billy Jones," said a child, "and he wants to fight you!"

"Go ahead," urged another companion, "show us some courage; show us some valor!"

Said the potential fighter, "Show me some way out!"

Values

1856

The value one takes out of education is directly proportional to the value one has placed on it and invested in it!

"Over the years," said the social studies teacher, "our country's values have changed."

"They sure have," volunteered one student. "This pack of bubble gum costs almost double what it did last year!"

Vanilla

1858

"The cafeteria is serving 'Vanilla Surprise' today."

"What's that?"

"If you can find any vanilla in it, they'll be real surprised!"

1859

"Was I supposed to put in three spoons of vanilla or three bottles?"

"Three spoons, of course," answered the home ec teacher.

"In that case," said the student, "would you like to try my 'Very, Very Vanilla' cake?"

Vanity

1860

"You see," commented the teacher, "I take a long time getting my hair and clothing just right. I call that a proper concern for one's appearance, except when others do it—then it's vanity!"

1861

"I heard Mr. Johnson is very vain," said one student.

"Oh, yes," commented another. "He has one on the side of his head that turns blue and pulses when he gets angry!"

Vase

1862

"Is it pronounced 'V-AH-SE' or 'V-AY-SE'?" asked a student.

"That depends," another child answered, "on whether the relative who gave it to your family is rich or poor!"

1863

"This is a very rare vase," stated the art teacher. "In fact, it's one of a kind."

At that, the teacher turned and accidentally knocked the vase from the table to shatter on the floor.

"Now," commented one student, "it's 273 of a kind!"

Vault

1864

The kindergarten class was being taken on a tour of the high school track and stadium.

"This is the area where we do the pole vault," explained the guide. "Who knows what a pole vault is?"

Answered one tike, "That's the safe where you keep those big sticks people jump with!"

1865

"You shouldn't carry that much money around," the teacher told the student. "Let us put it in the school vault for you."

"You don't understand," the pupil protested, "if it's in the school vault, then I can't bet it on the school races!"

Ventilation

1866

"Please open the window," said the teacher, "so we can get a little ventilation!"

"It's not going to matter," remarked a student. "The hot air outside is no match to what keeps coming in here!"

1867

"Kids," said the P.E. instructor, "we're taking a survey, and we want your comments on what would most improve the physical education program in this school."

Ninety-five percent responded, "An efficient ventilation system for the locker room!"

Venus

1868

"So," remarked the teacher, "Venus is considered the goddess of beauty."

"I don't think so," ventured a student. "I saw her statue, and without arms, she couldn't put on lipstick and mascara!"

1869

The teacher peered through the telescope and exclaimed, "I can see Venus! I can see Venus!"

"Mr. Johnson!" a student snapped indignantly, "at least have the decency to call her and tell her to pull down the shades!"

Verb

1870

"What's that quote about state of being verbs?"

"What quote about state of being verbs?"

"The Shakespeare thing—Oh, yeah, 'To be or not to be . . .'"

1871

"Give me an example of a transitive verb."

"AmTrak!"

"How is that a transitive verb?"

"It carries the action across, don't it?"

Verbose

1872

"I got an A+ in English grammar! Does that mean I'm now verbose?"

1873

"Do you think you might be a little verbose?"

"I can answer unequivocally and without hesitation, secure in the knowledge that the veracity of my statement remains unchallenged—no!"

Verse

1874

And I, when I was younger far,
Instead of smoke and curse,
Wrote poetry like this and made
The world a little verse!

1875

"Shall we attend the student poetry reading?"
"Please! Nothing could be verse!"

Veteran

1876

"Where did you get shot?" the student asked the teacher.

"Shot?" answered the teacher. "I was never shot. Who told you that I was?"

"Well," returned the child, "I heard the principal talking, and she told the guidance counselor that you were a veteran teacher!"

1877

"Mrs. Jones," said a student, "I heard the principal call you a veteran teacher, but a veteran is someone who has survived a great war . . . "

Answered Mrs. Jones, "Well?"

Vibration

1878

"You know that vibration in the school van that you told me to ignore," said the custodian to the maintenance worker, "Well, it stopped . . . "

"I told you so!"

" . . . right after the rear wheels fell off!"

1879

"What did you do when you first heard the vibration in your engine?" asked the shop teacher.

"I did what I was supposed to do," said the colleague who had come for advice, "I turned up the radio until I couldn't hear it!"

Vice-Principal

1880

Said the visitor, "I would like to speak to the main sinner."
"The main sinner?"
"You know, the vice-principal!"

1881

"I want to see the principal!" demanded the visitor.
"She's not here today; may I get you the vice-principal?"
"OK, but if you got a principal just for that, then things here are even worse than I heard!"

Victory

1882

The greatest victory is the one in which the child becomes the master of the page before him!

1883

"I have finally," stated the student, "achieved a total and complete victory over English grammar!"
"You mean," said the teacher, "that you studied it until you learned it?"
"No," shouted the victorious student, "I took the book out to the backyard barbecue and I burned it!"

Villain

1884

"Why do I misbehave?" stated the student. "I misbehave so that you can be a great teacher and straighten me out. Remember, there would be no heroes if there were no villains!"

1885

The class put on an "old-fashioned" melodrama, and when the child assigned to be the villain came out, the audience booed and hissed appropriately.

The child took a step or two, broke into tears, and exclaimed, "Whatever it is, I'm sorry, and I won't do it again! Can I please have a hug?"

Violence

1886

The school band got up on the stage and one boy rose, took out a hammer, and started pounding on the music stands and instruments.

"Stop!" yelled the music teacher. "I said we needed more violins—more VIOLINS!"

1887

"I want to rid this school of violence," said the student council president, "even if I have to beat up every violent kid in the school!"

Violin

1888

"How long did it take you to learn to play the violin?" one student asked another.

"I don't know," the first answered, "because according to my parents AND my music teacher, I ain't there yet!"

1889

"My mom wouldn't let me see that movie," lamented one child. "I guess it was too musical."

"Too musical?"

"Yeah, she said it had too much sax and violins!"

Virtue

1890

"You don't have what it takes to pass my class," said the teacher. "Sorry, but honesty is a virtue!"

"So is truthfulness," replied the student. "Your breath smells!"

1891

A garden filled with virtues,
Now wouldn't that be nice;
If we could cultivate the good
And weed out all the vice!

Visit/Visiting/Visitor

1892

Principal on telephone: "Honestly, Madam, it is not unusual for a child to threaten to lie down in the middle of rush hour traffic if his parents visit the school!"

1893

"So," said the teacher, "if anyone has long-range plans, I would appreciate it if you'd tell me."

"Mrs. Johnson," replied one girl very matter-of-factly, "my Mom is visiting school tomorrow, so I plan to die of embarrassment."

Vitality

1894

"Where do you get all that vitality?" a visitor asked a teacher. "You're always moving; always moving!"

"I have to," said the teacher. "If I ever stopped, they'd catch up!"

1895

"My Mom says I have such vitality because I eat a good breakfast each day!" said the student.

"Say," commented the teacher, "have I ever explained the theory of fasting until noon?"

Vocal

1896

"As a vocal music teacher," said the parent, "do you feel that my child's voice needs more training?"

"Training, no," replied the teacher, "more like a leash and muzzle!"

1897

"Why are you so vocal in class?" asked the teacher of the talkative student.

"My Mom," replied the child, "won't listen to me at home, so where else should I express myself!"

Vocabulary

1898

"Do you feel living overseas has increased your vocabulary?" the teacher asked the new child in class.

"Oh, yes," the student replied. "Now I can get thrown out of school in three languages!"

1899

"I am happy to report that your son has a vocabulary of 976 words."

"How wonderful!"

"Unfortunately, 853 of them are unprintable!"

Vote

1900

"You are about to vote for class president," said the teacher. "Remember to vote wisely; remember to vote for the best person . . . "

"And," interrupted a candidate, "remember whose father owns a candy store!"

1901

"So," concluded the student candidate, "on election day, vote for honesty; vote for integrity; vote for progress . . . "

"Hey!" whispered one of his cronies, "I thought we were supposed to vote for you!"

Vow

1902

Said the teacher, "Let us vow to do our homework; let us vow to study for tests; let us vow to come to class prepared."

"I don't know about you," said one student to a classmate, "but my mother told me never to swear!"

1903

"I vow to you to do all my assigned work," said the student.

"That's very good of you," replied the teacher.

"Now," the student added, "let's just hope you have a merciful and forgiving nature!"

Vulgar

1904

The boy came up to the teacher in the cafeteria and, with a mouthful of food, began, "Mmmmr. Johhhfmumpf! Urr flumpf ess . . . "

"Wait!" commanded the teacher. "It is very vulgar to speak with your mouth full. We will wait until you are finished!"

So, the man and the boy stood side by side for a good minute until the lad stopped chewing.

"Now," said the man, "what have you got to tell me?"

Said the boy, "Your zipper's open!"

1905

The girl reached over, grabbed a handful of cookies, and stuffed them into her mouth.

"How vulgar!" exclaimed a playmate.

"Listen," explained the girl, "we got nine kids in our family. What's better, vulgarity or slow starvation?"

Vulture

1906

"What is the bird that circles around dying people, waiting to pick their bones?"

"Relatives!"

1907

"Well, I know that vultures will never pick my bones!"

"Never going into the desert, eh?"

"No, I'm a teacher; too tough to pick!"

Wages

1908

"So," Mom and Dad quizzed their kindergarten child, "what's the first thing you learned in school?"

"I learned," proclaimed the tot, "that my allowance is WAY below minimum wage!"

1909

"Know what we studied in school, Dad? Wage negotiations!"

"Interesting, Son. Did you learn anything?"

"Oh, yes, Dad. In fact, I want to talk to you. What's all this management propaganda about allowances not going up?"

Wagon

1910

"So, every morning," said the student, "I deliver newspapers in a wagon."

Asked the teacher, "Station?"

Replied the student, "No, little red . . . "

1911

As the teacher walked home one afternoon, she saw one of her students pulling his brother about in a red wagon.

"How nice of you to do this for your brother," remarked the teacher.

"Yep!" said the little brother from the wagon, "and as long as he keeps it up, I won't tell Mom where he hid his report card!"

Wallpaper

1912

"Jones," said the plant manager, "I don't know if our company should manufacture a wallpaper designed to look like dirty hand prints."

"But," ventured Jones, "the school will eat it up! Now when the visitors see the walls, the school doesn't have to apologize; they can call it decor!"

1913

"No," commented the teacher to a student, "we cannot put wallpaper in the classroom so that decades from now some archeologist can discover your name written on the wall underneath!"

Waltz

1914

Grandma and Grandpa demonstrated a waltz for their granddaughter.

"Wow!" exclaimed the wide-eyed child, "you actually touched! How radical!"

1915

"So, the waltz went 1-2-3! 1-2-3!"

"You mean, you had to keep going around in circles just because you couldn't count higher than three?"

Want

1916

"Remember yesterday," said the student, "when you told the class that whatever we want the most, that we will accomplish!"

"Yes, I remember."

"Well," continued the pupil, "I just want you to know that you so inspired me that I went right out and cut all classes yesterday afternoon!"

1917

We often want what we need, but it is far less frequently that we need what we want!

Wash

1918

"Harry," said the teacher, "did you wash your hands?"

"Yes, Ma'am!"

"They don't look washed to me!"

"Honest, Ma'am, I did wash them . . . yesterday or the day before!"

1919

"Mrs. Jones," said one first-grader, "you're gonna be so happy! You know this morning when you said you were going to take your wrist watch to the jeweler to be cleaned? Well, you don't have to, because we took it from your desk at recess, and we washed it!"

Water

1920

"You want to go get a drink of water?" mused the teacher. "That's the sixth drink this period!"

"I know," said the student, "but they're showing this really neat movie in the room by the water fountain!"

1921

The child fell to the floor, grasped his throat with both hands and flailed violently from side to side.

"OK! OK!" sighed the teacher. "I get the message! You can get a drink of water!"

Wave

1922

"If you didn't know the answer," asked the teacher, "why did you raise your hand?"

"I was waving to YOU!" stated the child indignantly. "That's what I get for being friendly!"

1923

On the field trip to the beach, the teacher stood facing inland, observing the children. One child called, "Wave!" and the teacher waved to the child. Then another and another called, "Wave!" The teacher was standing there, determined that she would not respond, when—Pow!— she was hit by the biggest wave you ever saw!

Weather

1924

Teacher to student looking out window: "I'm sorry, but I can't give the weather detention for lack of cooperation!"

1925

"The weather," commented the teacher, "is a lot like my seventh-period class. There is no telling what it's going to do next, and it simply cannot be controlled."

Wedding

1926

When the class learned that their teacher was getting married, they wrote her special marriage vows, insisting that at her wedding she promise to love, honor, and never assign homework over a weekend!

1927

"Inviting your first-grade class to your wedding was a lovely idea," said the bride's friend, "but do you think it was wise to introduce them to your husband's side of the family for the first time by saying, 'I'd like you to meet my children'!"

Weekend

1928

The weekend is so popular that if we didn't have it where it is, we'd have to hold it in the middle of the week!

1929

"What did you do last weekend?"

"I made plans for this weekend, so I'd have all week to look forward to them!"

Weep

1930

As the teacher evoked the feeling of the poem, she asked, "Do you know what it is to truly weep?"

"Oh, yes," answered one student. "How do you think I got my skateboard?"

1931

Mother came in to Junior's room to find him crying in a corner.

"I've done three walls," sniffled the lad. "One more to go after this!"

"No, no!" said Mother, "I asked you to SWEEP up the room!"

Weight

1932

In our faculty lounge, we always have very weighty discussions. Somebody's always talking about one diet or another!

1933

Said the rotund teacher: "The principal just said that he wanted to talk to me, because he needed the opinion of someone who carried a lot of weight around this school! Now, what do you think he meant by that?"

Weight Control

1934

"I'm an expert on weight control," said the overweight teacher.
"Er . . . are you sure?"
"Of course," came the reply, "I can put on weight any time I want to!"

1935

"When it comes to weight control, I'm an expert," said the teacher. "I once lost 65 pounds in a single afternoon!"
"That's impossible!"
"No, it's not!" insisted the teacher. "The kid cut my class!"

Western

1936

"My teacher said I would be great in Western movies!"
"Did she really say that?"
"Well, no, but she did say that I was real good at horsing around!"

1937

It was a psychological Western. The hero was a marshall who was also a psychiatrist. He could bring law and order to any place on the frontier, but the town really had to WANT to change!

Wheelchair

1938

"May I borrow the school's wheelchair?" the student asked the school nurse.
"Why?" inquired the nurse. "Is someone injured?"
"Look," the student relied, "I got homework in every subject tonight, and if I can't use the wheelchair to carry those books out to the bus, I ain't gonna make it!"

1939

School nurse to student: "I'm sorry, but a hangnail does not qualify you to ride down the hall in a wheelchair so you can wave to your friends!"

Whistle

1940

The teacher explained to the class, "If I knock on my desk, I'm getting angry; if I slam a book, I am ready to explode; and, if I whistle, you will all get detention for a week! Any questions?"

"Just one," replied a student. "Could I offer you some of these salted crackers?"

1941

The student was trying to whistle, and after many tries finally managed a weak squeak. Just as he did, a fire whistle sounded from a nearby station.

"You see!" said his brother, "Somebody heard you!"

Whittling

1942

When the woodshop teacher got to class, there was a boy seated in the middle of the floor with a pile of wood shavings about him that easily reached his shoulders.

"Son," said the teacher, "not that I mind, but what are you whittling?"

Answered the student, "A toothpick!"

1943

"Which way to the room with the grand piano?" one small student asked a teacher in the hall.

"Over there," replied the teacher. "Why? Are you going to take up piano playing?"

"No," returned the child, "whittling!"

Wildlife

1944

"Today," said the teacher, "we are going to learn about wildlife!"
"Wow!' said one child, "a whole lesson, just on us!"

1945

On vacation in a national park, the teacher stopped to talk to a park ranger.

"I'm sure you'll enjoy experiencing the wildlife here," said the guide.

"I get enough wildlife in my class all year long!" replied the teacher. "I'm here for a rest!"

Will and Testament, Last

1946

Teacher to lawyer: "Come on! There has to be a way I can will my third-period class to the principal!"

1947

The true teacher who passes on leaves more than a piece of paper to dispose of his or her estate, for the will and testament of that educator has been written on the hearts and minds of those who have come within his or her scope.

They are a legacy no court or body of laws could ever frame!

Window

1948

"Bobby! Were you looking out the window?"

"No, Ma'am! I was looking THROUGH the window to get to that empty baseball field across the street!"

1949

"Let me explain to you one more time," said the principal to the student. "The windows of this school are to let light IN, and not to allow students to jump OUT!"

Wink

1950

A "WINK" is a "BLINK" with a hidden agenda!

1951

"Billy," said the teacher, "Mary claims that you are flirting with her; that you keep winking at her."

"Ma'am," said the child with a sigh, "were you ever a kid with allergies during hay fever season?"

Wisdom

1952

"WISDOM" is a rare commodity for which many people wrongly substitute learning!

1953

"There is no substitute for wisdom!" intoned the teacher.

"Yeah!" whispered one student, "but a couple million in tax-free bonds comes very, very close!"

Wit

1954

"I would like to have a battle of wits with you," said one student to another, "but you have only half your ammunition!"

1955

"Use WIT in a sentence?" asked one student of another.

Answered the other, "I went to school WIT my BRUDDER!"

Witness

1956

"Honest! I did my homework, but I lost it on the way to school. George saw it; he's my witness!"

"All right, bring George in here."

"Sure thing, Mr. Jones! Just let me have five minutes with him first!"

1957

"He started it; I'm a witness!" exclaimed the boy. "I know he started it, because I was there when my friend and I jumped him from behind a tree!"

Wood

1958

"As a student," asked the principal, "which would you rather have; the hard plastic desktop or real wood?"

"Real wood!"

"Gives you a warm feeling, eh?"

"No, it's just easier to carve your initials into!"

1959

"I know your family is well-to-do," said the shop teacher, "but I cannot really justify your building a birdhouse out of solid mahogany with teak inlays!"

Words

1960

The word "FEW" means an amount over five or six thousand, as in the sentence, "We will now hear a FEW words from our principal!"

1961

"There's nothing to writing," stated the student. "You put enough words together, and you know what you have?"

"Yes," answered the teacher, "an incredibly long line of words about which nobody cares!"

Work

1962

I love work; I can sit and watch it for hours!

1963

"When I go to work," remarked one student, "I want to work someplace where I'll be able to advance rapidly!"

"Like government service?" asked a friend.

"Of course not!" exclaimed the student, "like the business my father owns!"

World

1964

An article we studied in school said that soon mankind would be traveling to other planets to do there what we've done for this world . . . Gosh! You'd think we would know better by now!

1965

"As adults," said the teacher, "we must all make a contribution to the world!"

"Oh, no!" remarked one student, "you mean we now have city, state, property, federal, AND 'world' taxes?"

Worry

1966

My philosophy about teaching is to never worry about tomorrow—especially since I'm so neurotic today!

1967

"If I were you," said a student to her friend, "I wouldn't worry a bit about your parents punishing you for a bad report card."

"You wouldn't?"

"Nope! They'll probably die of heart attacks the moment they see it!"

Writers/Writing

1968

Then there was the teacher whose handwriting was so bad, she sent her son to the store with a note, and he came back with a bag of chocolate-chip cookies and an aardvark!

1969

"Name one of the best writers of our times," requested the teacher.

"Billy Jones!"

"But," remarked the teacher, "Billy Jones is a student in this school."

"Yeah!" explained the student, "but you should see the absentee notes he forges!"

X, The Letter

1970

"What is this?" questioned Dad. "This test paper has a big X drawn through the answer!"

"How about that!" said the child. "The teacher liked my answer so much, she kissed it!"

1971

"So, you see, the letter X stands for some unknown quantity in the equation. Now, if I solve that equation for X and write down the answer, what will happen?"

Answered one student, "You'll be X-cited?"

X-Ray

1972

"When I was in the hospital," said the student during show and tell, "they took some bad pictures of me!"

"Excuse me," the teacher interrupted, "what do you mean by 'bad pictures'?"

"Honest!" said the child. "I heard them talking, and they said my pictures were X-RAY-ted!"

1973

"Life has taught me many things, and the chief one is that to find life's answers, we must look within ourselves . . . "

"Gosh! Are you a philosopher?"

"No, I'm an X-ray tech!"

Xylophone

1974

"My music teacher doesn't think much of my musical ability," said the student.

"Come on," remarked another student, "you're in the band, aren't you?"

"Sure!" the first student commented, "but she insists I play the xylophone using ostrich feathers!"

1975

"My Dad wants me to join the marching band," said one youth, "so I'm going to sign up for the xylophone."

"But," commented a friend, "in most bands I've seen, they won't let you march with a xylophone."

Smiled the first student, "Precisely!"

Yacht

1976

"All you can think about is sailing! You never consider anything but sailing! You don't care about me, or anything but sailing! You are completely insensitive!"

"I am yacht!"

1977

Remember, a yacht is just a rowboat that's worked out in the gym!

Yard

1978

"How much is a yard?" the student asked.

The teacher explained in inches and centimeters.

"Now do you understand?" asked the teacher.

"Sure," the student answered, "but I sprayed grass killer all over our front lawn by mistake, and I'm going to have to replace that grass, so what I really want to know is—how much is a yard?"

"Yes," said the clerk, "this is very expensive fabric. Do you know how much a yard of this fabric is?"

"Of course," returned the shopper, "36 inches no matter how much it costs! Don't ask silly questions!"

Yarn

1980

Said the grandfather, "There's nothing I like better than a nice fire and a good yarn!"

So, for his birthday, his grandson got him a can of sterno and two skeins of top-quality red wool!

1981

"Many times," said the home ec teacher, "when people buy a skein of yarn, they roll it into a ball. Can anyone tell me why?"

Ventured one student, "It makes it easier for the cat to unwind?"

Year

1982

"How long is a year?"

"Ten months."

"When does it start and end?"

"Late August or early September, ending late May or June."

"Are you insane?"

"No, a teacher!"

1983

"I was once young like you," said the gray-haired, stooped-over, sallow-faced man. "Then I started to teach here, and you see what the years have done to me!"

"And," asked the younger teacher, "how many years have you been here?"

"This," the other replied, "is the end of my second!"

Yearbook

1984

I think that every yearbook ought to come with a label on the cover stating:

WARNING: Looking at this book more than 20 years after publication date may cause severe depression!

1985

I looked at my high school yearbook the other day, and I thought how young and inexperienced I appeared! It's amazing how a few decades, 100 pounds, and a thousand brush loads of missing hair can help correct that look!

Yellow

1986

"Billy Jones is YELLOW!" shouted a student.

At that, the teacher began to lecture the boy about calling other people names.

"Don't you EVER," the teacher concluded, "call another student YELLOW!"

Just then, Billy Jones walked in wearing lemon-yellow pants and the brightest yellow shirt you can imagine!

1987

"What a happy child she must be," stated the observer, "Her whole picture is in yellow!"

"Don't get carried away," remarked the teacher, "that's the only marker that hasn't dried out!"

Yes

1988

Children are "YES" from the beginning; a coiled mass of "YES" waiting to explode into a world of possibilities. The good teacher knows and loves the "YES" of each and every child!

1989

NO is a wall, but YES is a gate;
YES lets you go, and NO makes you wait.
Since I have the choice, then the better, I guess,
Is to tie down my NO's and let loose every YES!

Yielding

1990

"And this sign means that you yield the right of way," said the driving teacher.

With that, the student floored it and shot out into traffic.

"What are you doing?"

"Hey!" the student stated, "I ain't yielding nothing! If they want the right of way, they gotta TAKE IT FROM ME!"

1991

"Billy, when I told you that you had to stop fighting so hard and yield to learning, I did NOT mean that you could go to sleep behind your history book!"

Youth

1992

YOUTH is a period of insanity, frustration, pain, and uncertainty to which most people willingly long to return!

1993

My youth wasn't so hot as I lived it; thank goodness I can keep adding great things that never happened as I remember it!

Yowl

1994

If you cross a YELL with a HOWL, you will get a YOWL, a sound peculiar to cats and elementary school children!

The class was silently working when a blood-curdling yowl came from the back of the class.

"Martha!" snapped the teacher, "What in the world?"

"I'm going to be a black cat in the school play," said the child, "and I'm getting ready! You never heard of method acting?"

Yo-Yo

1996

I have a theory that the yo-yo was modeled after a typical day of teaching! Enough said!

1997

"Well, Betty," asked the teacher, "do you enjoy playing so long with that yo-yo?"

Answered the child, "I do . . . I don't . . . I do . . . I don't . . . "

Yule

1998

"What we need is an old-fashioned Holiday," smiled Grandpa, "with the yule log in the fireplace, flaming up, up, up!"

"What we have is a new-fashioned Holiday," sighed Father, "with the bills in the desk drawer, mounting up, up, up!"

1999

"Use the word YULE in a sentence."

"Eat whatever you want this holiday, but YULE pay for it later!"

Zeal

2000

Where can I find some zeal?" asked the teacher.

Answered one student in a French accent, "Zee zeal would be in zee water at zee zoo!"

2001

"For teaching in our school," said the principal to the faculty, "you need a great amount of zeal!"

Commented a member of the audience, " . . and a catcher's mask and a chest protector."

Zero

2002

"But, you must have known that Billy was doing poorly," said the teacher. "He's gotten a zero on every test he took!"

"Oh, no!" moaned the parent, "he told me those were happy faces, and you just forgot the eyes and smile!"

2003

"Remember," said the math teacher, "there is nothing lower than zero!"

"Oh, yeah," whispered a student. "Wait until she sees the math test we took today!"

Zest

2004

"Teaching's exciting
And fills you with zest!"
"Quite true," said the teacher,
"'Cause those kids never rest!"

2005

Said Dad, "What's lacking in your life, Son, is enthusiasm; you need more zest!"

"Come on, Dad!" said the lad, "In school, I get zested every Friday!"

Zipper

2006

"Which is better, zippers or buttons?"

"It really doesn't matter," stated the teacher, "that is no longer an open subject!"

2007

"Tommy has been gone to the lavatory for a long time," said the teacher, "go see if he's all right."

The boy was back in a minute. "He's all right, Ma'am," the student smiled. "But, he did get stuck in his zipper, and he says he ain't coming back until he can negotiate the conditions of his return!"

Zone

2008

The motorist pulled over and questioned the pedestrian.

"I didn't see any signs, but this is a school zone, isn't it?"

"Why, yes," said the walker, "how did you know?"

"Easy," the driver explained, "I could hear the screaming above the noise of the traffic!"

2009

The basketball coach often complained that his team employed a "School Zone" defense—every shot had to be voted upon by the alumni!

Zoo

2010

Said one tired teacher at the end of the field trip to the zoo, "Now I'm certain! The bars are there to protect the animals from us!"

2011

Said the principal, "Do you think our class should be taken to the zoo?"

"Oh, yes," said the teacher, "but I don't think the zoo would have facilities for them all; some are much too dangerous!"

2012

Composition by a third-grader: The zoo was fine! I like the monkey house. It made me think of our class!